you say

t mato

A Special Jessica's Biscuit Edition

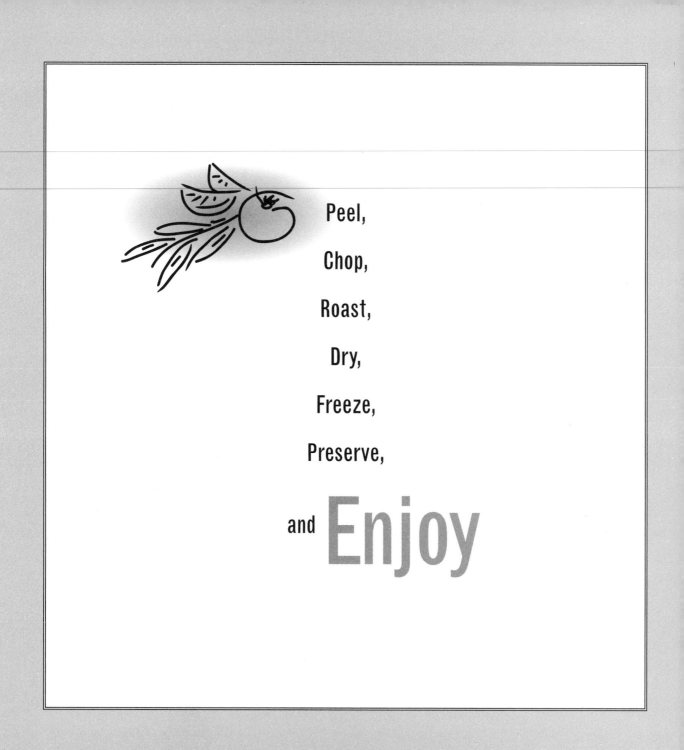

Peel,

Chop,

Roast,

Dry,

Freeze,

Preserve,

and **Enjoy**

you say
tomato

Joanne Weir

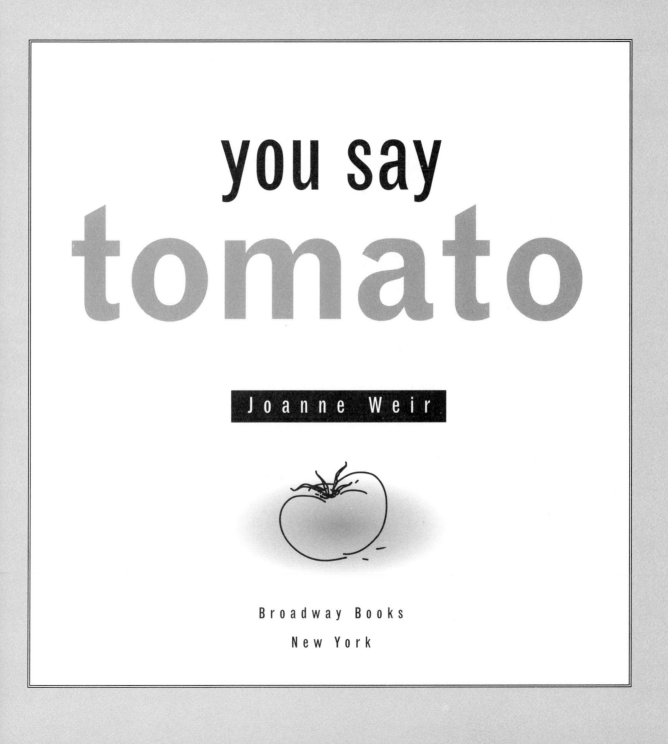

Broadway Books

New York

BROADWAY

Broadway Books titles may be purchased for business or promotional use or for special sales. For information, please write to: Special Markets Department, Bantam Doubleday Dell Publishing Group, Inc., 1540 Broadway, New York, NY 10036.

BROADWAY BOOKS and its logo, a letter B bisected on the diagonal, are trademarks of Broadway Books, a division of Bantam Doubleday Dell Publishing Group, Inc.

Library of Congress Cataloging-in-Publication Data

Weir, Joanne.
    You say tomato : peel, chop, roast, dry, freeze, preserve, and enjoy / Joanne Weir. — 1st ed.
        p.   cm.
    Includes index.
    ISBN 0-7679-0135-5
    1. Cookery (Tomatoes)   2. Tomatoes.   I. Title.
TX803.T6W45   1998
641.6'5642—dc21   97-31272
                                                               CIP

FIRST EDITION

Designed by Judith Stagnitto Abbate/ABBATE DESIGN

98 99 00 01 02 10 9 8 7 6 5 4 3

To Mom,
you taught me everything there is to know
about making the best tomato sandwich

Ode to Tomatoes

Pablo Neruda

The street
filled with tomatoes,
midday,
summer,
light is
halved
like
a
tomato,
its juice
runs
through the streets.
In December,
unabated,
the tomato
invades
the kitchen,
it enters at lunchtime,
takes
its ease
on countertops,
among glasses,
butter dishes,
blue saltcellars.
It sheds
its own light,
benign majesty.
Unfortunately, we must
murder it:

the knife
sinks
into living flesh,
red
viscera
a cool
sun,
profound,
inexhaustible,
populates the salads
of Chile,
happily, it is wed
to the clear onion,
and to celebrate the union
we
pour
oil,
essential
child of the olive,
onto its halved hemispheres,
pepper
adds
its fragrance,
salt, its magnetism;
it is the wedding
of the day,
parsley
hoists
its flag,

potatoes
bubble vigorously,
the aroma
of the roast
knocks
at the door,
it's time!
come on!
and, on
the table, at the midpoint
of summer,
the tomato,
star of earth, recurrent
and fertile
star,
displays
its convolutions,
its canals,
its remarkable amplitude
and abundance,
no pit,
no husk,
no leaves or thorns,
the tomato offers
its gift
of fiery color
and cool completeness.

Acknowledgments

You spend what seems like a lifetime writing a book. And if you're organized, you keep a file of everyone who has helped you along the way. And as you go along, the file gets thicker and thicker, and the list grows longer. Many people have been so helpful and giving of their time and information, my fear is I don't want to forget anyone.

To my literary agent, Judith Weber, thank you for taking my call in the first place and then walking me through the best publishing houses in New York. I am happy that *You Say Tomato* found a good home with Broadway Books. A very special thanks to my editor and friend, Harriet Bell. Without her enthusiasm and foresight, there wouldn't be a book in the first place. And with her efforts, this is a much better book. Thank you to Caitlin Connelly and everyone at Broadway Books for their support on this project.

When I was in the deepest throes of the book, I shared my kitchen with two excellent recipe testers, Mary Ann Mullen and Cathy Cogliandro Alioto. Both Mary Ann and Cathy brought inspiration, brilliance, and expertise to my kitchen each day. My heartfelt thanks goes out to them. And to the recipe testers from afar, Nan Kelley and Patty Padawer, thank you.

I couldn't have written this book without the help of Phyllis Palone Sturman. As a research assistant, her work was thorough, well executed, and invaluable. Phyllis and I would like to thank Andrew Smith, author of *The Tomato in America* and *Pure Ketchup*, which chronicle the history and lore of the tomato, incomparably, I might add. Thanks to Dan Strehl of the Los Angeles Public Library, Barbara Haber of Schlesinger Library at Radcliffe College, and Jan Langone of the Wine and Food Library, for pointing me in the right direction.

To those who contributed their favorite tomato recipes or offered inspiration and support, Emma Afra, Giovanna Ascari, Lisa Atwood, Hilda Barrera, Beaulieu Vineyards, Paul Bertolli, Elizabeth and Tony Boyle, Alanna Brady, Giovanni Capelli, Sue Condos, Jesse Cool, Sammie Daniels, Gary Danko, Lisa Ekus, Magaly Fabre, Susan Feniger, Rick Forrestal, Judy Witts Francini, Brett Frechette, Marcella Friel, Anna Hughes, Lauraine Jacobs, Madjur Jaffrey, Claudia Jeung, Michele Jordan, Laurence Jossel, Ariana Kumpis, Maria and Dimitri Likouressis, Carolyn Lockhart, Mary Sue Milliken,

Jan Newberry, Louise Nixon, Peggy O'Brien, Charlie Rick, Gwenda Robb, Charlotte Robinson, Filipe Rojas-Lombardi, Gabriella Salas, Pia Scavia, Phillip Searle, Shelley Sorani, Angel Stoyanof, David Tanis, Pedgi Taylor, Becky Tenanes, Jean Tenanes, Giovanna Tenati, Howard Twelftree, Frances Walker, Alice Waters, and Kathy, David, and LaRea Weir.

To Angela and Scott Crandall, who dropped green tomatoes on my doorstep on more than one occasion, and to Nigel and Frances Walker of Eatwell Farms, for their kind and generous donation of time and tomatoes, tomatoes, tomatoes.

To the "Office Party Club," Pamela Altieri, Barbara Ignatius, Linda Pratt, and Kraemer Winslow for their loyalty and friendship over the years. A special thanks to Max Evans for being just a thought away.

I can't imagine what I would do without my family, Jean and John Tenanes, John, Becky, Sara and Cory Tenanes, Nancy, David, Liz and Niki Gokey, Jinny and Jack Reilly, and Beth Harubin. Thanks for your love, encouragement, and understanding. May the joys of the table be ours always.

For her invaluable inspiration in the kitchen and classroom, my heartfelt thanks goes to my teacher, friend, and mentor, Madeleine Kamman. And to Alice Waters and everyone at Chez Panisse, I thank you for inspiring all of us with utmost care, love, and respect on how to bring the garden to the table.

I am so grateful to my producer, Linda Brandt, and the *Now Weir Cooking* television crew, who understand my breakneck schedule and constantly adjust their own to accommodate me.

And finally, my special love to Paul. Thank you for building me a terrace to grow tomatoes, painting my sky the loveliest blue, and letting the sun shine every single day. Without you, life wouldn't be the same.

Contents

Introduction

Botanically a fruit but legally in America a vegetable, the omnipresent *Lycopersicon esculentum,* or, as we know it, the garden tomato, has survived multiple names, transformations, disingenuous descriptions, and a long migration from the New World to the rest of the world and back to become one of the most popular foods in American cuisine. Not only do we like to eat tomatoes, but between twenty-five and forty million of us love to grow hundreds of varieties in gardens, containers, and window boxes. There's a tomato for just about every personality, space, and climate.

The Early Years

The ancestor of our garden tomato started as a small red fruit on a long vine that most resembled the currant and cherry tomatoes of today. It grew wild—as many types of tomatoes still do—in the Andes region of Peru and the coastal highlands of western South America hundreds of years ago. Whether or not the Incas used the berries for food is disputable; however, we do know that once the tomato seeds were carried to the Galapagos Islands and then to Central America, the Mayans, among other native inhabitants, cultivated the small wild fruit and serendipitously produced a large, lumpy specimen. Farther north, the Aztecs soon adopted the new plant, which resembled a small husked fruit that grew in the Mexican highlands. The husked fruit and other small plump round fruits were called *tomatl.* The Aztecs called the new large version of the round fruit *xitomatl.* It was used in a sauce, or salsa, with chiles and ground squash seeds, and served with fish, seafood, venison, and other meats.

After Cortés led the Spanish Conquest in 1519, the conquerors lumped the *tomatl* and *xitomatl* plants together under the name *tomate.* They introduced the *tomate* throughout their empire, including the Caribbean and the Philippines. The *tomate* continued its migration through Southeast Asia, and eventually the rest of Asia, where it didn't exactly become part of the cuisine. However, the *tomate* plants—actually the *xitomatl* plant—quickly adapted to the Mediterranean climates of Spain, southern France, and Italy, where the fruit was cooked with olive oil and onions for sauce, and combined with cucumbers for salads. In England for many years and in early colonial America, the British had reservations about eating the *tomate,* but they did grow the fruit for medicinal applications such as cool wet dressings for skin inflammations and headaches. The smooth-skinned red *tomates* were used for decorative purposes.

A Tomato by Any Other Name

In the first known reference to the *tomate* in Europe, Italian herbalist Pietro Andrae Matthioli referred to the *tomates* as *mala aurea,* or golden apples, because the first *tomates* brought to Europe were yellow. Later he used the Italian version of the term, *pomi d'oro,* which is still used today.

But as Europe was inundated with new plants from the Americas, Africa, and Asia during the 1500s, confusion seemed inevitable as the *tomate* received numerous names in different languages. Botanists, herbalists, and physicians did their best to name and classify the new plants according to their original location (*pomi de Peru),* classical Greek and Roman texts (*glaucium* and *lycopersicon,* or wolf's peach), myths, (*poma amoris,* or love apple), religious beliefs, and the latest medical theories. The name love apple stuck and was usually associated with the small pretty red *tomate.* But "love apple" was not necessarily a favorable moniker. The love apple was grouped with the mandrake plant, which had its own damage control problems as a member of the nightshade family, which includes toxic belladonna, henbane, and tobacco, plus the edible eggplant, potatoes, and peppers.

The actual word *tomato* may have come from Jamaica, where the Spanish had introduced the *tomate.* And although we don't know exactly how the word *tomato* was pronounced, it was spelled *tomawto* in colonial South Carolina, where slaves from the Caribbean were brought.

The Tomato in America

It is impossible to pinpoint the exact time the love apple came to North America, or the people who brought it. It is probable that the early Spanish explorers or later arrivals, such as the British colonists and French Huguenot refugees, brought seeds and plants. Or the slaves taken from the West Indies

> # ". . . the spread of American food crops to Europe, Asia, and Africa."
>
> These crops included maize [corn], potatoes, sweet potatoes, tomatoes, peanuts, manioc, cacao, as well as various kinds of peppers, beans, and squashes. All of them were totally unknown outside of the Americas before the time of Columbus. If you can imagine the Italians without tomatoes, the Chinese without sweet potatoes, the Africans without maize, and the Irish, Germans, and Russians without potatoes to eat, the importance of American food crops becomes self-evident."
>
> From Herman J. Viola and Carolyn Margolis, *Seeds of Change*

and Caribbean islands by colonial traders may have introduced the tomato along with their cooking customs. Whoever was responsible for its arrival, the settlers of the South and the southeastern seaboard of North America were the first to accept and cultivate the tomato. Coastal towns and cosmopolitan areas, both of which often served as trade centers, continued to adopt the tomato more quickly than the inland regions of America, both eating the fruits raw and using them for cooking.

Doubting Tomatoes

While gardeners in the Mediterranean and warm-weather regions of colonial America enjoyed fruitful and delicious tomatoes, their cold-climate counterparts were at a clear disadvantage. Outside the boundaries of hot sun and long growing seasons, a good tomato was hard to grow or find; what was available was no doubt similar in taste to our lackluster out-of-season tomatoes. There was just no point in eating a tomato when it didn't taste good as a result of poor growing conditions or lack of culinary preparations. And people were suspicious of new fruits and vegetables, often associating them with illness or poisoning. In reality, it was probably the water the fruits or vegetables were washed in that made people sick. So, regardless of the fact that many people ate tomatoes, and lived to cook another day, many preferred to grow them simply for decoration. And others couldn't get past the strong, unpleasant smell of the foliage.

The Tomato Takes Off in America

Momentum for the tomato, whose popularity was still stronger in the South, began to change in the late 1790s and early 1800s when newly opened French-owned restaurants started to feature tomato dishes on their menus. The tomato's profile was enhanced when Thomas Jefferson grew tomatoes at Monticello, and the tomato was listed in the census of plants in "The American Gardener." Soon people recognized how versatile tomatoes were. And tomato plants were prolific. Too many tomatoes? Feed them to the livestock.

The tomato's popularity increased exponentially during and after the Civil War—so much so that America was importing tomatoes from Bermuda, the Bahamas, and other Caribbean Islands. By 1870, factories in eastern Pennsylvania and New Jersey were processing thousands of acres of local produce, making tomatoes one of the top three canned vegetables.

> However, if they were cooking with tomatoes in Africa . . . it would have been due to the Portuguese, who had been in West Africa since the fifteenth century and who early and enthusiastically took to the tomato. . . . It is amusing to think that the black slaves may have brought tomatoes to the South; it is there that we first hear of their use in the United States, and Jefferson reported in 1782 that they were common in Virginia gardens."
>
> From John L. Hess and Karen Hess,
> *The Taste of America*

Which leads us to how the tomato became a vegetable: In the early 1890s, when the United States began to import significant amounts of vegetables, Congress levied a 10 percent tariff on vegetables only to protect American growers. A U.S. Customs agent at the port of New York claimed the tomato was a vegetable subject to tariff, but to avoid paying taxes, a West Indian importer claimed his tomatoes were a fruit. After a few years in the court system, the case reached Supreme Court Associate Justice Horace Gray who mandated, "Botanically speaking, tomatoes are the fruit of a vine, just as are cucumbers, squashes, beans, and peas. But in the common language of the people, whether sellers or consumers of provisions, all these are vegetables which are grown in kitchen gardens, and which, whether eaten cooked or raw, are like potatoes, carrots, parsnips, turnips, beets, cauliflower, cabbage, celery, and lettuce, usually served at dinner in or after the soup, fish, or meat which constitute the principal part of the repast, and not like fruits generally, as dessert." To this day, the tomato remains classified as a vegetable.

Ketchup

In 1896 the *New York Tribune* cited tomato ketchup as the national condiment. I specify tomato ketchup because this condiment, in the tradition of the tomato, evolved from a litany of languages, places, and ingredients. Versions of ketchup/catsup had been used for hundreds of years throughout East India and Malaya, China, Spain, Portugal, France, and Britain. Andrew Smith, author of *The Tomato in America,* says that English explorers and traders came across a "fermented soy-based fish sauce" in Asia that served as the precursor for their ketchup. Different versions included nuts, fish, brine, or mushrooms plus numerous herbs, spices, and sometimes vinegar or wine.

For years, ketchup was always homemade, and with a few minor exceptions was virtually the same as tomato sauce. Eventually, American manufacturers developed the ketchup of consumer preference: a thick, smooth, bright red tomato ketchup, with generous portions of salt, vinegar, sugar, and spices.

Ketchup has long been used for coloring and flavoring soups, gravies, and sauces and as a condiment. In the 1950s, ketchup became the universal companion for meat loaf, hamburgers, hot dogs, fries, and hash browns. Ketchup and ketchup bottles are used in art form, in humor, and in social commentary. Perhaps the extensive advertising campaigns of the big three ketchup-producing companies, Heinz, Hunt, and Del Monte, in the 1950s and early 60s had that great an impact. Maybe it's not that complicated. Maybe we just liked the taste. And when we found the right blend of sweet, sour, salt, and zest, we put ketchup on everything!

Ketchup does have competition these days: tomato salsa. While Americans still consume about ten billion ounces of ketchup compared to four billion ounces of salsa, salsa's sales figures are higher because it is more expensive. And its popularity continues to grow.

The Tomato Today

Today we have hundreds of varieties of tomatoes in different shapes, sizes, and colors. Although they are not always at their best flavor, tomatoes are available year-round in markets everywhere. Nothing compares with the succulent taste of vine-ripened, garden-fresh tomatoes, but commercial tomatoes maintain a reserved spot at the market.

Generally, tomatoes fall into four main categories: beefsteak (large, irregular, pumpkin-shaped), plum (excellent for cooking and particularly for making sauces), cherry (a perfect addition to a salad), and a medium-sized category (a good slicing tomato), with numerous varieties within each group. (See pages 257–262.)

Take Two and Call Me in the Morning

The biggest boost toward what became the first wave of tomato mania came from a Dr. John Cook Bennett in 1834, whose claims helped solidify the tomato's acceptance as a culinary vegetable. He reported that tomatoes were "the most healthy article of the Materia Alimentary." Fancy as this sounds, all he was saying was that eating them helped in the treatment of diarrhea, violent bilious attacks, indigestion, and cholera. He urged his readers to eat as many tomatoes as possible and predicted that the active ingredients in tomatoes would soon be available in pill form. And indeed, not long after his pronouncement, tomato pills were everywhere.

In 1837, a second wave of tomato mania gained momentum when Archibald Miles of Cincinnati began marketing a pill he called the Compound Extract of Tomato, promising it to be an elixir for many diseases. A few months later, Guy Phelps of Hartford turned out his version, Compound Tomato Pills, supposedly the cure for everything from inflammation of the lymph glands and joints, indigestion, jaundice, bilious disease, colds, flu, and fever to nervous disease, glandular swelling of all kinds, constipation, colic, and headaches. Just two years later, issues of every newspaper from Hartford to Cincinnati included advertisements for tomato cures that took up almost a third of the entire newspaper. Miles and Phelps had become fierce competitors, each claiming that his pill was the best and the other was a fraud. This massive media campaign came to an end with the demise of both companies in 1839. Still, tomato mania continued throughout the next decade.

Most of our commercial tomatoes are hybrids. They are grown by traditional, hothouse, or hydroponic (in water, without dirt) methods. Simply put, hybridization or cross-planting takes the best characteristics of two closely related plants to make a new variety. The variety bears resemblance to both parent plants, but it has its own identity. New varieties of tomatoes were, and continue to be, bred for disease-resistance, size, and adaptability to various growing seasons and climates. New varieties can be formulated quickly if true breeding varieties exist; but producing the desired traits can take several generations of planting.

The tomatoes you find in your grocery stores were picked green and stored, for possibly weeks, in refrigerated quarters, then blasted with ethylene gas—which is the natural ripening gas in tomatoes—to redden them for market. Oftentimes they may be red, but they definitely are not ripe!

A modern growing process that is faster and more specific than hybridization produces the bioengineered or genetically altered tomato. These tomatoes have had specific genes altered to achieve a certain trait that will become inherent in future offspring. They have been developed to stay on the vine longer, to bear up under shipping and handling without damage, and to have a longer shelf life.

> If you believe you are allergic to tomatoes and get a rash every time you even taste one, the symptoms are not those of allergies at all. Instead, the tomato acts as a cleanser and brings out impurities in your system.

What Is This Flavr Savr Gene?

Developed and patented by Calgene, a biotechnological company that genetically engineers plants and plant products for food and seed in Davis, California, the Flavr Savr gene was supposed to give us luscious tomatoes year-round. But since Calgene's Flavr Savr tomato received FDA approval in 1994, as well as regulatory clearance in Canada, Mexico, and the United Kingdom, the company has curtailed Flavr Savr growing operations. Calgene, which is now part of Monsanto Company, the company that developed a genetically engineered bovine growth hormone, is currently using the Flavr Savr gene with traditionally grown plants in an effort to produce varieties that not only have more flavor, but also are more economically and agriculturally feasible to grow and produce.

Calgene, an agricultural biotech firm in Davis, California, developed Flavr Savr, a bio-tech tomato that gained Food and Drug Administration (FDA) approval in 1994. DNA Plant Technology Corporation in Oakland, California, is also at work on a genetically altered tomato. Purdue University, Indiana, is developing a tomato for ketchup and sauces that will yield more pulp and more tomatoes with less processing. Yes, they have minimized some of the imperfections, but have they engineered a better tomato? I don't think so.

Perhaps in response to the commercial tomato, in search of a mouthwatering tomato, or a longing to connect to our agricultural heritage, there has been a resurgence of interest in heirloom vegetables. An heirloom, Webster's dictionary tells us, is "any treasured possession handed down from generation to generation." As for the tomato, countless original tomato varieties were lost fifty to one hundred years ago. Instead, hybrid tomatoes, old, faithful varieties like Early Girl, Better Boy, and Big Boy, took over. It was only logical—heirloom tomatoes do not ship as well, do not keep as long, and are less disease-resistant. But whatever their deficiencies, heirloom tomatoes make up for them in flavor, tenderness, and diversity.

This preoccupation with gardening and tomatoes started in the 1970s when baby boomers found the fruits of their labor in their own backyards. It was a way of getting back to nature. In the 1980s, with greater interest in food, the tomato craze hit its stride. We were exposed to a wide variety of tomatoes in restaurants; now we wanted to have the same choices at home. Since then, numerous seed catalog and supply companies and organizations now specialize in the preservation and sale of heirloom seeds.

Take Care of Your Tomatoes, Because They Take Care of You!

When you bring your prized possessions home from the farmers' market or, better yet, from your own garden, store the tomatoes at room temperature, out of direct sunlight, with the stem end up to prevent bruised shoulders. To preserve the flavor, avoid refrigeration.

In addition to its culinary attributes, the tomato boasts certain nutritious elements. Tomatoes are low in calories—about 30 to 35 for one medium tomato. One tomato supplies half of our daily supply of vitamin C, which is one of the cancer-fighting antioxidants. Recently, lycopene, another tomato antioxidant that is part of the carotenoid family, has shown significant promise in fighting prostate cancer. Vitamin A and potassium are also found in tomatoes.

> Just how the name 'apples of love' became attached to the tomato is not certain. One story is that Sir Walter Raleigh gave a plant to Queen Elizabeth, telling her it was an 'apple of love.' Still another theory holds that the French name *pomme d'amour* was a phonetic derivation from the Italian *pomo di mori*, meaning 'apple of the Moors,' as the Italians still called the Spanish. Or it may have been because the tomato, like cacao beans and the vanilla pod, was rumored to be wickedly, even dangerously, aphrodisiac. Yet the French were [initially] as unenthusiastic as the English; it was not until the Empress Eugénie in the nineteenth century introduced Spanish tomato dishes into France that the tomato became at last an important part of the French cuisine."
>
> From Betty Wilson,
> *Cooks, Gluttons, and Gourmets*

Why the Tomato Is So Wonderful

More than any other fruit or vegetable, the tomato has changed the face of modern cuisine. Most of us have a few cans of tomatoes in the pantry. And no matter where we live, we look forward to growing our own tomatoes or to buying them fresh at the farmers' market. No other fruit or vegetable is anticipated with such enthusiasm. There is hardly a summertime pleasure greater than taking your first bite of a ripe, juicy red tomato fresh off the vine.

tomat

techniques

and **basics**

Peel it, seed it, chop it . . . these are all terms we take for granted. But what do they mean? Do you use a knife to peel a tomato? How long do you boil a tomato so that the skin can be removed easily? How do you seed a tomato? In this chapter, you will find out just what these terms mean, what to do with the tomatoes to get them ready for your recipe, and just how simple cooking with tomatoes can be.

Tomato Glossary

Beefsteak tomato: A large, bright red tomato, slightly elliptical in shape; also known as a slicing tomato or slicer; good raw or cooked.

Canned tomatoes: Come in many forms including chopped, diced, peeled, whole, crushed, stewed; some have herbs, such as oregano or basil, added.

Cherry tomato: Red, orange, green, or yellow, round in shape, and about 1 inch in diameter. The red tomato has a more pronounced flavor than the others; used for salads, garnish, quick sautés, or eating out of hand.

Chili sauce: Puree of tomatoes, sugar, and vinegar cooked until thick; similar to ketchup except the seeds are not removed.

Currant tomato: Sweet red and yellow; about 1/2 inch in size; these look like berries or currants.

Dried tomatoes: Tomatoes dried by the sun, baking, or other means; dark red, sweet, chewy, and highly flavorful. They can be stored in oil or dry packed in cellophane. The dry packed can be reconstituted in hot water or other liquid. Their intense flavor is a delicious addition to soups, sauces and relishes, sandwiches, salads, and pasta dishes in particular. Can be sliced into small strips and eaten with soft cheeses, such as mozzarella, Fontina, or Havarti on bread.

Globe tomato: Medium in size, firm, and juicy; a good tomato for slicing.

Green tomato: Picked before ripe, often available in the autumn when tomatoes won't ripen for lack of sun and warmth or just before the first frost. Its sharp taste makes it excellent for frying and broiling and a good addition to relishes.

Passata: Canned sieved tomatoes. Useful, along with canned tomatoes and tomato paste, for winter soups and sauces.

Pear tomato: Yellow, red, or orange, shaped like a small pear or teardrop; smaller than the cherry tomato; used like cherry tomatoes.

Plum tomato: Also called Roma or Italian tomato; egg-shaped red or yellow tomato. They are good for cooking and canning; they have a lot of pulp, which renders them perfect for sauces.

Purple tomatoes: Assorted varieties that range from a dusky pink and dark pink to purple; their flesh ranges from red to brownish purple-pink.

Salsa: Translates as sauce in Spanish and Italian; in Mexican cooking, this is a spicy condiment; the best-known one is traditionally made with raw tomatoes, cilantro, jalapeños, onions, and lime juice, often served with tortilla chips.

Stewed tomatoes: Canned sliced or cut-up tomatoes cooked with onions, celery, bell peppers, sugar, and spices.

Striped tomatoes: Tomatoes that have rather orange or green and yellow skin with slight colored striations.

Tomatillo: Sometimes referred to as Mexican green tomato or jamberry; part of the tomato family, it looks like a small green tomato with a thin, parchment-like husk, similar to its relative the Cape gooseberry. Tomatillos are used when green and firm; husking and simmering for about five minutes enhances their flavor. Popular in Mexican and Southwestern cooking, they are used in guacamole, sauces, salads, and fresh salsas.

Tomato concassé: From the French verb *concasser,* meaning to break up or crush. Condiment of raw tomatoes that have been peeled, seeded, and chopped, sometimes seasoned with salt; used as a base for other sauces.

Tomato coulis: Peeled and seeded fresh tomatoes that have been drained well and cooked down to a thick, intensely flavored reduction. In French *coulis* means sauce.

Tomato juice: Juice from fresh tomatoes, cooked for a short time, pureed, and strained; available in bottles and cans.

Tomato ketchup: A thick, spicy tomato-based condiment.

Tomato paste: Tomatoes cooked for many hours, strained, and reduced to a deep red, intensely flavored concentrate; available in cans and tubes.

Tomato puree: A thick liquid from tomatoes that have been cooked for a short time and strained.

Tomato sauce: A thinner version of puree. This canned product is often used as the base for other sauces; seasonings and herbs are frequently added.

Tree tomato or tamarillo: Not a member of the tomato family, this egg-shaped fruit is native to South America. Can be eaten fresh or cooked, in sweet and savory dishes; commonly used for making pies and jelly. The tart, flavorful golden pink flesh is covered with a tough, bitter skin of red, purple, amber, or yellow.

Tomato Sizes and Yields

(When a recipe calls for a specific size of tomato, use these approximate weights or amounts.)

Size	Weight	Cups chopped
cherry	1 ounce	about 1 tablespoon
		1 cup = about
		5 ounces
plum	2 to 3 ounces	about 1/3 cup
small tomato	3 to 5 ounces	about 2/3 cup
medium tomato	6 to 8 ounces	about 3/4 cup
large tomato	9 to 12 ounces	about 1 1/4 cups
extra-large		
tomato	13 to 16 ounces	about 2 cups
1 can tomatoes	15 ounces	about 1 1/2 cups
1 can tomatoes	28 ounces	about 3 cups,
drained		

Tomato Nutrition

A whole tomato fresh from the garden, eaten raw, juice running down your chin and over your paws, will most likely weigh 5 to 8 ounces, have about 32 calories, 1/4 grams of protein, 6 grams of carbohydrate, .6 grams of fiber, .2 grams of fat, 1,100 International Units of vitamin A, 28 of vitamin C, rags and tags of the B vitamins, a little bit of iron, 16 milligrams of calcium, 33 of phosphorus, 4 of sodium and 300 of potassium."

From Sharon Nimitz and Ruth Cousineau, *The Tomato Imperative*

Peeling, Coring, and Seeding Tomatoes

Bring a large saucepan of water to a boil. With a small sharp knife, cut an X in the bottom of each tomato. Drop the tomatoes into the boiling water for 15 to 20 seconds. Remove with tongs or a slotted spoon. Cool enough to handle, then peel off the skins. Forget the ice water bath sometimes recommended after boiling or blanching tomatoes—it just dilutes the flavor.

Alternatively, tomatoes can be peeled with a very sharp vegetable peeler, sawing with a back-and-forth motion.

To remove the core, cut a V-shaped indentation with a small knife and lift it out.

You can seed fresh or canned tomatoes using the same easy method. Cut each tomato crosswise in half. Cupping each tomato half in the palm of your hand, hold it cut side down and squeeze the seeds into a bowl. Discard the seeds.

Tomato Tools

When it comes to tomatoes, you don't need many special kitchen tools. There are, however, two that will make your life much easier: first, a high-quality high-carbon stainless steel slicing knife, preferably serrated, and second, a stainless steel food mill, for pureeing tomatoes for sauces and soups.

Roasting Peppers

Peppers and tomatoes have a culinary affinity for one another, and many recipes use roasted peppers.

Roast the peppers under the broiler, using tongs directly over a gas flame, gas grill, or charcoal fire, turning occasionally, until the skin is completely black. Place the peppers in a plastic bag and let steam for 10 minutes to help loosen the skins. Place a strainer over a bowl to catch the juices from the peppers. Remove and discard the black skin, seeds, and membranes by scraping with a knife. Reserve the juices and use in salad dressings or sauces. Bits of charred skin left on the peppers are acceptable.

For red pepper puree, pound or puree the peppers in a mortar and pestle, food processor, or blender to a fine paste.

Making Sun-Dried Tomatoes

First off, you will need a stretch of dry days and a drying box. To make one, stretch a clean piece of window screen over a wooden wine crate and staple it securely in place. Halve the tomatoes and arrange them cut side up on the screen. Place the tomatoes in the direct sunlight. Remember to bring them in at night or if there's rain. If you have a problem with flies, you will need to make a screen cover that rests above the tomatoes, without touching them at all. Cherry tomatoes will be ready in a day, plum tomatoes in a few days. They are ready when they are leathery, but not brittle.

To store sun-dried tomatoes, pack them into clean jars, cover with olive oil, and refrigerate, or freeze them in zip-lock bags.

What is the best way to store tomatoes?
Harold McGee, author of *On Food and Cooking: The Science and Lore of the Kitchen,* replies: "Tomatoes came originally from warm desert areas along the western coast of South America. Both the plants and their fruit can survive fairly cold temperatures, but not without suffering. Temperatures below about 50°F disrupt cell membranes in the fruit, and this physical damage throws the chemical ripening machinery out of balance. Instead of liquefying, the cell walls become merely spongy, and flavor compounds are generated in far smaller quantities. Whether it's left on the vine in cold weather or stored in the refrigerator, a chilled tomato becomes mealy and tasteless.

"A few chill-resistant tomato varieties have been developed and may turn out to be more tolerant of refrigerator storage. In the meantime, our harvest will stay delicious only as long as we make it feel at home. The ideal place to store tomatoes is an out-of-the-way spot—in the basement, or a closet, or a garage—that remains cool but never falls below 55°F or so. Even a warm kitchen counter is preferable to the refrigerator. Some fruit may get overripe and spoil there, but at least the remainder will still taste like home-grown tomatoes!"

From "Q&A," *Kitchen Garden,* August/September 1996

Making Oven-Dried Tomatoes

Makes 2 to 2¼ cups

3 pounds plum tomatoes, cored and cut
   lengthwise in half
1 tablespoon coarse salt

Place the tomatoes, cut side up, on a baking sheet and sprinkle with salt. Let sit for 1 hour.

Preheat the oven to 250°F.

Bake the tomatoes until they are almost dry yet still slightly soft and plump, 5 to 6 hours.

To store oven-dried tomatoes, pack them into clean jars, cover with olive oil, and refrigerate, or freeze them in zip-lock bags.

Roasting Tomatoes

Stick a fork into a tomato. Hold the tomato over a gas or outdoor barbecue flame and turn until the skin is scorched on all sides, 30 to 60 seconds. Let the tomato cool enough to handle, then peel.

Alternatively, heat a dry cast-iron skillet over medium-high heat until very hot. Add whole tomatoes and cook, turning occasionally, until the skins are lightly blackened and blistered, 10 to 12 minutes. Let the tomatoes cool enough to handle, then peel.

Oven-Dried Tomatoes in Herb Oil

Makes 2¼ to 2½ cups

¾ cup extra virgin olive oil
1 sprig fresh rosemary
4 sprigs fresh thyme
2 sprigs fresh oregano
1 bay leaf
1 recipe Oven-Dried Tomatoes (this page)

Place the olive oil in a small saucepan and heat until warm. Remove from the heat, add the rosemary, thyme, oregano, and bay leaf, and let sit for 1 hour.

Pack the cooled tomatoes into a jar and cover with the oil, turning the jar over several times to distribute the oil. Store in the refrigerator for up to 3 weeks.

> I f a wood fire is burning, you can pierce the tomatoes at the stem end with a long-handled kitchen fork and turn them around for a few seconds over the embers—this loosens the skin and gives the tomatoes a nice smoky taste."
>
> Lulu Peyraud, quoted in Richard Olney,
> *Lulu's Provençal Table*

For Charley Rick, tomatoes are his life. Since 1942, he's been studying tomatoes at the University of California at Davis. Why, you ask? Seems he studied asparagus and endive for years until an older member of the Department of Vegetable Crops suggested he examine "bull" tomato plants, those plants with lots of foliage and no fruit—and after that, the rest was history. Charley heads up the Tomato Genetic Resource Center, basically a tomato seed library, studying and cataloging seed samples for investigators and developing ways to improve the tomato through breeding. He's just completed his fifteenth trip to the Andes, researching the original wild species, which, surprisingly, hasn't veered too far from its beginnings, tiny, mostly green fruit, some being very sweet, some not good at all. But Charley's not there for the culinary experience, he's there to study what makes tomatoes disease- and insect-resistant, to improve their quality, color, and flavor, and to develop species more tolerant of environmental stresses.

When I asked Charley about the most unusual tomato name he had come across, he let out a laugh. He caught himself and got a bit more serious. In the Midwest in the early sixties, a colleague came across a rare beefsteak tomato, one with white streaks on the foliage, that the grower called Mama Loves Papa. Seems that when he asked the grower for seeds, the man declined. Realizing that he'd have to do a little fancy footwork, Charley's colleague then asked if he might taste Mama Loves Papa. With a special tomato knife, he dissected the tomato, cutting it into many pieces until he had just what he wanted—a few seeds clinging to the blade of the knife. He swiped the knife across the leg of his pants and smiled all the way out the door.

In his own home garden, one of Charley's personal favorite tomato varieties is Enchantment. This variety happens to be exactly the right size and shape for the feed tube of his food processor, the perfect machine to slice tomatoes to quarter-inch slices, which he then dehydrates. Celebrity is another favorite. From the first tomato he plucks from his vines in July until his last straggler in December, tomatoes constitute 50 percent of his diet.

My final question to this doctor of tomatoes: What is your favorite recipe? Without pause, he said, "You know, these days if I'm feeling ambitious, I toast up a couple of slices of heavy wheat bread, paint it with mayonnaise, add fresh chopped dill, and a big slab of tomato. Don't forget the salt."

Canning Tomatoes

6 to 8 quarts

20 pounds ripe red or yellow tomatoes
Coarse salt
White wine vinegar or lemon juice

Wash the jars, lids, and rubber seals in hot soapy water and rinse. Place the jars and lids in boiling water for 30 seconds to sterilize them. Wash a large canner and lid as well and dry. Peel and core the tomatoes and cut into halves or quarters. *For the raw-pack canning method,* pack the raw tomatoes into canning jars to 1/2 inch from the top. Add 1 teaspoon salt and 2 teaspoons white wine vinegar or lemon juice to each quart of tomatoes. *For the hot-pack method,* bring the raw tomatoes to a boil in a stainless steel pot. Then pack into jars to 1/2 inch from top. Add 1 teaspoon salt and 2 teaspoons white wine vinegar or lemon juice to each quart. Be sure the tomatoes are covered with their juice. For either method, wipe the necks and tops of each jar, fit each with a rubber seal and lid, and seal.

Fill the canner (it should be deep enough that the level of the water will be 3 to 4 inches above the tops of the sealed jars) two-thirds full with water. Place a rack inside the canner so the jars won't touch one another or the sides of the canner. Bring to a boil. Place the jars in the rack and process raw-pack tomatoes for 50 minutes, hot-pack tomatoes for 45 minutes.

Immediately remove the jars from the boiling water and let sit several inches apart on a cooling rack or a kitchen towel, away from drafts, until cool.

After the jars have cooled, check the seals to see that the top resists the pressure of your finger. If there is some give, chances are high that it is not properly sealed. In that case, either eat the tomatoes immediately or transfer to another sterilized jar and process again.

Label the jars and store in a dry dark place.

Here's how they preserved tomatoes in 1839 according to Lettice Bryan, author of *The Kentucky Housewife*

"To Keep Tomatoes through the Winter

"Select those that are large and ripe, but firm, and perfectly free from blemish. Wipe them clean with a cloth, taking care not to bruise them in the least; put them in a jar of the best vinegar, with a large handful of salt, adding no spices as the design is to retain the pure flavor of the tomatoes as much as possible. They will be found fine for soups and gravies, and may be dressed in any way that fresh ones can, except for preserves or jellies. The jar should be closed securely."

Making Tomato Paste

One case of tomatoes will make 2 to 2½ cups paste

To make your own tomato paste, peel tomatoes and puree them in a blender until smooth. For each 4 cups pureed tomatoes, use 1 teaspoon salt. Place the tomatoes and salt in a large pan and bring to a boil over high heat. Immediately reduce the heat to low and simmer, stirring occasionally, until the mixture is very thick, 1½ to 2 hours. Spread the paste on nonaluminum baking sheets and allow to cool. Cover with cheesecloth and put the baking sheets in the hot sun and dry weather. For the next 3 to 4 days, stir and spread the paste to ensure that it dries evenly. When it is the consistency of peanut butter, place in sterilized jars and top with olive oil.

If you live in a humid climate, put the baking sheets in a 250°F oven for 4 to 5 hours.

When you slice a tomato horizontally, a lovely flower-like pattern is revealed. Red tomato flesh envelops segments of a jelly-like substance that contains the tiny tomato seeds. It is in the "jelly" that you find the highest concentration of vitamin C and most of the tomato's flavor.

How Phillip Searle Looks at the Tomato

Phillip Searle is an Australian culinary wizard, chef, and master of the tomato. When it comes to a tomato, he can use every single part.

Give him a box of tomatoes and the first thing he does is core them. He processes them in the food processor until they are coarsely chopped, then places them in a large stainless steel pot and boils them for twenty minutes. Next they are strained through a cheesecloth-lined coarse strainer. He reduces the juice, or as Phillip calls it, "tomato essence," over a low flame until it is one tenth the original volume. This can be used to enhance sauces; it also freezes well.

Phillip puts the pulp that's left in the strainer through a food mill fitted with the finest blade. Then he heats a tablespoon or two of virgin olive oil in a saucepan and cooks the pulp with a pinch of sugar until it is very thick. You can use this tomato puree anytime you're looking for a concentrated tomato flavor, perhaps with pasta.

Finally, he spreads the pulp that's left in the food mill on a baking sheet and dries it in a 200°F oven until completely dry, 2 to 3 hours. Once it's cool, he pulverizes the dried pulp in a spice grinder. You can add this tomato powder to pasta dough, soups, and vinaigrettes to enhance the flavor. Phillip does not believe in waste.

Freezing Tomatoes

On the day the tomatoes are picked, peel, seed, and chop them. (Plum tomatoes are the best choice.) Do not drain. Place the tomatoes in plastic containers with tight-fitting lids or in zip-lock bags. Freeze for 2 to 3 months. Use for sauces or in any recipe calling for canned tomatoes.

Tomato Dust

What to do with all those leftover tomato skins after peeling tomatoes? Why, make tomato dust. Place the skins on a baking sheet in a single layer and bake in a 200°F oven until completely dry, $1^{1}/_{2}$ to 2 hours. Then pulverize them in a spice grinder to make a fine powder or dust. Use the dust as a flavor enhancer when making fresh pasta dough, or add to vinaigrettes, sauces, and soups.

sauces

Peak-Season Tomato Sauce

This is the sauce to make at the height of the season and freeze in containers to use later in the year during tomato-less months. Starting all of the ingredients in one pot at the same time is the secret. Use any type of tomato except cherry tomatoes. Serve this sauce with creamy polenta and grilled sausages or your favorite pasta.

Makes about 4 cups

4 pounds ripe plum tomatoes, cored and
  halved
1 small red onion
6 garlic cloves, halved
3 sprigs fresh basil
Coarse salt and freshly ground black pepper

Place the tomatoes, onion, garlic, basil, and $1/2$ teaspoon salt in a large pot and bring to a boil over high heat. Reduce the heat to medium-high and cook, stirring occasionally, until the tomatoes collapse, about 15 minutes. Reduce the heat to low and simmer until the sauce is thick, 1 to $1^{1}/_{2}$ hours.

Pass the sauce through a food mill fitted with the finest blade. Season to taste with salt and pepper if necessary.

This sauce can be refrigerated for 1 week or frozen for 2 months.

Summer Tomato Sauce with Basil and Black Olives

Summer tomato sauces, full of flavor, cook in minutes. For this one, choose a pasta with a lot of surface area, such as gemelli, fusilli, or penne.

Makes about $4^{1}/_{2}$ cups

1 tablespoon extra virgin olive oil
1 medium red onion, minced
3 garlic cloves, minced
4 medium ripe red tomatoes, diced
1 cup coarsely chopped fresh basil
$1/3$ cup pitted and chopped cured black olives,
  such as Kalamata or Niçoise
Coarse salt and freshly ground black pepper

Heat the olive oil in a large skillet over medium heat. Add the onion and cook, stirring occasionally, until soft, about 7 minutes. Add the garlic and cook, stirring, for 1 minute. Add the tomatoes and cook, stirring occasionally, for 3 minutes.

In the meantime, mix together the basil and olives.

Add the tomatoes to the basil and olives. Season to taste with salt and pepper. Reheat before serving.

The sauce can be stored in the refrigerator for up to 2 days and in the freezer for up to 2 months.

Oven-Roasted Plum Tomato Sauce

Slowly oven-roasting plum tomatoes to partially dry them and remove some, but not all, of the water content, results in sweet, intensely flavored tomatoes, which, in turn, make a tomato sauce ideal for tossing with fedelini, linguine, spaghetti, and other long pastas. Top with plenty of grated Pecorino and Parmigiano-Reggiano. Make plenty of this one at the peak of the season and you'll not be sorry a couple of months later to find it in the freezer.

Makes about 4¹/₂ cups

5 pounds ripe plum tomatoes, cored and
    halved
2 tablespoons coarse salt
3 tablespoons extra virgin olive oil
1 medium yellow onion, minced
¹/₂ teaspoon chopped fresh thyme
¹/₂ teaspoon chopped fresh rosemary
¹/₂ teaspoon chopped fresh oregano

Place the tomatoes, cut side up and close together, on a baking sheet. Sprinkle with the salt and let sit for 1 hour.

Preheat the oven to 300°F.

Place the tomatoes in the oven and cook until they are partially dried but still moist, about 3 hours. Remove the tomatoes from the oven. (These can be baked 3 to 4 days ahead of time and refrigerated until ready to proceed.)

Heat the oil in a large saucepan over medium heat. Add the onion and cook, stirring occasionally, until soft, about 7 minutes. Add the tomatoes, thyme, rosemary, oregano, and 1 cup water and cook, stirring occasionally, until the tomatoes have fallen apart and the water has evaporated, about 30 minutes. Pass the sauce through a food mill. The sauce can be kept in the refrigerator for 3 to 4 days.

> Making the year's supply of tomato sauce is the most important domestic ritual in the Sicilian summer, and each housewife believes in the efficacy of her favorite method with fervor equal to that with which she believes in the efficacy of her favorite saint. There are basically two rival schools of thought: The one favors passing the scalded tomatoes through the food mill, then sterilizing the filled and capped bottles in boiling water; the other prefers to heat up the empty bottles, fill them with boiling hot tomato sauce, and then lay them in a nest of woolen blankets, so well wrapped that they will take several days to cool off."
>
> From Mary Taylor Simeti,
> *On Persephone's Island*

Tomato-Herb Sauce

When I was testing tomato recipes, I realized I had a ton of very ripe tomatoes that were just waiting to be made into sauce, so I cored them and tossed them into a big pot with lots of the summer herbs that were flourishing on my deck garden. Two hours later, I had a new sauce.

Makes about 5 cups

8 large ripe red tomatoes, cored and halved
20 fresh chives
3 sprigs fresh rosemary
4 sprigs fresh thyme
4 sprigs fresh oregano
2 sprigs fresh spearmint
1 sprig fresh savory
Coarse salt and freshly ground black pepper

Place the tomatoes in a large pot, bring to a boil, and boil until they have released their juices, about 10 minutes. Reduce the heat to low.

In the meantime, tie the herbs together into a bundle with kitchen string.

Add the herb bundle to the pot. Simmer slowly until the sauce has reduced by two thirds and is thick, about 2 hours.

Remove the herb bundle and discard. Pass the sauce through a food mill fitted with the finest blade. Season to taste with salt and pepper.

The sauce can be refrigerated for up to 2 days or frozen for 2 months.

Stewed Plum Tomato Sauce

Plum tomatoes have lots of flesh and pulp, great for making sauce. They also have a generous amount of acidity that balances well with their natural sweetness.

Makes about 2 1/2 cups

6 pounds ripe plum tomatoes, cored and halved
10 sprigs fresh basil, tied together with kitchen string
Coarse salt and freshly ground black pepper

Place the tomatoes, basil, and 1/2 cup water in a large pot and bring to a boil over high heat. Boil for 10 minutes, then reduce the heat to medium. Cook until the tomatoes collapse, about 10 minutes. Reduce the heat to low and simmer slowly, stirring occasionally, until the sauce is thick, about 2 hours. Remove the basil and discard.

Cool the sauce and pass through a food mill into a bowl. Season to taste with salt and pepper.

You can store this in the refrigerator for up to 3 days and in the freezer for up to 1 month.

Smoky Yellow Tomato Sauce

Grilling the tomatoes on an open fire gives this tomato sauce a very smoky flavor. Use as you would any tomato sauce, or add a couple of tablespoons of it to a vinaigrette to serve with grilled tuna steaks or swordfish. I like to use it in a lasagne layered with roasted peppers and eggplant and smoked Scamorza or smoked mozzarella. If this sauce is stored for more than a day, it will lose some of the smokiness.

Makes about 2 cups

5 to 6 large ripe yellow tomatoes
Coarse salt and freshly ground black pepper

Preheat an outdoor grill.

Grill the tomatoes 4 inches from the flame, turning occasionally, until they are black on all sides, 15 to 20 minutes. The skins will burst and some juices will escape. Remove from the grill and let cool enough to handle.

Core the tomatoes and coarsely chop. Place the tomatoes in a large skillet and bring to a boil over high heat. Reduce the heat to low and simmer until the sauce is reduced by about one third and thickened, 15 to 20 minutes. Pass through a food mill fitted with the finest blade into a bowl. Season to taste with salt and pepper.

This sauce can be refrigerated for up to 1 day, but no longer.

Green Tomato Sauce

Toss strips of grilled chicken and hot linguine or fettuccine with this tart sauce.

Makes about 4 cups

2 tablespoons extra virgin olive oil
1 large yellow onion, minced
2 garlic cloves, minced
5 medium green tomatoes, chopped
2 bay leaves
Coarse salt and freshly ground black pepper

Heat the olive oil in a large skillet over medium-high heat. Add the onion and cook, stirring occasionally, until soft, about 7 minutes. Add the garlic and stir until fragrant, about 1 minute. Add the tomatoes, bay leaves, and salt and pepper to taste and simmer until the tomatoes are soft, 10 to 15 minutes.

This sauce can be refrigerated for up to 3 days or stored in the freezer for up to 2 months.

Picante Tomato Sauce

Try this mellow-yet-hot sauce with burritos or enchiladas, grilled rib-eye steaks, or ribs. If you prefer it hotter, double the amount of jalapeños and cayenne.

Makes about 4 cups

4 mild dried red chiles, such ancho, guajillo, or árbol
1 tablespoon corn oil
1 large yellow onion, minced
1 jalapeño or serrano pepper, halved, seeded, and minced
5 garlic cloves, minced
2 pounds ripe plum tomatoes, diced
$1/8$ to $1/4$ teaspoon cayenne
Coarse salt and freshly ground black pepper

Place the dried chiles in a bowl and cover with boiling water. Let sit until the chiles soften, about 30 minutes.

Drain the chiles, reserving the soaking liquid. Remove the stems and seeds, coarsely chop, and process in a blender or food processor with just enough of the soaking liquid to form a thick paste. You should have approximately 3 tablespoons.

In a large skillet, heat the oil over medium heat. Add the onion, jalapeño, and garlic and cook, stirring, until soft, about 7 minutes. Add the red chile paste, the tomatoes, and cayenne and stir together. Cover and cook, stirring frequently, until the tomatoes have given off some of their juice, 5 minutes. Remove the cover, stir, and cook, uncovered, until

the liquid has evaporated slightly, about 5 minutes. Season to taste with salt and pepper. Cool for 10 minutes.

Puree the sauce in the blender or food processor until smooth.

Store this sauce in the refrigerator for up to 3 days or freeze for up to 1 month.

Love-Apple Sauce

In 1814, Richard Alsop was the first American to publish a tomato sauce recipe.

"Take the ripest and best tomatoes, carefully strip them of their outer peel, and cut out the insertion of the stalk and any spots may be upon them, divide them into eight parts or slices, and take out a part if not the whole, of the seeds. Put them into a saucepan, or even spider, with a very little butter previously melted, and cover them close, in order to keep in the steam; when nearly done, add to them salt and pepper to taste, and replacing the cover, let them stand a little longer. Should it be desirable to thin the sauce, add a little water to it just before it is done."

From Richard Alsop, *The Universal Receipt Book or Complete Family Direction by a Society of Gentlemen in New York*

Sicilian Tomato Pesto

Pesto is traditionally made with basil, garlic, olive oil, and plenty of Parmigiano-Reggiano, but in Sicily, fresh chopped tomatoes are added. The combination is memorable.

Makes about 2½ cups

¼ cup pine nuts
4 cups fresh basil leaves
3 garlic cloves, minced
⅓ cup extra virgin olive oil
½ cup freshly grated Parmigiano-Reggiano
⅛ teaspoon crushed red pepper flakes
2 large ripe red tomatoes, peeled, seeded, chopped, and drained
Coarse salt and freshly ground black pepper

Heat a small skillet over medium-high heat and add the pine nuts. Cook, stirring constantly, until golden, 3 to 4 minutes. Immediately remove from the pan.

Place the basil leaves, garlic, pine nuts, and olive oil in a blender or food processor and process until smooth. Stop and scrape down the sides. Add the cheese and crushed red pepper and pulse a few times to make a thick paste. Transfer to a bowl and fold in the tomatoes. Season with salt and pepper.

Sofregit

From Catalonia, the northern region of Spain that borders on France, comes this savory-sweet sauce, sweet not from sugar but from the caramelized onions and the inherent sweetness of tomatoes. Use this as a base for paella or fish soups, or on its own as a pasta sauce with steamed shrimp, clams, scallops, or mussels or hot sausage.

Makes about 3 cups

3 tablespoons extra virgin olive oil
3 large yellow onions, minced
2½ cups peeled, seeded, and chopped tomatoes
Coarse salt and freshly ground black pepper

Heat the olive oil in a large skillet over low heat. Add the onions and cook until very soft and light golden, about 45 minutes.

Add the tomatoes and cook until the liquid has evaporated, 10 to 12 minutes. Season to taste with salt and pepper.

The sauce can be stored in the refrigerator for up to 2 days or in the freezer for up to 1 month.

Spicy Tomato Sauce, Tuscan Style

Spicy hot and packed with a punch, this sauce is called salsa di pomodoro forte *in Italy,* forte *meaning hot. This version was inspired by Judy Francini, a California transplant now firmly planted in Florence, who gets her inspiration from the San Lorenzo market that she can see from her kitchen window. Serve with linguine, spaghetti, or fettuccine.*

Makes about 5 cups

5 large ripe red tomatoes, peeled, seeded, and
    chopped
1 large onion, coarsely chopped
1 large carrot, coarsely chopped
1 stalk celery, coarsely chopped
2 tablespoons chopped fresh flat-leaf parsley
10 large fresh basil leaves
Coarse salt
1 tablespoon extra virgin olive oil
10 garlic cloves, thinly sliced
$1/2$ teaspoon crushed red pepper flakes, or to
    taste
1 tablespoon unsalted butter at room
    temperature
Freshly ground black pepper

Place the tomatoes, onion, carrot, celery, parsley, basil, and $1/2$ teaspoon salt in a large saucepan, cover, and bring to a boil over high heat. Reduce the heat to low and cook, covered, stirring occasionally, until the tomatoes fall apart and the carrots are very tender, 1 hour. Cool for 30 minutes.

Puree the tomato sauce in a blender, food processor, or food mill until smooth.

In a small skillet, heat the olive oil over medium heat and cook the garlic and red pepper flakes, stirring, until the garlic is soft, about 30 seconds. Add to the tomato sauce along with the butter. Stir well and season to taste with salt and pepper.

The sauce can be stored in the refrigerator for up to 3 days and in the freezer for up to 1 month.

Romesco Sauce

The Spanish word romesco *has three meanings: a seafood dish, a hot red pepper that grows in Catalonia, in the northeast corner of Spain, and this sauce. Serve with grilled trout and roasted new red or Yukon Gold potatoes.*

Makes about 2 cups

15 skinned hazelnuts
4 medium ripe red tomatoes
5 garlic cloves, unpeeled
2 dried red chile peppers, such as ancho chiles
$^1/_4$ teaspoon crushed red pepper flakes
$^1/_4$ cup plus 3 tablespoons red wine vinegar
$^1/_4$ cup plus 1 tablespoon extra virgin olive oil
1 slice white bread
15 blanched almonds
1 teaspoon sweet paprika
Coarse salt and freshly ground black pepper

Preheat the oven to 350°F.

To peel the hazelnuts, place them on a baking sheet and bake them in a 350°F oven until the skins crack, 5 to 7 minutes. Remove them from the oven and place them in a kitchen towel. Rub them vigorously to remove as much skin as possible.

Place the tomatoes and garlic in an ungreased roasting pan and roast until the tomatoes are soft, about 30 minutes. When cool enough to handle, peel, core, and seed the tomatoes; set aside. Peel the garlic and set aside.

In the meantime, place the dried red peppers and crushed red pepper in a saucepan with $^3/_4$ cup water and $^1/_4$ cup of the vinegar. Bring to a boil over high heat, reduce the heat to low, cover, and simmer slowly for 10 minutes. Turn off the heat and let steep for 30 minutes. Drain the peppers, discard the seeds and liquid, and finely chop them.

Heat 1 tablespoon of the oil in a small skillet and fry the bread until golden on both sides. Transfer to a food processor or blender. Add another 1 tablespoon oil to the pan and sauté the almonds and hazelnuts until golden. Add the nuts to the processor, along with the peppers, tomatoes, garlic, and paprika.

With the motor running, gradually pour in the remaining 3 tablespoons olive oil and 3 tablespoons vinegar, and season with salt and pepper. Process until smooth. Strain through a coarse strainer. Let sit at room temperature for 2 hours before serving.

The sauce can be refrigerated for up to 1 day. Bring to room temperature before serving.

Sonoran Tomato Sauce

From the Sonora area of northern Mexico, this sauce is a very common one, typically served with carne asada, *or steaks cooked over a wood fire, or with grilled fish, clams, or oysters caught in the neighboring gulf.*

Makes about 2 cups

4 medium ripe red tomatoes
1/2 teaspoon cumin seeds
1 teaspoon coriander seeds
1 tablespoon chopped fresh cilantro
1/2 cup minced yellow onions
3 canned green chiles, diced
2 teaspoons white wine vinegar
Coarse salt and freshly ground black pepper

Preheat a broiler or an outdoor grill.

Place the tomatoes on a baking sheet and broil 4 inches from the heat source, turning occasionally, for 5 minutes. Or place them directly on the grill 4 inches from the heat source and grill them, turning occasionally, for 5 minutes. Cool the tomatoes enough to handle, then core and peel them.

Puree the tomatoes in a blender or food processor until smooth. Place in a saucepan and bring to a boil over medium-high heat. Reduce the heat to low and simmer until reduced to 2 cups, about 10 minutes.

In the meantime, place the cumin and coriander seeds in a small skillet over medium-high heat and stir until fragrant, 1 to 2 minutes. Grind in a spice grinder or mortar and pestle to a powder.

Add the spices to the tomato sauce, along with the cilantro, onions, green chiles, and vinegar. Remove from the heat. Season to taste with salt and pepper. Let sit for 30 minutes before serving.

This sauce can be refrigerated for up to 3 days or frozen for up to 1 month.

Grated Tomato Sauce

No-cook sauces are a breeze. Frances Walker of Eatwell Farm in Winters, California, was this inspiration for this one. She and her husband, Nigel, raise a daunting array of glorious heirloom tomatoes at their farm they call "the tomato wonderland." Serve this on a pasta such as radiatore or fusilli, with lots of nooks and crannies to collect the hot sauce.

Makes about 2 1/2 cups

6 medium ripe red or yellow tomatoes
2 garlic cloves, minced
1/3 cup chopped fresh basil
2 tablespoons extra virgin olive oil
Coarse salt and freshly ground black pepper

Cut the tomatoes crosswise in half. Cupping a tomato half in one hand, cut side out, and using the coarse holes of a grater, grate the tomato into a bowl. Discard the peel. Repeat with the remaining tomatoes. Add the garlic, basil, and olive oil. Season to taste with salt and pepper.

Use within 24 hours.

Uncooked Tomato Sauce

Delicate fresh no-cook tomato sauces like this one are a perfect foil for fresh poached shellfish tossed with spaghetti, linguine, or fettuccine.

Makes about 3 cups

3 large ripe red or yellow tomatoes, diced
1 garlic clove, minced
2 tablespoons chopped fresh basil
$\frac{1}{2}$ small red onion, diced
2 tablespoons balsamic vinegar
1 tablespoon chopped fresh flat-leaf parsley
1 tablespoon extra virgin olive oil
Coarse salt and freshly ground black pepper to taste

Place all of the ingredients in a large bowl and mix together. Leave at room temperature for at least 2 hours before serving. Use the sauce the same day that you make it. Refrigerate but bring to room temperature before serving.

Marinara Sauce

This flavorful sauce was originally made by Italian fishermen, who cooked it in minutes on charcoal braziers on the decks of their fishing boats. But don't think they ate just pasta and sauce—they often threw in whatever they had left of the sea's harvest: squid, clams, shrimp, tiny fish, or mussels. This sauce also makes a great base for San Francisco–style cioppino or fish soup.

Makes about 4 cups

2 tablespoons extra virgin olive oil
1 large yellow onion, chopped
1 carrot, diced
2 garlic cloves, coarsely chopped
Two 28-ounce cans Italian plum tomatoes, chopped and drained
3 tablespoons chopped fresh flat-leaf parsley
1 teaspoon dried oregano
Coarse salt and freshly ground black pepper

Heat the olive oil in a large saucepan over medium heat. Add the onion, carrot, and garlic and cook until soft, about 7 minutes. Add the tomatoes, parsley, and oregano, increase the heat to high, and bring to a boil. Reduce the heat and simmer until reduced by one quarter, about 20 minutes.

Pass the sauce through a food mill fitted with the finest blade into another saucepan. Simmer gently over low heat for 15 minutes. Season to taste with salt and pepper.

This can be stored in the refrigerator for up to 3 days and in the freezer for up to 1 month.

Nonna's Winter Tomato Sauce

This is a silky-smooth sauce to make during the cold tomato-deprived months. Be sure to buy the best-quality canned plum tomatoes. Serve with any type of pasta.

Makes about 5 cups

2 tablespoons extra virgin olive oil
1 large yellow onion, diced
4 garlic cloves, coarsely chopped
Three 28-ounce cans Italian plum tomatoes, chopped
1 cup dry red wine
2 tablespoons tomato paste
3 tablespoons chopped fresh flat-leaf parsley
2 teaspoons dried basil
1 teaspoon dried oregano
Coarse salt and freshly ground black pepper

Heat the olive oil in a large saucepan over medium heat. Add the onion and cook, stirring, until soft, about 7 minutes. Add the garlic and continue to stir for 1 minute. Add the tomatoes, wine, tomato paste, parsley, basil, oregano, and 1 cup water. Increase the heat to high and bring to a boil. Reduce the heat and simmer until the sauce is reduced by half, 1 to 1^1/$_2$ hours.

Pass the sauce through a food mill fitted with the finest blade. Season to taste with salt and pepper.

You can store this sauce in the refrigerator for up to 3 days or in the freezer for up to 1 month.

Quick 1–2–3 Tomato Sauce

In one of my classes, an older Italian woman, dressed in black and with a strong accent, raised her hand and proceeded to tell me and everyone in the class that to make good tomato sauce requires hours and hours of simmering. Minutes later, after tasting this simple-to-make sauce, she gave me a smile and a little wink, as if we shared a secret, and asked for a second helping. When time is of the essence, this simple-to-make tomato sauce is the solution.

Makes about 2 cups

2 tablespoons extra virgin olive oil
3 cups peeled, seeded, and chopped fresh or canned tomatoes
^{1}/$_2$ teaspoon dried oregano
Large pinch of crushed red pepper flakes
^{1}/$_4$ cup dry red wine
2 tablespoons balsamic vinegar
1 tablespoon tomato paste
1 teaspoon sugar
Coarse salt and freshly ground black pepper
1 to 2 teaspoons red wine vinegar

Heat the olive oil in a large skillet over medium-high heat. Add the tomatoes, oregano, red pepper flakes, red wine, balsamic vinegar, tomato paste, and sugar. Cook and stir occasionally until the liquid begins to evaporate and the sauce thickens slightly, 4 to 5 minutes. Puree the sauce in a blender or food processor until smooth. Season to taste with salt and pepper and the red wine vinegar.

Puttanesca Sauce

In Naples, they add grated orange and canned oil-packed tuna to the traditional puttanesca sauce of tomatoes, anchovies, capers, crushed red pepper flakes, and garlic. It makes a more substantial sauce for serving with linguine or spaghetti. But you can leave out the orange and tuna and still have a terrific sauce for a piece of grilled salmon. There's no need to serve grated cheese with this.

Makes about 4 cups

2 tablespoons extra virgin olive oil
1 small red onion, thinly sliced
4 garlic cloves, minced
2¹/₂ cups peeled, seeded, chopped, and drained
    fresh or canned plum tomatoes
4 anchovy fillets, soaked in water for 10
    minutes, drained, patted dry, and finely
    chopped
3 tablespoons capers, chopped
¹/₂ cup cured black olives, such as Kalamata or
    Niçoise, pitted and coarsely chopped
1 tablespoon tomato paste
¹/₂ teaspoon grated orange zest
¹/₂ cup fresh orange juice
¹/₄ to ¹/₂ teaspoon crushed red pepper flakes
Freshly ground black pepper
One 6-ounce can Italian tuna packed in oil,
    drained
2 tablespoons chopped fresh flat-leaf parsley

Heat the olive oil in a large skillet over medium heat. Add the onion and cook, stirring, until soft, about 7 minutes. Add the garlic and cook, stirring occasionally, for 1 minute. Add the tomatoes, anchovies, capers, olives, tomato paste, orange zest, orange juice, crushed red pepper, and black pepper to taste. Simmer slowly, stirring occasionally, until the liquid evaporates, about 5 minutes. Add the tuna and parsley and simmer for 30 seconds.

This can be stored in the refrigerator for up to 1 day or frozen for up to 2 months..

Amatriciana Sauce

Bursting with flavor, salsa amatriciana comes from the tiny village of Amatrice, tucked into the green slopes of the Tronto Valley in Lazio, outside Rome. Traditionally, amatriciana is served over bucatini, fat spaghetti with a hole in the center.

Makes about 3½ cups

2 tablespoons extra virgin olive oil
7 ounces pancetta, thinly sliced and diced
1 large red onion, thinly sliced
¾ teaspoon crushed red pepper flakes
4 garlic cloves, minced
1 cup dry white wine
4 cups peeled, seeded, and chopped fresh or
    canned tomatoes
¼ cup chopped fresh flat-leaf parsley
Coarse salt and freshly ground black pepper

Heat the olive oil in a large skillet over medium heat. Add the pancetta and onion and cook, stirring occasionally, until soft and light golden, 10 to 15 minutes. Add the red pepper and garlic and cook, stirring, for 3 minutes. Increase the heat to high, add the wine, and simmer until most of the wine evaporates, 3 to 4 minutes.

Pass the tomatoes through a food mill and add the tomatoes and parsley to the pan. Bring to a boil, reduce the heat, and simmer until the sauce reduces by one quarter, 30 to 35 minutes. Season with salt and pepper.

This keeps in the refrigerator for up to 3 days or in the freezer for up to 1 month.

Corsican Creamy Tomato Sauce with Spearmint

I met Josie in the village of Porto Vecchio on the French island of Corsica. She made me a dish of pasta with a tomato sauce scented with fresh herbs from the surrounding hillside. The tomato sauce was so heavenly I asked her secret. She bent over and whispered in my ear, "I can't let the village people know. I put a splash of cream into the tomato sauce. It brings out the sweetness."

Makes about 3 cups

2 tablespoons extra virgin olive oil
1 small yellow onion, minced
3 garlic cloves, minced
6 cups peeled, seeded, chopped, and drained
    fresh or canned plum tomatoes
⅓ cup heavy cream
3 tablespoons chopped fresh spearmint
Coarse salt and freshly ground black pepper

Heat the olive oil in a large skillet over medium heat. Add the onion and cook, stirring, until soft, about 7 minutes. Add the garlic and cook until fragrant, about 1 minute. Add the tomatoes and cook until the liquid has reduced by about half and the sauce is thick, 20 to 30 minutes.

Puree the sauce in a blender or food processor or put it through a food mill fitted with the finest blade. Add the cream and spearmint and season to taste with salt and pepper.

You can refrigerate this sauce for up to 1 day or store in the freezer for up to 1 month.

Fiery Spanish Tomato Sauce

Patatas bravas, *literally, "brave potatoes," are a favorite tapa in Spain, made with crispy roasted or fried potatoes and this spicy hot tomato sauce. Oftentimes allioli, Spain's version of aïoli, or garlic mayonnaise (see page 38), is drizzled over the top. The mayonnaise melts into the hot tomato sauce and potatoes.*

Makes about 2 cups

2 tablespoons olive oil
$1/4$ cup minced yellow onion
2 garlic cloves, minced
2 cups peeled, seeded, and chopped fresh or
 canned tomatoes
$1/2$ cup dry Spanish sherry
2 tablespoons chopped fresh flat-leaf parsley
$1/4$ teaspoon chopped fresh thyme
$1/4$ to $1/2$ teaspoon crushed red pepper flakes
1 bay leaf
Coarse salt and freshly ground black pepper
1 tablespoon red wine vinegar

Heat the olive oil in a large skillet over medium heat. Add the onion and garlic and cook, stirring, until soft, about 7 minutes. Add the tomatoes, sherry, 1 cup water, the parsley, thyme, red pepper flakes, and bay leaf. Simmer slowly until the liquid is reduced by one quarter, about 20 minutes. Cool for 10 minutes.

Remove the bay leaf and discard. Puree the sauce in a blender or food processor until smooth. Season with salt and pepper and the vinegar.

You can refrigerate the sauce for up to 3 days or freeze for up to 1 month.

Searching for the Best Tomatoes

Paul Ferrari, of Ultra Lucca Italian food importer in northern California, is in continual pursuit of the perfect tomato. Actually, finding quality fanatics in every food category is the goal of his travels. His search for the "Great Tomato" took him to the warm South of Italy, especially the regions of Campania and Calabria. He found tomato heaven, however, in the obscure Adriatic region of Molise, where the Di Majo family invited him for a simple farmhouse lunch. The tomatoes waiting on the counter for the pasta sauce were the most beautiful he'd ever seen, and the sauce the best he'd ever tasted. He discovered that the family had experimented with forty-eight varieties of tomatoes before judging this one the best.

But tomatoes are only a sidelight of the Di Majo wine-growing estate, and Paul is still trying to persuade them to can enough of these pomodori for him to feature in his stores. In their usual Italian way, the family seems to be in no hurry, and supplying the extended family takes precedence over commercial considerations. But Paul hasn't given up, and he manages a lunch invitation as often as possible.

Lamb, Red Pepper, and Tomato Sauce

This easy-to-prepare lamb sauce requires minimal effort for great results. Heat the oil and flavor it with bay leaves, garlic, and rosemary, then throw in the lamb, peppers, tomatoes, and white wine and stew until the sauce is thick and packed with sweet flavor. Toss it with any pasta and sprinkle with grated Parmigiano-Reggiano.

Makes 2½ to 3 cups

2 tablespoons extra virgin olive oil
3 garlic cloves, crushed
2 bay leaves
2 sprigs fresh rosemary
1¼ pounds lean boneless lamb, cut into ½-inch cubes
1 cup dry white wine
3½ cups peeled, seeded, and chopped fresh or canned tomatoes
2 large red bell peppers, cored, seeded, and diced
Coarse salt and freshly ground black pepper

In a large saucepan, heat the olive oil over medium-high heat. Add the garlic, bay leaves, and rosemary and cook, stirring, until the garlic is golden brown, about 1 minute. Remove the garlic, bay leaves, and rosemary and discard.

Add the lamb and cook until golden on all sides, about 5 minutes. Increase the heat to high, add the white wine, and simmer until reduced by one half, 1 to 2 minutes. Reduce the heat to low, add the tomatoes, bell peppers, and salt and pepper to taste, and simmer until the sauce is thick, 1½ to 2 hours. Add water if necessary during the cooking to thin the sauce.

The sauce can be refrigerated for up to 3 days or frozen for up to 1 month.

Ragù

In Italy, this is called sugo di carne, *the richest of all tomato sauces. In Bologna, half a cup heavy of cream is added at the end to make an even richer sauce. Enjoy this with pappardelle, penne, or rigatoni; it makes enough for a pound of pasta.*

Makes about 5 cups

1 ounce dried porcini mushrooms
2 tablespoons extra virgin olive oil
1 medium yellow onion, minced
1 large carrot, minced
1 stalk celery, minced
3 ounces prosciutto, finely diced
1 pound ground sirloin
1 cup dry red wine
6 cups peeled, seeded, and chopped fresh or canned tomatoes
Coarse salt and freshly ground black pepper
Freshly grated nutmeg

Cover the mushrooms with 1 cup boiling water. Let sit until the water is cool, about 30 minutes. Remove the mushrooms from the soaking liquid, strain, and coarsely chop; reserve the liquid.

In the meantime, in a large skillet over medium heat, heat the olive oil. Add the onion, carrot, and celery and cook until the onion turns golden brown, about 20 minutes. Add the prosciutto and ground sirloin, increase the heat to medium-high, and cook, breaking up the meat with a wooden spoon, until the meat is lightly browned, 8 to 10 minutes. Add the red wine and simmer until reduced by three quarters, about 5 minutes.

Add the porcini mushrooms, the reserved porcini water, and the tomatoes and bring to a boil. Season to taste with salt and pepper. Reduce the heat to low, cover, and simmer, stirring occasionally, until the flavors have melded and the sauce has thickened, about 2 hours. Taste and season with nutmeg.

This keeps in the refrigerator for up to 3 days and freezes well for up to 1 month.

Ketchup versus Salsa

Heinz conducted a survey in which they discovered 67 percent of those questioned misidentified ketchup as a vegetable, 16 percent said it was a fruit, and only 12 percent knew that it was a condiment. Sad state of affairs.

Heinz has known this all too well. In 1993, ketchup sales decreased 1.7 percent and salsa sales rose a whopping 10.5 percent. Tomato ketchup still sells much more in quantity but salsa costs more per ounce. Americans consume about four billion ounces of salsa compared to ten billion ounces of ketchup.

From Andrew Smith, *Pure Ketchup*

Summer Nectarine, Tomato, and Red Onion Salsa

The essence of summer comes through in the floral flavors of nectarines mixed with the sweetness of tomatoes. Serve this colorful salsa very simply with tortilla chips, or with grilled chicken breasts or butterflied poussin.

Makes about 2 cups

1 large ripe red tomato, diced
2 small ripe nectarines, halved, seeded, and diced
1/2 small red onion, diced
1 1/2 tablespoons thinly sliced fresh basil
1 1/2 tablespoons thinly sliced fresh mint
1 1/2 tablespoons coarsely chopped fresh cilantro
1/2 jalapeño or serrano pepper, seeded and minced
1 tablespoon fresh orange juice
1 tablespoon fresh lime juice
Coarse salt and freshly ground black pepper

In a medium bowl, toss together the tomato, nectarines, red onion, basil, mint, cilantro, jalapeño, orange juice, and lime juice. Season to taste with salt and pepper. Use within 2 hours.

Five-Tomato Salsa Cruda

The colors, flavors, and aroma of this fresh salsa ring with summer. Serve with tortilla chips or grilled fresh tuna steaks or swordfish, or as a topping for quesadillas or burritos. If a variety of tomatoes is unavailable, use all red tomatoes. Serve this the same day you make it.

Makes about 3¹/₂ cups

2 cups assorted cherry tomatoes of different
    sizes and colors (green, red, yellow, and
    orange), halved
1 large ripe red tomato, diced
1 large ripe yellow or orange tomato, diced
2 jalapeño or serrano peppers, seeded and
    minced
¹/₃ cup chopped fresh cilantro
¹/₄ cup plus 2 tablespoons fresh lime juice, or
    more if needed
3 green onions (white and green part), thinly
    sliced
Coarse salt

In a large bowl, mix together all the tomatoes, the jalapeño, cilantro, lime juice, green onions, and 1 teaspoon salt. Taste and season with additional lime juice and salt if needed.

Roasted Tomatillo and Avocado Salsa

This salsa goes well with simple seafood dishes such as grilled skewered shrimp or scallops, and with quesadillas, burritos, or tostadas. If fresh tomatillos are unavailable, you can substitute two twelve-ounce cans, drained and chopped. Use this the same day it is made.

Makes about 2¹/₂ cups

1 pound tomatillos, husked and rinsed
¹/₄ cup chopped fresh cilantro
1 garlic clove, minced
¹/₄ cup minced red onion
1 ear fresh corn, kernels removed and blanched
    in boiling water for 30 seconds
2 tablespoons fresh lime juice
1 jalapeño or serrano pepper, seeded and
    minced
1 medium avocado, halved, pitted, and diced
Coarse salt and freshly ground black pepper

Heat a cast-iron pan or ridged grill over medium-high heat for 15 minutes. Add the tomatillos and cook, shaking the pan occasionally, until golden on all sides and soft, about 20 minutes. Remove from the pan and cool completely.

Place the tomatillos in a food processor and process until almost smooth.

In a large bowl, mix together the tomatillos, cilantro, garlic, red onion, corn kernels, lime juice, and jalapeño. Add the avocado and stir gently. Season to taste with salt and pepper.

Chipotle Sauce

The first bite is deceptive. . . . The tomatoes offer a sweetness that seems to temper the heat, but then this smoked jalapeño sauce creeps up on you. This Mexican sauce is best served with beef or chicken enchiladas, drizzled with lots of sour cream and melted Jack cheese, or mixed with mayonnaise and slathered on a roast pork sandwich. Make it well in advance and store in the refrigerator or in the freezer for up to a month. Chipotles are dried jalapeños that are smoked over a fragrant wood fire. They are often canned in a spicy adobo sauce and are available at any store specializing in Mexican ingredients.

Makes 2 cups

1 tablespoon vegetable oil
1 small yellow onion, minced
1 garlic clove, minced
3 cups peeled, seeded, and chopped fresh or
    canned tomatoes
2 canned chipotle peppers in adobo, chopped
$1/2$ teaspoon dried oregano
Coarse salt

Heat the oil in a large saucepan over medium heat. Add the onion and garlic and cook, stirring, until soft, about 7 minutes. Add the tomatoes, chipotles, and oregano and simmer, uncovered, until thick, about 10 minutes.

Place the sauce in a blender and process until smooth. Season to taste with salt.

Salsa Verde

Salsa verde, literally "green sauce," is an Italian blend of all sorts of herbs, anchovies, capers, garlic, lemon juice, and virgin olive oil, served with bollito misto, *or mixed boiled meats. With the addition of chopped green tomatoes, it becomes a sensational sauce for crispy fried or grilled fish, chicken, or veal chops. Use this within two hours of making it.*

Makes about 3 cups

2 anchovy fillets, soaked in water for 10
    minutes, drained, and patted dry
2 medium green tomatoes, diced
$3/4$ cup chopped fresh flat-leaf parsley
$1/4$ cup snipped fresh chives
1 teaspoon chopped fresh thyme
1 teaspoon chopped fresh oregano
$1/2$ teaspoon chopped fresh sage
3 tablespoons capers, chopped
2 garlic cloves, minced
$1/4$ cup fresh lemon juice
$1/4$ cup extra virgin olive oil
Coarse salt and freshly ground black pepper

In a medium bowl, mash the anchovies with a fork. Add the tomatoes, parsley, chives, thyme, oregano, sage, capers, garlic, lemon juice, and olive oil, mix well, and season to taste with salt and pepper.

Green Tomato Raita

Raita, an Indian sauce with many variations, is designed for two purposes—to cool your mouth after eating spicy foods and to act as a digestive. (And it tastes good too!) Serve this with grilled lamb chops, spicy stewed chicken, or as a sauce for steamed basmati rice.

Makes about 3 cups

2 cups plain yogurt
1 small cucumber, peeled and diced
Coarse salt
1 teaspoon cumin seeds
1 garlic clove, minced
2 teaspoons grated fresh ginger
$1/2$ serrano pepper, seeded and minced
Freshly ground black pepper
1 large green tomato, diced

Place the yogurt in a cheesecloth-lined strainer set over a bowl. Let drain for at least 2 hours, or overnight.

Place the cucumber in a colander and salt lightly. Let sit for 15 minutes. Rinse and pat dry.

Place the cumin seeds in a small skillet set over medium-high heat, and stir until fragrant, 1 to 2 minutes. Remove from the pan and cool. Grind to a powder in a spice grinder or mortar and pestle.

Place the yogurt, cucumbers, cumin, garlic, ginger, and serrano pepper in a bowl and mix together. Season to taste with salt and pepper. Let sit for 1 to 4 hours before serving. Just before serving, stir in the tomato.

Mayonnaise

This can be stored in the refrigerator for up to one week. Nothing beats a fresh-off-the-vine tomato and homemade mayo sandwich.

Makes about 1 cup

$1/2$ cup olive oil
$1/2$ cup peanut oil
1 large egg yolk
1 teaspoon Dijon mustard
2 to 3 tablespoons fresh lemon juice
Coarse salt and freshly ground black pepper

In a 2-cup measure, combine the olive and peanut oils.

In a small bowl, whisk the egg yolk, mustard, and 1 tablespoon of the combined oils together until the mixture is thick and emulsified. Drop by drop, add the remaining oil, whisking constantly. After half of the oil has been added, add the remaining oil in a steady stream, whisking, until all of the oil has been added. Do not add the oil too quickly, or the mayonnaise will separate. Add the lemon juice and salt and pepper to taste.

Aïoli (Garlic Mayonnaise) Prepare the mayonnaise, adding 2 to 3 minced garlic cloves with the lemon juice. Although the basic mayonnaise can be made up to a week in advance, do not add the garlic until the day you will be serving it.

2 to 3 garlic cloves, minced

Rouille
("Rusty" Garlic Mayonnaise)

Rouille *means rust in French and that describes the reddish orange color of this spicy, garlicky mayonnaise. Add the cayenne pepper to taste, but it should have a little jolt of heat. Make this the same day you will be using it. Stir a large spoonful of rouille into a bowl of hot bouillabaisse for a classic French favorite.*

Makes 2 cups

3 garlic cloves
1 slice coarse white bread, crusts removed
2 tablespoons bottled clam juice, fish stock, or
   water
Large pinch of saffron threads
$^1/_4$ to $^1/_2$ teaspoon cayenne
$^3/_4$ cup olive oil
$^3/_4$ cup peanut oil
1 tablespoon Dijon mustard
2 large egg yolks, at room temperature
3 to 4 tablespoons fresh lemon juice
$^1/_4$ cup chopped fresh flat-leaf parsley
1 tablespoon tomato paste
1 large red bell pepper, roasted and pureed
   (page 13)
Coarse salt and freshly ground black pepper

Mash the garlic in a mortar and pestle or mince it with a knife, and set aside.

Put the bread in a bowl, drizzle with the clam juice, and sprinkle with the saffron and $^1/_4$ teaspoon cayenne. Add the mashed garlic and mash with a fork to make a paste.

In a 2-cup measure, combine the olive oil and peanut oil. In a large bowl, whisk together the mustard, egg yolks, and 1 tablespoon of the combined oils until an emulsion is formed and the mixture is homogeneous. Drop by drop, add the oil, whisking constantly. Do not add the oil too quickly; be sure that the emulsion is homogeneous before adding more oil.

Add the lemon juice, parsley, tomato paste, red pepper puree, and mashed bread. Season to taste with additional cayenne, salt, and pepper.

Tomato Mayonnaise with a Kick

Just what it says, a good old-fashioned homemade garlicky mayonnaise pushed to the edge with cayenne. If you
are squeezed for time, use one cup of prepared mayonnaise
as the base. Serve with grilled fresh tuna burgers, grilled
summer vegetables, or roasted potatoes. This will keep
well for up to a week; however, if you make it ahead,
don't add the garlic until the day of serving.

Makes about 1¼ cups

½ cup olive oil
½ cup vegetable, sunflower, or safflower oil
1 large egg yolk
1 tablespoon Dijon mustard
2 garlic cloves, minced
2 tablespoons fresh lemon juice
¼ cup tomato paste
1 teaspoon sweet paprika
Cayenne to taste
2 tablespoons snipped fresh chives
Coarse salt and freshly ground black pepper

Combine the olive oil and vegetable oil in a measuring cup.

In a small bowl, whisk together the egg yolk, mustard, and 1 tablespoon of the combined oils until an
emulsion is formed. Drop by drop, begin to add the
oil to the emulsion, whisking constantly. After half
of the oil has been added, continue to add the oil in
a steady stream, whisking constantly, until all of
the oil has been incorporated; do not add the oil too
quickly. Add the garlic, lemon juice, tomato paste,
paprika, cayenne, and chives and season with salt
and pepper.

firsts

Grilled Bread with Tomatoes and Olive Oil

In every village in Spain, they make a simple tapa called pan con tomate, *bread with tomatoes. Thick slabs of country-style bread are toasted over a wood fire until lightly golden. Then tomato halves are smeared all over the toast, leaving the seeds, juice, and pulp, and the bread is rubbed with garlic and fruity Spanish olive oil. As an optional garnish, thin slices of Manchego cheese can be added. Manchego cheese is a sheep's milk cheese available in many well-stocked cheese shops. Also Spanish olives, anchovies, or Spanish ham or prosciutto make a nice garnish.*

Serves 6

2 garlic cloves
Coarse salt
1/4 cup extra virgin olive oil
Twelve 3/4-inch-thick slices country-style bread
6 very ripe red tomatoes, halved
Freshly ground black pepper

■ optional garnish, choose one or a combination
1/2 cup green Spanish olives
12 anchovy fillets, soaked in cold water for 10
   minutes, drained, and patted dry
6 paper-thin slices Spanish ham or prosciutto
12 paper-thin slices Manchego

Preheat the broiler or an outdoor grill.

In a mortar and pestle, mash the garlic with a pinch of salt. Mix in the oil.

Broil or grill the bread until golden brown. Cup a tomato half in your palm, rub both sides of one toast with the tomato, squeezing slightly as you go to leave the pulp, seeds, and juice. Repeat with the remaining tomatoes and toasts.

Drizzle the olive oil over one side of the toasts and sprinkle with salt and pepper. Serve immediately, with the optional garnishes, if desired.

Grilled Bread with Roasted Tomato and Garlic Puree

Oven-roasted tomatoes and a healthy dose of roasted garlic make a simple puree that can be spread on grilled bread and served as a first course. You can also use the puree as a sauce for grilled chicken breasts, swordfish, or pork chops. Make it several hours in advance if you like, but don't spread it onto the grilled bread until you are ready to serve it.

Serves 6

8 plum tomatoes (about 1¼ pounds), cored and
   cut lengthwise in half
3 garlic bulbs
2 tablespoons extra virgin olive oil
½ teaspoon fresh lemon juice
Pinch of cayenne
1 tablespoon chopped fresh flat-leaf parsley,
   plus sprigs for garnish
1 teaspoon chopped fresh oregano, plus sprigs
   for garnish
Coarse salt and freshly ground black pepper
Twelve ½-inch-thick slices coarse-textured
   bread

Preheat the oven to 450°F.

Oil a baking sheet and place the tomatoes cut side down on the baking sheet. Bake until soft and lightly browned, about 45 minutes. Turn the tomatoes over and continue to bake until very soft and just slightly moist, about 45 minutes longer. Remove from the oven and cool for 10 minutes.

Meanwhile, place the garlic bulbs in a small baking dish. Drizzle with the olive oil and 1 tablespoon water and cover with foil. Bake until the garlic is soft, about 40 minutes.

Pass the garlic through a potato ricer or a food mill, and discard the skins. Reserve the garlic pulp and the garlic oil.

Peel the tomatoes and discard the skins. Chop the tomatoes and put in a small bowl. Add the reserved garlic and garlic oil, the lemon juice, cayenne, parsley, and oregano, and mix well. Season to taste with salt and pepper.

Under the broiler, toast the bread until light golden. Spread with the tomato-garlic puree and place on a platter. Serve immediately, garnished with oregano and parsley sprigs.

Grilled Bread with Red Relish

Mix roasted red and yellow peppers and ripe tomatoes together, flavor them with a good dose of garlic, harissa or cayenne, ground cumin, and lemon, and you get a full-flavored, versatile spread. Serve this with grilled tuna steaks or with toasted pita chips, or mix it with mayonnaise and spread it onto grilled chicken sandwiches. The relish can be made one day in advance; however, do not add the garlic until ready to use. Harissa can be purchased in a can or tube at most well-stocked grocery stores.

Serves 6

2 large red bell peppers (see page 12), peeled,
   seeded, and cut into $1/2$-inch dice
1 large yellow bell pepper (see page 12),
   peeled, seeded, and cut into $1/2$-inch dice
3 medium ripe red tomatoes, peeled, seeded,
   and chopped
2 garlic cloves, minced
$1^1/2$ teaspoons ground cumin
$1/4$ teaspoon harissa or cayenne
1 tablespoon extra virgin olive oil
2 tablespoons fresh lemon juice
$1/4$ cup chopped fresh flat-leaf parsley
Coarse salt and freshly ground black pepper
1 baguette, cut on a sharp diagonal, into
   $1/2$-inch slices, about 18 to 24

Preheat an outdoor grill or preheat the broiler.

Place the tomatoes in a frying pan and cook over high heat, stirring, until the liquid has evaporated, 6 to 8 minutes. Transfer the tomatoes to a bowl.

Add the red and yellow peppers, garlic, cumin, cayenne, olive oil, lemon juice, and parsley to the tomatoes. Mix well. Season to taste with salt and pepper. Place in the center of a serving dish.

Grill or broil the slices of bread on each side until light golden. Place the bread around the relish on the serving dish and serve.

Winter Tomatoes

Magaly Fabre cooks from her heart. She and her husband, Raymond, and their two sons operate Domaine de Mont Redon, a winery in Châteauneuf-du-Pape. One January Sunday, I had a lunch with Magaly that turned into an all-day affair. We ate stuffed tomatoes for lunch and later, as the sun was setting, I asked her for her secret for vine-ripened tomatoes in the middle of winter. Curiously enough, she told me, when the summer season ends, she tugs all of her tomato plants from the ground and hangs them, vine and all, in the cellar. Then, throughout the winter, she plucks almost-summer-like tomatoes from the dried vines.

Crostini Rossi

"Red toast" is made in Tuscany at the height of tomato season and served as a celebration of the most glorious of fruits. Be sure to choose tomatoes that are ripe, sweet, and fresh off the vine. Mashed anchovies and chopped black olives are a nice addition to the tomato mixture.

Serves 6

2 large ripe red tomatoes, peeled, cored, seeded, and chopped
1 slice country-style bread
3 tablespoons red wine vinegar, or more to taste
3 tablespoons extra virgin olive oil
1 tablespoon capers
1 garlic clove, chopped
3 tablespoons chopped fresh flat-leaf parsley, plus a few sprigs for garnish
2 teaspoons chopped fresh thyme, plus a few sprigs for garnish
Pinch of crushed red pepper flakes
Coarse salt and freshly ground black pepper
6 large $^{1}/_{4}$-inch-thick slices country-style bread

Place the tomatoes in a strainer set over a bowl and let drain for 15 minutes.

Place the slice of sourdough bread on a plate and drizzle the vinegar over the top. Let sit for 1 minute, and then gently wring it out. Put the bread, 2 tablespoons of the olive oil, the capers, garlic, parsley, thyme, crushed red pepper, and tomatoes in the bowl of a food processor and pulse

a few times. Season with salt and pepper. (This can be done up to 4 hours ahead. Taste and season with salt, pepper, and vinegar if necessary before serving.)

Preheat the oven to 425°F or preheat an outdoor grill.

Brush the slices of bread lightly with the remaining 1 tablespoon olive oil and toast or grill until golden on each side. Spread the crushed tomatoes on top of the toasts, garnish with parsley and thyme sprigs, and serve immediately.

Fried Green Tomato "Sandwiches"

*T*ake green tomato slices and sandwich herbed goat cheese *in between them, fry them, and you have a sumptuous first course. If you'd like, serve them with homemade garlic mayonnaise (page 38) made spicy-hot with a dash of cayenne. Try adding other ingredients to the filling in place of the herbs: thin slivers of sun-dried tomatoes, chopped black olives, capers, or sliced green onions.*

Serves 6

4 ounces fresh goat cheese
1/4 cup finely snipped fresh chives
1 tablespoon chopped fresh flat-leaf parsley,
    plus a few sprigs for garnish
2 teaspoons chopped fresh thyme, plus a few
    sprigs for garnish
2 teaspoons chopped fresh oregano, plus a few
    sprigs for garnish
1 teaspoon finely grated lemon zest
Coarse salt and freshly ground black pepper
5 to 6 medium green tomatoes (about 2 1/2
    pounds), cut into 1/4-inch slices
1 cup all-purpose flour
3 large eggs, beaten
2 tablespoons milk
1 1/2 cups yellow or white cornmeal
2 tablespoons olive oil

In a small bowl, mash together the goat cheese, chives, parsley, thyme, oregano, and lemon zest. Season to taste with salt and pepper. Place the tomatoes in a single layer on paper towels and salt lightly.

Place the flour in a bowl. Place the eggs and milk in a separate bowl. Place the cornmeal in a third bowl. Season all three with salt and pepper. With paper towels, pat the tomatoes dry. Place half of the tomatoes in a single layer on a work surface. Spread the cheese mixture evenly over the slices. Top with the remaining tomato slices, making sandwiches. One by one, place the tomato sandwiches in the flour. Press down lightly, turn to coat, then tap off the excess. Next dip in the egg mixture to coat completely, then dip in the cornmeal and tap off the excess. (You can prepare the tomatoes several hours in advance to this point.) Set aside on a plate.

Preheat the oven to 375°F.

Heat 2 tablespoons of the olive oil in a large skillet over medium-low heat until rippling. Cook the tomato sandwiches in batches, in a single layer, until they are golden on each side and the walls of the tomatoes are fork-tender, 10 to 12 minutes. Remove from the pan and drain on paper towels, then place the sandwiches on a baking sheet and keep warm on the top rack of the oven until all of the sandwiches are cooked.

To serve, place the tomato sandwiches on a platter and garnish with the herb sprigs.

Polenta and Tomato Gratins

Sun-dried tomatoes, Fontina, and mozzarella baked in between layers of polenta make a terrific first course or vegetarian main course. These can be assembled several hours or even a day in advance and baked just before serving.

Serves 6

Coarse salt
2 cups polenta or coarse cornmeal
3 tablespoons unsalted butter, at room
     temperature
Freshly ground black pepper
1½ cups coarsely grated Fontina (about 6
     ounces)
1½ cups coarsely grated mozzarella (about 6
     ounces)
½ cup freshly grated Parmigiano-Reggiano
¾ cup thinly sliced Sun-Dried (page 13) or
     Oven-Dried Tomatoes (page 14)

Bring 8 cups water to a boil in a large saucepan over high heat and add 1 teaspoon salt. Lower the heat to medium and slowly add the polenta, whisking constantly. Continue to whisk until the mixture thickens, 4 to 5 minutes. Change to a wooden spoon and simmer over low heat, stirring occasionally, until the polenta is very thick and a spoon stands in the center, 20 to 25 minutes.

Add the butter and mix well. Remove from the heat. Season to taste with salt and pepper.

Meanwhile, preheat the oven to 425°F. Butter six 4-inch round gratin dishes.

In a bowl, mash the Fontina, half of the mozzarella, and half of the Parmigiano together with a fork. Season with pepper.

Spread half of the hot polenta in the gratin dishes, distributing it evenly. Spoon the cheese mixture on top of the polenta, distributing it evenly. Top with the tomatoes. Spread the remaining polenta on top and sprinkle with the remaining mozzarella and Parmigiano. (The gratins can be prepared 1 day ahead of time; store in the refrigerator. Bring to room temperature before baking.)

Bake on the top rack of the oven for 10 to 15 minutes, until the gratins are heated through and the edges are bubbling and golden.

Preheat the broiler. Place the gratins under the broiler and broil until golden, 1 to 2 minutes; watch them very closely. Serve immediately.

Tomato-Rice "Olives"

These aren't olives at all, but instead small balls of deep-fried rice the size of an olive. A favorite in northern Italy, they are crispy and golden on the outside, creamy and sweet/tangy in the center. This makes lots, so invite a crowd.

Makes about 60

2 tablespoons extra virgin olive oil
$1/2$ cup finely minced onions
1 cup arborio rice
$1^1/4$ cups Chicken Stock (page 78)
$1^1/4$ cups milk
$2/3$ cup tomato paste
Coarse salt and freshly ground black pepper
$1/4$ cup freshly grated Parmigiano-Reggiano
1 cup all-purpose flour
4 large eggs
4 cups toasted fresh bread crumbs, finely ground
Vegetable and olive oil for frying

Heat the extra virgin olive oil in a large saucepan over medium heat. Add the onions and sauté until soft, about 5 minutes. Add the rice and cook, stirring constantly, for 2 minutes.

Meanwhile, place the chicken broth and milk in a saucepan and heat just to a simmer.

Add the hot broth mixture to the rice, along with half of the tomato paste and salt and pepper to taste. Bring to a simmer, reduce the heat to low, cover, and cook slowly until the rice is tender, about 20 minutes. If the rice dries out during cooking, add hot water as necessary.

Stir in the remaining tomato paste and the Parmigiano-Reggiano. Cool completely.

Form the rice mixture into small olive-size balls, using slightly less than a tablespoon of mixture for each one. Place the flour in a bowl. Whisk the eggs and $1/2$ cup water in another bowl. Place the bread crumbs in a third bowl.

Roll the rice olives in the flour, then the egg, then the bread crumbs, coating them completely. Place on a baking sheet until you are ready to cook them. (These can be prepared up to 1 day in advance up to this point.)

In a deep pan, heat 1 inch of a combination of vegetable oil and olive oil to 375°F. Fry the rice olives in batches until golden on all sides, 1 to $1^1/2$ minutes. Drain and serve immediately.

Vegetable Garden Soufflés

One day you walk out to the garden to find juicy sun-ripened tomatoes of every shape, size, and color and sweet red, green, and yellow bell peppers all ripening on the vine. What to do?! Gather them into the basket, bring them into the kitchen, and stew them together. Fold the stew into a soufflé base to make individual soufflés to serve as a fresh and light first course or as a lunch main course with a green salad. If you make the stew a couple of days ahead so that the flavors meld, it's even better.

Serves 6

2 tablespoons extra virgin olive oil
1 small yellow onion, minced
1 garlic clove, minced
2 small bell peppers, any color, cored, seeded, and diced
2 large ripe tomatoes, any color, peeled, seeded, and chopped
Coarse salt and freshly ground black pepper
4 tablespoons unsalted butter
$1/4$ cup all-purpose flour
$1^1/2$ cups half-and-half
6 large eggs, separated
1 cup freshly grated Parmigiano-Reggiano
Pinch of cayenne

Heat the olive oil in a large frying pan over medium-high heat. Add the onion, garlic, and peppers and cook until soft, about 10 minutes. Reduce the heat to medium-low, add the tomatoes, and cook, covered, stirring occasionally, for 10 minutes. Remove the cover and cook until the liquid has reduced by half, 1 to 2 minutes. Let cool for 15 min-

utes. Season to taste with salt and pepper. (The vegetables can be prepared up to 2 days in advance; cover and refrigerate. Bring to room temperature before proceeding.)

Meanwhile, preheat the oven to 450°F. Grease six individual 1-cup soufflé dishes. Make an aluminum foil collar for each one by folding a sheet of foil lengthwise in half and then in half again. Butter one side of the foil well, wrap it around the soufflé dish so it extends 1 to $1^1/2$ inches above the rim, and secure by tying a piece of string around the foil.

Melt the butter in a medium saucepan over medium heat. Whisk in the flour and let the mixture bubble for 2 minutes. Meanwhile, in a small saucepan, scald the half-and-half.

Add the half-and-half to the flour/butter, whisking rapidly. Cook, stirring, for a few minutes, until thick and smooth. Add the tomato mixture and stir well. Remove the saucepan from the heat and add the egg yolks one at a time, stirring well after each addition. Add $1/2$ cup of the Parmigiano-Reggiano and the cayenne. Season to taste with salt and pepper.

In a large bowl, with an electric mixer beat the egg whites until stiff. Fold half of the whites into the egg yolk mixture to lighten it, then fold in the remaining whites. Distribute the mixture evenly among the soufflé dishes. Sprinkle with the remaining $1/2$ cup Parmigiano. Place the soufflé dishes on a baking sheet. Bake in the center of the oven until the tops are well browned and the soufflés do not jiggle when shaken, 10 to 15 minutes. Serve immediately.

Grilled Potatoes with Tomato Harissa

Red and sweet potatoes roasted with garlic and herbs are good in themselves, but here they are really just a vehicle for eating the delicious hot pepper and tomato sauce. The sweetness of stewed sun-dried tomatoes tempers the heat of harissa, the spicy North African red pepper condiment. And tomato harissa is wonderfully versatile: Try it as a dipping sauce for other roasted vegetables, as a sauce for skewers of grilled fish, chicken, or pork, or as a flavoring for mayonnaise for a roasted lamb sandwich.

Serves 6

3/4 cup sun-dried tomatoes in oil (about 4
    ounces), drained and patted dry
1 1/2 to 2 tablespoons harissa
1 small garlic clove, minced, plus 5 garlic
    cloves, unpeeled, halved
Coarse salt and freshly ground black pepper
4 medium red potatoes (about 1 1/4 pounds), cut
    into 1-inch pieces
2 large sweet potatoes (about 1 1/4 pounds), cut
    into 1-inch pieces
1 tablespoon extra virgin olive oil
2 sprigs fresh oregano
2 sprigs fresh thyme

Bring 1 1/2 cups water to a boil in a small saucepan. Add the tomatoes, reduce the heat, and simmer slowly until the tomatoes are soft, 10 minutes. Cool slightly.

Transfer the tomatoes with their liquid to a blender and process until very smooth. Add the harissa, minced garlic, and salt and pepper to taste and process until smooth. Thin with just enough water to make a barely fluid paste. Set aside. (This sauce can be made 2 days in advance and stored in the refrigerator. Bring to room temperature before proceeding.)

Preheat the oven to 375°F.

Rinse the potatoes and, while still wet, place in a single layer in a baking dish. Drizzle with the oil and turn the potatoes to coat. Add the unpeeled garlic and the herb sprigs and season with salt and pepper. Cover with foil and cook until tender, 45 to 60 minutes. Remove from the pan. (The potatoes can be prepared 1 day ahead of time to this point.)

Meanwhile, preheat an outdoor grill or a ridged cast-iron grill.

Brush the potatoes with olive oil, place them on the grill or in the grill pan, and cook, turning occasionally, until golden and crisp, 4 to 5 minutes.

To serve, place the potatoes on a platter and drizzle with the tomato harissa sauce or serve it on the side.

Mussels with Tomato and Feta

In *Greece, the first course is called* meze, *oftentimes an elaborate array of cold and hot dishes, and this sizzling-hot casserole of briny mussels, tomatoes, and feta cheese is a favorite. Place it in the center of the table with a big basket of crusty rolls to sop up the sauce. The success of this simple dish depends upon impeccably fresh shellfish, flavorful tomatoes, and pungent imported feta; shrimp or clams can be substituted for the mussels.*

Serves 6

2 tablespoons olive oil
1/3 cup minced yellow onion
4 large ripe red tomatoes, peeled, seeded, and
    chopped, or 5 cups seeded and chopped
    canned tomatoes
1 cup dry white wine
1/4 teaspoon dried oregano
Pinch of crushed red pepper flakes
1 teaspoon red wine vinegar
2 pounds mussels, scrubbed and beards
    removed
6 ounces feta cheese, crumbled
Coarse salt and freshly ground black pepper
1 tablespoon coarsely chopped fresh flat-leaf
    parsley

Heat the olive oil in a large, deep skillet over low heat. Cook the onion until soft, about 7 minutes. Increase the heat to high, add the tomatoes, white wine, oregano, crushed red pepper, and vinegar and bring to a boil. Stir well, reduce the heat to low, and simmer, uncovered, until thick, 20 to 25 minutes.

Add the mussels, cover the pan, and cook until the mussels open: Remove the cover periodically and remove the mussels from the pan with tongs as they open, placing them in a bowl. Set the skillet aside and cool the mussels. Discard any mussels that have not opened.

Preheat the oven to 400°F.

Remove the mussels from the shells and discard the shells. Add the mussels to the tomato sauce, add the feta, and stir well. Season to taste with salt and pepper. (This dish can be made up to 1 day in advance to this point and stored in the refrigerator.)

Place the mussel mixture in a 2-quart baking dish and bake until it bubbles around the edges, about 10 minutes or 15 minutes if refrigerated. Garnish with the parsley and serve.

Clams Mexicana

The natural acidity of tomatoes gives shellfish a real boost. You see the shellfish-tomato combination all over the world, in hundreds of different dishes, from pasta to shellfish soups and stews. Here, small briny clams are stewed with tomatoes, garlic, cilantro, marjoram, and jalapeños and served with warm flour tortillas to collect the flavorful juices.

Serves 6

1 cup dry white wine
3 pounds Manila or littleneck clams, scrubbed
2 tablespoons olive oil
1 medium yellow onion, chopped
3 garlic cloves, minced
3 medium ripe red tomatoes, peeled, seeded, and chopped, or 2 cups seeded and chopped canned tomatoes
2 tablespoons chopped fresh flat-leaf parsley
2 tablespoons chopped fresh cilantro, plus whole sprigs for garnish
$1/2$ teaspoon dried marjoram
$1/2$ teaspoon ground coriander
2 jalapeños, seeded and chopped
Coarse salt and freshly ground black pepper
Warm flour tortillas

Heat the white wine in a large skillet. Add the clams, cover, and cook over high heat until they open, 3 to 5 minutes. Remove the clams from the pan, discarding any that have not opened, and set aside. Reserve the cooking liquid.

Heat the oil in another large skillet over medium heat. Add the onion and garlic and cook until soft, about 7 minutes. Increase the heat to high, add the reserved clam liquid, and simmer until reduced by half, 2 to 3 minutes. Add the tomatoes, parsley, cilantro, marjoram, coriander, and jalapeños and cook until the sauce thickens slightly, about 5 minutes. Season to taste with salt and pepper. Add the clams and stir together until hot, 1 minute.

To serve, spoon the clams into a large bowl and garnish with cilantro sprigs. Serve with warm flour tortillas.

Tomato Statistics

The fruit that we now call a vegetable, despite or in spite of a myriad of appellations and clouds of mystery, has become one of the most popular foods on the globe.

Consider these statistics:

- Well over one and a half billion tons of tomatoes are grown worldwide.
- The United States commercially produces the largest share, 16 percent of the world's tomatoes.
- Twenty-five to forty million Americans grow tomatoes.
- Americans eat more than twelve million tomatoes each year.
- The average American eats eighteen pounds of fresh tomatoes each year.
- The average American eats seventy pounds of processed tomatoes each year.
- The United States imports four hundred thousand tons of tomatoes yearly, mostly from Mexico.
- The dollar worth to American farmers is more than one and a half billion dollars.

From Andrew Smith, *The Tomato in America*

Oysters with Fresh Tomato Horseradish

Opening oysters isn't the easiest job, but once you've mastered the task, nothing could be simpler and more refreshing than serving a platter of ice-cold oysters on the half-shell with this tart and hot sauce made from chopped tomatoes, shallots, grated horseradish, and plenty of coarsely cracked black pepper. Alongside, serve buttered rye bread and chilled glasses of Champagne.

Serves 6

1/3 cup dry white wine
3 tablespoons Champagne vinegar or white
    wine vinegar, or more to taste
2 medium shallots, finely minced
1 large ripe red tomato, peeled, seeded, and cut
    into 1/4-inch dice
1 tablespoon grated fresh horseradish
1/4 teaspoon coarsely ground black pepper
36 oysters, scrubbed
Lemon wedges
Fresh flat-leaf parsley

In a small serving bowl, combine the wine, vinegar, shallots, tomato, horseradish, and pepper. Season with additional vinegar if needed. (This sauce can be made several hours in advance and set aside at room temperature until ready to use.)

Place the bowl of tomato horseradish on a platter and surround it with a bed of crushed or shaved ice.

With an oyster knife, carefully open the oysters. Discard the top shells and detach the oysters from the bottom shells, reserving the liqueur in the shell. Place the oysters in the half-shell on the ice. Serve immediately, garnished with lemon wedges and parsley

Smoked Shrimp Quesadillas with Tomato-Lime Salsa

Cooked black beans, diced avocado, and/or fresh corn can be added to this easy cherry tomato salsa. If smoked shrimp are unavailable, substitute flaked smoked trout or smoked mussels or scallops.

Serves 6

6 ounces smoked shrimp
³/₄ cup coarsely grated mozzarella (about 3 ounces)
³/₄ cup coarsely grated pepper-Jack cheese (about 3 ounces)
³/₄ cup coarsely grated white Cheddar (about 3 ounces)
5 green onions, thinly sliced
Six 8- to 9-inch flour tortillas
1 recipe Tomato-Lime Salsa (recipe follows)

Combine the smoked shrimp, mozzarella, Jack cheese, Cheddar, and green onions in a bowl and mix well. Distribute the mixture evenly among 3 of the tortillas, and top with the remaining tortillas. (The quesadillas can be assembled up to a day in advance.)

Heat a nonstick skillet over medium heat, add a quesadilla, and cook until the cheese melts, 2 to 3 minutes. Flip the quesadilla and cook for 2 to 3 minutes longer. Transfer to a plate, cover to keep warm, and continue with the remaining quesadillas.

Cut each quesadilla into 6 wedges and serve immediately, with the salsa.

Tomato-Lime Salsa

Makes 2¹/₂ cups

1 pound assorted yellow, orange, and red cherry tomatoes, quartered
¹/₄ cup plus 1 tablespoon chopped fresh cilantro
¹/₄ cup minced red onions
3 tablespoons fresh lime juice
1 jalapeño or serrano pepper, seeded and minced
Coarse salt and freshly ground black pepper

Place the tomatoes, cilantro, red onions, lime juice, and chile pepper in a bowl. Mix well and season with salt and pepper.

Orzo-and-Scallop-Stuffed Tomatoes

Growing up, when I visited my grandparents' farm in the Berkshire Hills of Massachusetts, my grandfather often made stuffed tomatoes for Saturday lunch during the summer. We kids considered stuffed tomatoes "old folk's food." Not anymore. In this sophisticated version, peak-of-the-season tomatoes are stuffed with tiny orzo beads, scallops, crunchy cucumbers, sweet corn, and dill. You can prepare them a few hours ahead and store them in the refrigerator until serving time.

Serves 6

$^3/_4$ cup orzo
3 tablespoons extra virgin olive oil
6 large firm but ripe red tomatoes
Coarse salt
6 ounces bay or sea scallops, side muscle
    removed
Freshly ground black pepper
1 cup fresh corn kernels, blanched in boiling
    water for 2 minutes
$^1/_2$ cup diced peeled cucumbers
$^1/_3$ cup thinly sliced green onions
2 tablespoons fresh lemon juice
$^1/_4$ cup chopped fresh dill, plus a few sprigs for
    garnish

Bring a large saucepan of salted water to a boil. Add the orzo and cook until tender, 5 to 8 minutes. Drain the orzo and immediately toss it with 1 tablespoon of the olive oil. Cover and refrigerate until well chilled, 1 hour or up to 24 hours.

In the meantime, cut a $^3/_4$-inch slice off the stem end of each tomato; save the tops. With a spoon, carefully scoop out the pulp and reserve for another use. Sprinkle the inside of the tomatoes with salt and place the tomatoes upside down on paper towels to drain for 1 hour.

If using sea scallops, slice them into $^1/_4$-inch slices.

Heat 1 tablespoon of the olive oil in a large frying pan over medium-high heat. Add the scallops and cook until almost firm to the touch, 2 minutes. Season with salt and pepper, remove from the pan, and cool.

In a large bowl, mix the orzo, scallops, corn, cucumbers, green onions, lemon juice, dill, and the remaining 1 tablespoon olive oil. Season to taste with salt and pepper.

Spoon the orzo and scallop mixture into the tomatoes, distributing it evenly. Place the tops on the tomatoes and chill for at least 30 minutes or up to 6 hours.

To serve, place the tomatoes on serving plates and garnish with dill sprigs.

Miss Judy's Rice-Stuffed Tomatoes

*H*ere's another spin on stuffed tomatoes given to me by *Judy Witts Francini from Florence, Italy. As the starchy short-grain white rice cooks inside hollowed-out tomatoes, it absorbs all the sweet flavors of the tomatoes and fresh basil. These can be assembled up to a day in advance and baked just before they are to be served.*

Serves 6

6 large ripe red tomatoes
Coarse salt
3/4 cup short-grain arborio rice
1/4 cup extra virgin olive oil
2 garlic cloves, crushed
3 tablespoons fresh basil leaves torn into small
    pieces
1/2 teaspoon dried oregano
Freshly ground black pepper

Cut a 3/4-inch slice off the stem end of each tomato; save the tops. With a spoon, carefully scoop out the pulp. Chop it and set it aside in a bowl. Sprinkle the inside of the tomatoes with salt and place the tomatoes upside down on paper towels to drain for 1 hour.

Bring 2 cups of water to a boil in a saucepan. Add 1/4 teaspoon salt. Add the rice, reduce the heat to low, and cook, covered, until the rice is almost tender, about 10 minutes. Drain the rice.

Combine the rice, 2 tablespoons of the olive oil, the garlic cloves, basil, oregano, the reserved tomato pulp, and salt and pepper to taste in a bowl. Mix well and let sit for 1 hour.

Preheat the oven to 350°F.

Sprinkle the inside of the tomatoes with pepper. Remove the garlic cloves from the rice and distribute the rice evenly among the tomatoes. Cover with the reserved tops. Place in a baking dish, drizzle with the remaining 2 tablespoons olive oil, and bake until soft, about 45 minutes.

Serve warm or at room temperature.

Tomatoes Stuffed with Tuna, Capers, and Herbs

Tomatoes filled with tuna-mayo-celery salad used to be de rigueur at ladies' luncheons. Here, capers, pine nuts, and herbs update and revitalize this classic. Serve as a first course or as a light entrée with a mixed green salad.

Serves 6

6 medium firm but ripe red tomatoes
Coarse salt
$^1/_3$ cup capers, drained
$^1/_4$ cup pine nuts, toasted
$^2/_3$ cup chopped fresh flat-leaf parsley
1 teaspoon chopped fresh oregano
2 garlic cloves, minced
$^1/_4$ cup extra virgin olive oil
1 tablespoon fresh lemon juice
Two 5-ounce cans Italian tuna packed in oil,
    drained
Freshly ground black pepper

Cut a $^3/_4$-inch slice off the stem end of each tomato; save the tops. With a spoon, carefully scoop out the pulp and discard. Sprinkle the inside of the tomatoes with salt and place the tomatoes upside down on paper towels to drain for 1 hour.

In a medium bowl, mix together the capers, pine nuts, parsley, oregano, garlic, olive oil, and lemon juice. Add the flaked tuna and mix together gently. Season to taste with salt and pepper.

Sprinkle the inside of the tomatoes with pepper. Distribute the tuna evenly among them, cover with the reserved tops, and serve. (These can be made several hours in advance and refrigerated; bring to room temperature before serving.)

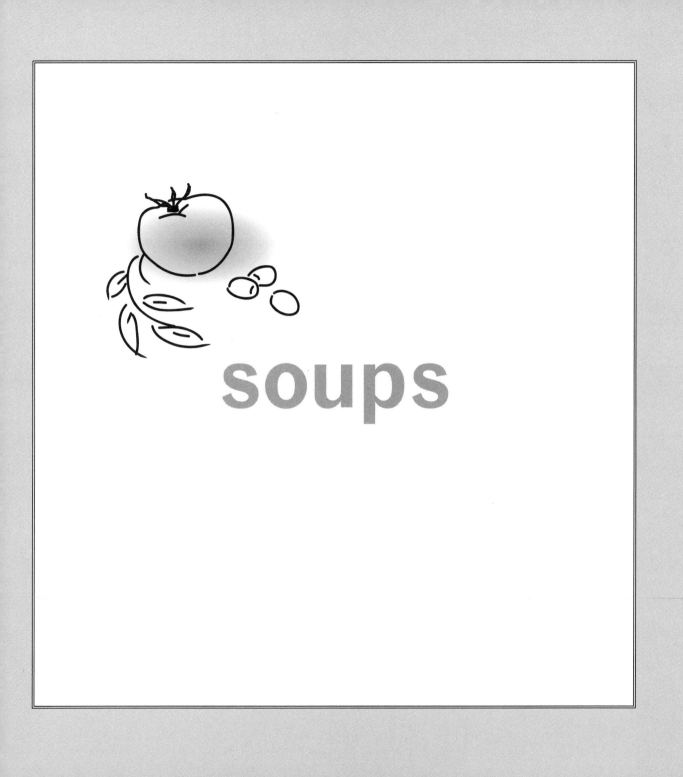

soups

Tomato-Basil Soup with Crispy Polenta Sticks

Is there any better combination of flavors in summertime than sweet, fresh ripe tomatoes and tender basil, plucked from the garden? Red or yellow tomatoes can be used.

Serves 6

1 tablespoon olive oil
1 medium yellow onion, chopped
8 sprigs fresh basil, tied together with kitchen string, plus ¹/₂ cup loosely packed fresh basil leaves, cut into thin strips
8 large ripe tomatoes, peeled, seeded, and chopped
4 cups Chicken Stock (page 78)
Coarse salt and freshly ground black pepper

Heat the olive oil in a large soup pot over medium-high heat. Add the onion and cook, stirring occasionally, until soft, about 7 minutes. Add the basil sprigs, tomatoes, chicken stock, and 1 cup water and bring to a boil over high heat. Reduce the heat to medium-low and simmer until the liquid is reduced by one quarter, about 20 minutes. Cool for 10 minutes. Remove the basil and discard.

In a blender, puree the soup in several batches un-til smooth, 2 to 3 minutes per batch. Strain into a clean pot and bring to a simmer over medium heat. Season to taste with salt and pepper. (The soup can be made up to 1 day in advance and stored in the refrigerator until ready to serve. Reheat the soup over medium heat until hot, about 5 minutes.)

To serve, ladle the soup into bowls and garnish with the basil leaves or with 3 to 4 crispy polenta sticks.

Crispy Polenta Sticks

Coarse salt
¹/₂ cup polenta or coarse cornmeal
¹/₄ cup freshly grated Parmigiano-Reggiano
1 teaspoon chopped fresh rosemary
1 tablespoon unsalted butter, at room temperature
Freshly ground black pepper
About 2 cups all-purpose flour
4 cups canola oil

Bring 3 cups water to a boil in a medium saucepan over high heat and add ¹/₂ teaspoon salt. Lower the heat to medium and slowly add the polenta, whisking constantly. Continue to whisk the mixture for 10 minutes. Change to a wooden spoon and continue to simmer, stirring periodically, until the spoon stands in the polenta, 20 to 25 minutes.

Add the Parmigiano-Reggiano, rosemary, and butter and mix well. Season with salt and pepper. Spread the hot polenta in a buttered 9 × 5-inch loaf pan. Smooth the top with a rubber spatula and let cool in the refrigerator until firm. (The polenta can be made up to 5 days in advance.)

About 30 minutes before you're ready to serve the soup, cut the polenta into sticks 1/2 inch thick and 3 inches long; this will make 18 to 24 sticks. Remove from the pan and toss the polenta sticks carefully in flour to dust them lightly.

Heat the canola oil in a deep heavy saucepan to 375°F. Drop the polenta sticks into hot fat, a few at a time. Do not overcrowd the pan. Fry until golden brown, 1 to 2 minutes. Remove with a slotted spoon and drain on paper towels. (If you need to reheat the polenta sticks, place them on a baking sheet in a single layer and heat in a 400°F oven until hot, 10 minutes.)

Pappa al Pomodoro

Pappa al pomodoro is a rich Tuscan tomato and garlic soup made with torn pieces of stale Tuscan bread, which is always unsalted, and plenty of basil. Pappa means mush, which describes this thick soup.

Serves 6

1/4 cup extra virgin olive oil
12 garlic cloves, thinly sliced
5 large very ripe red tomatoes, peeled, seeded, and diced
6 ounces stale coarse-textured country-style bread
3 cups Chicken Stock (page 78)
Coarse salt and freshly ground black pepper
1/3 cup fresh basil leaves, finely torn into 1/4- to 1/2-inch pieces
1 teaspoon chopped fresh oregano

Heat the olive oil in a large soup pot over medium heat. Add the garlic and stir for 30 seconds. Add the tomatoes and bread and cook until the bread falls apart, 5 to 10 minutes. Increase the heat to high, add the stock, 2 cups water, and salt and pepper to taste, and bring to a boil. Reduce the heat and simmer for 15 minutes, stirring occasionally. Turn the heat off, cover, and let sit for 5 minutes.

Add the basil and oregano and stir well. Season to taste with salt and pepper. (This soup can be made 1 day in advance; reheat over medium-low heat before serving.)

Ladle into bowls and serve immediately.

Tomato and Orange Soup with Orange Butter

The zesty flavor combination of orange and dill brings a simple tomato soup alive. Both the soup and orange butter can be made well in advance.

Serves 6 to 8

1 tablespoon olive oil
1 medium yellow onion, chopped
Zest of 1 orange, removed with a vegetable peeler (see Note), plus 1½ teaspoons grated orange zest
8 large ripe red tomatoes, peeled, seeded, and chopped
4 cups Chicken Stock (page 78)
3 tablespoons unsalted butter at room temperature
3 tablespoons plus 1 teaspoon fresh orange juice
4 tablespoons chopped fresh dill
Coarse salt and freshly ground black pepper

Heat the olive oil in a large soup pot over medium-high heat. Add the onion and cook, stirring occasionally, until soft, about 7 minutes. Add the strips of orange peel, the tomatoes, chicken stock, and 1 cup water. Bring to a boil over high heat. Reduce the heat to medium-low and simmer until the liquid is reduced by one quarter, about 20 minutes. Cool for 10 minutes.

In the meantime, in a small bowl, mash together the grated orange zest, butter, 1 teaspoon of the orange juice, and 1 tablespoon of the dill until smooth. Season to taste with salt and pepper. Place the butter in the center of a small piece of plastic wrap and shape it into a log ¾ inch in diameter. Wrap the plastic wrap over the butter and roll to make a sausage-like shape. Twist the ends of the plastic wrap in opposite directions to seal, and refrigerate. (This can be made up to 1 week in advance.)

In a blender, puree the soup in several batches until smooth, 2 to 3 minutes per batch. Strain into a clean pot and bring to a simmer over medium heat. Add the remaining 3 tablespoons dill and 3 tablespoons orange juice and season with salt and pepper. (The soup can be made up to 2 days in advance and stored in the refrigerator until ready to serve. Reheat the soup over medium heat until hot, about 5 minutes.)

To serve, ladle the soup into bowls and top each with a slice of the orange butter.

NOTE: *Use a vegetable peeler to remove the peel from the orange in strips. If any white pith remains on the back of the orange peel, scrape it away with a knife.*

Tomato-Garlic Soup

When my farmers' market is brimming with ripe tomatoes, braids of new garlic, and herbs such as rosemary, thyme, and oregano, I make this soup. Because it's so simple, its success depends upon the very freshest and most flavorful summer ingredients; it's not one to make in the winter. Don't be hesitant about seasoning it well with salt, which enhances both the natural acidity and the sweetness of tomatoes.

Serves 6

4 ounces dried small pasta shells
1 teaspoon olive oil
1 tablespoon extra virgin olive oil
1 small red onion, minced
$^1/_2$ cup garlic cloves, coarsely chopped
4 medium ripe red or yellow tomatoes, peeled, seeded, and chopped
4 cups Chicken Stock (page 78)
1 tablespoon chopped fresh flat-leaf parsley
1 tablespoon snipped fresh chives
1 teaspoon chopped fresh oregano
1 teaspoon chopped fresh thyme
$^1/_4$ teaspoon chopped fresh rosemary
1 tablespoon red wine vinegar
Coarse salt and freshly ground black pepper

In a large pot, bring 3 quarts water and 2 tablespoons salt to a boil. Add the pasta and cook until al dente, 7 to 10 minutes. Drain the pasta and immediately toss it with the 1 teaspoon olive oil.

In a soup pot, heat the extra virgin olive oil over low heat. Add the onion and garlic and sauté slowly, stirring occasionally so the garlic doesn't burn, until the onions are soft, about 10 minutes. Add the tomatoes, stock, 1 cup water, the parsley, chives, oregano, thyme, and rosemary, bring to a simmer, and simmer for 20 minutes.

Add the pasta, vinegar, and salt and pepper to taste. Simmer until the pasta is warm, 2 minutes.

Ladle the soup into individual bowls and serve immediately.

Andy Warhol, Pop Art, and Campbell's Soup

Pop artist Andy Warhol and the Campbell's soup can became almost synonymous after Warhol painted the Campbell's logo over and over again in the early sixties. When Campbell decided to redesign the label in 1994, they sponsored a contest to search for a new design and the "next Andy Warhol."

Creamy Tomato Bisque

Tomato bisque is a thick soup of vine-ripened summer tomatoes and a dose of cream for sweetness. Puree this soup in a blender, rather than a food processor, to give it a velvety texture.

Serves 6

1 tablespoon olive oil
1 medium red onion, chopped
8 large ripe red tomatoes, peeled, seeded, and chopped
4 cups Chicken Stock (page 78)
1 teaspoon sugar
1 cup heavy cream
Coarse salt and freshly ground black pepper
$^1/_4$ cup chopped fresh mint

Heat the olive oil in a large soup pot over medium-high heat. Add the onion and cook, stirring occasionally, until soft, about 7 minutes. Add the tomatoes, chicken stock, and sugar and bring to a boil over high heat. Reduce the heat to medium-low and simmer until the liquid is reduced by one quarter, about 20 minutes. Cool for 10 minutes.

In a blender, puree the soup in several batches until smooth, 2 to 3 minutes per batch. Strain into a clean pot and bring to a simmer over medium heat. Turn off the heat and stir in the heavy cream. Season to taste with salt and pepper. Reheat gently over low heat. (This can be made up to 2 days in advance; cover and refrigerate.)

To serve, ladle the soup into bowls and garnish with the fresh mint.

Tomato and Corn Chowder

This is a creamy chowder made sweet with tomatoes and corn, showcasing the best of summer. It is also good made with shrimp—see the variation below.

Serves 6

$^3/_4$ pound (about 2) baking potatoes, peeled and cut into $^1/_2$-inch dice
1 tablespoon unsalted butter
1 medium yellow onion, minced
6 medium ears fresh corn, shucked and kernels cut off
3 cups Chicken Stock (page 78)
$^1/_2$ cup heavy cream
Coarse salt and freshly ground black pepper
4 medium ripe red tomatoes, peeled, seeded, chopped, and drained
1 tablespoon finely snipped fresh chives

Bring a large saucepan of salted water to a boil. Add the potatoes and cook until tender, about 10 minutes. Drain and set aside.

Melt the butter in a large soup pot over medium-high heat. Add the onion and cook, stirring occasionally, until soft, about 7 minutes. Add all but 1 cup of the corn, the chicken stock, and 4 cups water, bring to a boil, reduce the heat, and simmer until the liquid is reduced by one quarter, about 15 minutes. Puree the soup in batches in a blender until very smooth, 2 to 3 minutes per batch. Strain through a fine sieve into a clean pan.

Add the cream, the reserved corn, and the potatoes. Season to taste with salt and pepper. Heat over medium-high heat just until hot, 3 to 4 minutes. Add the tomatoes and cook for 1 minute.

Ladle into bowls and serve immediately, garnished with the chives.

Variation: Shrimp, Tomato, and Corn Chowder

Use the shrimp broth in place of the chicken stock and water as the base of the soup.

1 pound jumbo shrimp
3 cups bottled clam juice or Fish Stock
  (page 80)
1 cup dry white wine
4 fresh thyme sprigs
3 bay leaves

Peel the shrimp, reserving the shells, and cut each shrimp in half down the back. Refrigerate the shrimp.

Place the shells, clam juice, 4 cups water, the white wine, thyme sprigs, and bay leaves in a soup pot. Bring to a boil over high heat, reduce the heat to medium-low, and simmer for 20 minutes. Strain the broth, and proceed with the above recipe. Add the shrimp along with the cream, corn, and potatoes.

> The crooked little tomato branches, pulpy and pale as if made of cheap green paper, broke under the weight of so much fruit; there was something frantic in such fertility, a crying-out like that of children frantic to please."
>
> John Updike

Roasted Yellow Pepper and Garlic Soup

With their sweetness and hint of smoke, roasted yellow peppers pair well with yellow tomatoes and garlic in a summery soup. Serve it with crusty bread and a salad on a hot night. You can make it a day in advance and reheat just before serving.

Serves 6

2 tablespoons extra virgin olive oil
2 yellow onions, chopped
8 garlic cloves, minced, plus 1 whole garlic
    clove
4 pounds yellow bell peppers, cut in half and
    roasted (see page 13)
5 cups Chicken Stock (page 78)
4 ripe yellow tomatoes, cored and diced
Coarse salt and freshly ground black pepper
6 long diagonal slices baguette
2 tablespoons snipped fresh chives

In a large soup pot, heat the olive oil over medium heat. Add the onions and cook until soft, about 7 minutes. Add the minced garlic and stir for 1 minute. Add the peppers and cook, stirring occasionally, for 3 minutes. Increase the heat to high, add the stock and tomatoes, and bring to a boil. Turn the heat down to low and simmer until the tomatoes fall apart, about 30 minutes. Cool for 20 minutes.

In batches, puree the soup in a blender until smooth, 2 to 3 minutes per batch. Strain through a fine strainer into a clean pot. Season to taste with salt and pepper.

To serve, toast the baguette slices until golden and rub with the whole clove of garlic. Reheat the soup and ladle into bowls. Top with the toasted bread and sprinkle with the chives.

Autumn Vegetable and Rice Soup

When your fall garden is chock-full of ripe vegetables, make a big pot of this hearty vegetable soup. Serve it either hot or at room temperature, topped with a dollop of pesto, or pass a small bowl of pesto at the table so your guests can help themselves.

Serves 6 to 8

1 cup dried navy beans, picked over and rinsed
2 tablespoons plus $1/3$ cup extra virgin olive oil
1 medium onion, finely chopped
2 carrots, diced
2 stalks celery, diced
1 bunch Swiss chard, stems removed and cut
    into $1/2$-inch pieces
3 medium ripe red tomatoes, peeled, seeded,
    and chopped, or 2 cups seeded and chopped
    canned tomatoes
7 cups Chicken Stock (page 78) or water
$1/4$ cup Arborio or other short-grain rice
Coarse salt and freshly ground black pepper
5 garlic cloves, minced
$2^1/2$ packed cups fresh basil leaves
1 cup freshly grated Parmigiano-Reggiano

Place the beans in a bowl, add plenty of water to cover, and let soak for about 3 hours; drain.

Heat 2 tablespoons oil in a soup pot. Add the onion, carrots, and celery and sauté slowly over medium-low heat until the vegetables are soft, about 15 minutes. Add the chard, tomatoes, stock, and beans and simmer, uncovered, until the beans are tender, 45 to 60 minutes. About 20 minutes before the soup is served, add the rice and simmer until the rice is tender. Season with salt and pepper.

In the meantime, place the garlic, basil, and $^1/_2$ cup of the Parmigiano in a blender or food processor. Process until a rough paste is formed. Add the remaining $^1/_3$ cup olive oil and salt and pepper to taste and process until the paste is smooth.

Ladle the soup into bowls and place a large spoonful of the basil puree on the top of each. Garnish with the remaining $^1/_2$ cup Parmigiano and serve immediately.

Chilled Tomato-Yogurt Soup

This refreshing chilled soup makes a perfect first course on a steamy hot day. It is light, refreshing, low in calories, and, best of all, simple to prepare. Once you eat the first spoonful, you can't stop. Serve it the day it's made.

Serves 6

3 cups whole-milk yogurt
3 medium ripe red tomatoes, peeled, seeded, and chopped
2 garlic cloves, minced
1 tablespoon extra virgin olive oil
3 tablespoons chopped fresh dill, plus 6 small sprigs
$1^1/_4$ cups cold milk
3 tablespoons white wine vinegar or fresh lemon juice
Coarse salt and freshly ground black pepper

Place the yogurt in a cheesecloth-lined strainer set over a bowl and let drip for 2 hours. Discard the water and place the yogurt in the bowl.

Add the tomatoes, garlic, olive oil, dill, and the milk and combine well. Puree in batches in the blender until smooth. Pour into a bowl, add the vinegar, and season to taste with salt and pepper. Chill for at least 1 hour.

To serve, ladle the soup into bowls and garnish with the dill sprigs.

Gazpacho

If you had thirty Spanish cooks in a kitchen, there would be thirty different versions of gazpacho. But one thing every Spanish cook agrees on is that gazpacho must contain soaked bread. A cool soup known as gazpacho arrived in southern Spain via the Moors and a version of the original is still made today with green grapes, stale bread, almonds, olive oil, and plenty of garlic. But in the early sixteenth century, when Columbus returned to Spain with the tomato from the New World, the face of gazpacho changed and took on a rosy hue.

This combination soup-salad is served cold or at room temperature to revive the spirit during the furnace-like summers in Spain. Sometimes it is made with a good pinch of pimenton, a smoked pimento powder that is available in markets that carry Spanish ingredients.

Serves 6

6 large ripe red tomatoes, peeled, seeded, and chopped
1 yellow or green bell pepper, cored, seeded, and coarsely chopped
1 yellow onion, coarsely chopped
1 large cucumber, peeled, halved, seeded, and coarsely chopped
3 large garlic cloves, minced
$1/4$ cup plus 2 tablespoons white wine vinegar
3 tablespoons extra virgin olive oil
1 slice stale Italian or French bread, crusts removed, soaked in water, and squeezed dry
Coarse salt and freshly ground black pepper

1 tablespoon unsalted butter
1 tablespoon extra virgin olive oil
3 garlic cloves, crushed
6 slices sourdough bread, crusts removed and torn into $3/4$-inch pieces
$1/4$ cup diced green bell pepper
$1/4$ cup peeled, seeded, and chopped cucumber
$1^1/2$ cups red or assorted cherry tomatoes, quartered
$1/4$ cup diced red onion

In a bowl, mix the tomatoes, bell pepper, onion, cucumber, garlic, vinegar, olive oil, and bread together. In batches, puree the mixture in a blender until very smooth, about 3 minutes per batch. Strain through a coarse strainer into a bowl and season with salt and pepper. Place in the refrigerator and chill for at least 1 hour or up to 8 hours.

Preheat the oven to 375°F.

For the garnish, melt the butter with the olive oil in a small saucepan over medium-high heat. Add the crushed garlic and cook, stirring occasionally, until light golden, 1 minute. Remove from the heat and discard the garlic.

Place the bread in a single layer on a baking sheet. Drizzle with the butter and oil and toss well. Bake, tossing the bread cubes occasionally, until golden, 10 to 12 minutes.

To serve, ladle the chilled soup into bowls and garnish with the toasted bread or croutons, bell pepper, cucumber, tomatoes, and red onion.

Aquacotta with Peppers

Like stone soup, the ancient Italian soup aquacotta— *which translates literally as "cooked water"—is a poor man's dish made from almost nothing. There are a million versions, but this one with sweet red and yellow bell peppers is particularly satisfying.*

Serves 6

2 tablespoons extra virgin olive oil
2 medium yellow onions, finely chopped
2 red or yellow bell peppers (or 1 of each),
    cored, seeded, and cut into thin 1-inch strips
1 large stalk celery, finely chopped
2 carrots, finely chopped
2 garlic cloves, minced
4 medium ripe red tomatoes, peeled, seeded,
    and chopped
Coarse salt and freshly ground black pepper
3 large eggs
1/2 cup freshly grated Parmigiano-Reggiano
6 slices coarse-textured Italian bread, toasted

Heat the olive oil in a large heavy soup pot over medium heat. Add the onions and cook until soft, about 10 minutes. Add the bell peppers, celery, carrots, garlic, and tomatoes, cover, and cook until the vegetables are very tender, about 30 minutes.

Add 6 cups boiling water and simmer for 5 minutes. Season to taste with salt and pepper. (This soup can be made 2 days in advance to this point and stored in the refrigerator until ready to serve; bring to a simmer before proceeding.)

In a small bowl, whisk together the eggs and Parmigiano-Reggiano. Add to the simmering soup and stir together. Immediately remove the soup from the heat. Season to taste with salt and pepper.

To serve, place a slice of bread in the bottom of each bowl and ladle the soup over the bread.

Gaspacha 1824

was surprised to find this recipe in an old recipe book, dated 1824, by Mary Randolph, called *The Virginia Housewife*. Her recipe for gazpacho may very well be the first published in the United States. Even Mary knew the common denominator for gazpacho is that it contain soaked bread.

Put some soft biscuit or toasted bread in the bottom of a salad bowl, put in a layer of sliced tomatas with skins taken off, and one of sliced cucumbers, sprinkled with pepper, salt, and chopped onions; do this until the bowl is full, stew some tomatas quite soft; strain the juice, mix in some mustard and oil, and pour over it; make it two hours before it is eaten.

Crab and Tomato Bisque

This velvety, creamy crab bisque can also be made with one and a half pounds of shrimp or two lobsters with equally delicious results. Serve it as an elegant first course on New Year's Eve, with glasses of Champagne.

Serves 8

2 Dungeness crabs (1 to 1½ pounds each) or 2 to 3 pounds blue crabs, cooked
3 tablespoons unsalted butter
1 medium yellow onion, diced
2 stalks celery, diced
1 carrot, diced
1 teaspoon chopped fresh tarragon or ½ teaspoon dried tarragon
2 medium ripe red tomatoes, peeled, seeded, and chopped, or 1½ cups seeded and chopped canned tomatoes
1 small red bell pepper, cored, seeded, and coarsely chopped
1 bay leaf
1 cup dry white wine
3 cups Fish Stock (page 80) or bottled clam juice
¼ cup long-grain white rice
1 cup heavy cream
Coarse salt and freshly ground black pepper
1 teaspoon fresh lemon juice, or to taste
2 tablespoons snipped fresh chives

Bring a large pot of salted water to a boil. Add the crabs and simmer until bright red, about 8 to 10 minutes for Dungeness crabs and 5 minutes for blue crabs. With tongs, remove the crabs from the water and cool. Clean and crack the crabs by first twisting off the claws and legs. Turn each crab on its back, pull up the flap apron, and twist it off. Put your thumb in the small crevice between the shell and the body and lift off the top shell. Remove the spongy white gills and intestines and discard. Snap each crab body in half. With a mallet, crack the claws and body, and remove the meat. Slice the large pieces of claw meat for garnish. With heavy shears, cut the crab shells into small pieces. Refrigerate crabmeat until ready to use.

Melt the butter in a large soup pot over medium-low heat. Add the onion, celery, carrot, and tarragon and cook slowly until the vegetables are very soft, about 15 minutes. Add the crab shells, tomatoes, bell pepper, bay leaf, wine, fish stock, and 1½ cups water. Increase the heat to high and bring to a boil. Reduce the heat to low, cover, and simmer slowly for 20 minutes. Cool for 15 minutes.

Place about one third of the crab broth and shells in a blender and pulse a few times. Line a fine strainer with cheesecloth and strain the broth through it into a large saucepan, pressing against the shells and then scraping the bottom of the strainer to extract as much liquid as possible. Continue with all of the crab broth and shells.

Combine the rice and 2 cups of the crab broth in a small pan, cover, bring to a boil, and boil until the rice is tender, about 20 minutes. Place the rice in the blender with a cup of the broth and blend until smooth.

Add the rice mixture to the remaining crab broth and bring to a simmer over medium heat.

Add the cream and season to taste with salt and pepper and the lemon juice. Strain once again through a cheesecloth-lined fine strainer. Add the reserved crabmeat, except the claw meat, and stir well.

To serve, ladle into bowls and garnish with the reserved sliced crab and the chives.

Pasta e Fagioli

Pasta e fagioli, *pasta and beans, is a staple of the Tuscan diet. It is more of a porridge than a soup, made thick with cannellini beans. Cook the beans separately before adding them to the tomatoes; the acid in the tomatoes would prevent the beans from cooking. A great make-ahead dish, pasta e fagioli is equally good made with fresh tomatoes in the summer or canned ones in the winter.*

Serves 6

1 cup dried cannellini or navy beans, picked
    over and rinsed
5 tablespoons extra virgin olive oil
1 medium yellow onion, finely chopped
3 garlic cloves, minced
3 cups peeled, seeded, and chopped fresh or
    canned tomatoes
3 cups Chicken Stock (page 78)
Coarse salt and freshly ground black pepper
1½ teaspoons chopped fresh rosemary
1 cup small dried semolina pasta, such as
    elbows or tiny shells

Place the beans in a bowl, add plenty of water to cover, and let soak for about 3 hours.

Drain the beans and place in a saucepan with water to cover by 2 inches. Bring to a boil, reduce the heat to low, and simmer gently, uncovered, until the skins begin to crack and the beans are tender, 45 to 60 minutes. Drain and set aside.

In a soup pot heat 2 tablespoons of the olive oil over medium-low heat. Add the onion and garlic and sauté slowly, stirring occasionally, until the onion is soft, about 10 minutes. Add the tomatoes, chicken stock, 2 cups water, the beans, and salt and pepper to taste, cover, and simmer for 30 minutes.

In the meantime, in a small saucepan, heat the remaining 3 tablespoons olive oil over medium heat. Add the rosemary and immediately remove the pan from the heat. Let steep until the soup is ready to be served.

Add the pasta to the soup and simmer until the pasta is tender, 12 to 15 minutes.

Ladle the soup into individual bowls, drizzle with the rosemary oil, and serve immediately.

Tortilla and Tomato Soup

Tortilla soup is a satisfying blend of flavors and textures, with creamy melting cheese, sour cream, and avocado against crispy, crunchy strips of fried tortillas. Tomatoes add sweetness and a splash of lime perks up the dish. With some hot corn bread, you have a meal.

Serves 6

2 tablespoons vegetable oil
2 large yellow onions, quartered and thinly sliced
5 garlic cloves, minced
One 3 1/2-pound chicken, cut into 6 pieces and skin removed
3 large ripe red tomatoes, peeled, seeded, and chopped
1 tablespoon ground cumin
2 teaspoons chili powder
1/2 teaspoon chopped fresh oregano
2 bay leaves
Juice of 1 lime, or to taste
Coarse salt and freshly ground black pepper
Corn oil for frying the tortillas
5 corn tortillas, cut into 1/4-inch strips
1/2 cup coarsely grated mozzarella (about 2 ounces)
1/2 cup coarsely grated Monterey Jack (about 2 ounces)
1 large avocado, peeled, seeded, and diced
1/4 cup sour cream

Heat the oil in a large soup pot over medium heat. Add the onions and cook, stirring occasionally, until soft, about 7 minutes. Add the garlic and cook, stirring, for 1 minute. Add the chicken, tomatoes, cumin, chili powder, oregano, bay leaves, and 8 cups water. Bring to a boil, reduce the heat to low, and simmer, uncovered, until the chicken is very tender, about 1 hour. (You should have approximately 6 to 7 cups broth remaining.) Remove and discard the bay leaves.

Remove the chicken from the pot. Remove the meat from the bones, dice it, and return it to the pot. Season to taste with the lime juice and salt and pepper.

Heat 1/2-inch of corn oil in a deep heavy pan to 375°F. Add the tortilla strips in batches and cook until crispy, about 1 minute. Remove from the pan and drain on paper towels.

To serve, reheat the soup until hot. Ladle into bowls and garnish with the mozzarella, Monterey Jack, and avocado. Top each with a spoonful of sour cream and some tortilla strips.

Nabia's Tomato-Lentil Soup

All over the world, tomatoes and legumes are commonly cooked together. In this Lebanese tomato soup, garlic, mint, cilantro, and lemon set off the soothing taste of lentils.

Serves 6

1 cup brown lentils, picked over and rinsed
2 pounds lamb soup bones
2 tablespoons olive oil
1 large onion, minced
4 garlic cloves, minced
4 medium ripe red tomatoes, peeled, seeded, and chopped
$^1/_2$ cup chopped fresh cilantro
$^1/_4$ cup chopped fresh mint
2 tablespoons fresh lemon juice
Coarse salt and freshly ground black pepper
Lemon wedges

Place the lentils in a large soup pot with the lamb bones and 8 cups water. Bring to a boil, cover, and simmer until the lentils are tender, 30 to 35 minutes.

In the meantime, heat the oil in a medium frying pan over medium heat. Add the onion and cook, stirring occasionally, until soft, about 7 minutes. Add the garlic and cook for 2 minutes. Remove from the heat and set aside.

When the lentils are tender, remove the lamb bones and discard. Add the sautéed onions, the tomatoes, cilantro, and mint to the lentils. Stir well, add the lemon juice, cover, and simmer slowly for 10 minutes. Season to taste with salt and pepper. (The soup can be made a day in advance and reheated just before serving. Adjust the seasonings with more lemon juice, salt, and/or pepper if necessary just before serving.)

To serve, ladle the soup into bowls and garnish with lemon wedges.

As for tomatoes, I prefer to leave them in their skins, except for a sauce or soup or stew in which the pieces of surprisingly tough peel will roll into mean little sticks, not pretty or good. Otherwise I think tomato skins are part of the whole somewhat brutal smell and texture of most dishes I use them in, much as the papery pink or yellow skin of little new potatoes can add a special quality to eating them whole. They crackle, almost as if one could and would bite through an amazing new kind of egg in its shell."

From M. F. K. Fisher,
With Bold Knife and Fork

Summer Vegetables and Orzo in Lamb Broth

If you have trouble finding lamb bones, substitute beef bones. Kefalotyri cheese is a sheep's or goat's milk cheese, available in specialty cheese shops; if it is unavailable, substitute Parmigiano-Reggiano.

Serves 6

3 pounds lamb bones
1 large onion, quartered
1 large carrot, coarsely chopped
12 sprigs fresh parsley
2 sprigs fresh thyme
1 bay leaf
3 tablespoons olive oil
2 medium yellow onions, diced
2 leeks (white and 2 inches of green part),
    quartered lengthwise and diced and washed
3 stalks celery with leaves, diced
2 carrots, diced
$^1/_2$ cup green beans, trimmed and cut into
    $^1/_2$-inch pieces
2 small zucchini, halved, seeded, and diced
3 medium ripe red tomatoes, peeled, seeded,
    and chopped, or 2 cups seeded and chopped
    canned tomatoes
1 teaspoon chopped fresh oregano
Coarse salt and freshly ground black pepper
$^1/_2$ cup orzo
$^1/_2$ cup grated kefalotyri cheese
$^1/_4$ cup chopped fresh flat-leaf parsley

For the broth, place the lamb bones in a stockpot and cover with water. Bring to a boil and immediately drain. Place the lamb bones back in the stockpot and add the onion, carrot, parsley, thyme, bay leaf, and 8 cups water. Bring to a boil, reduce the heat, and simmer very slowly, uncovered, for 2 hours. As the liquid evaporates, replenish it to maintain the original level in the stockpot.

Strain the stock and discard the bones. Skim off the fat. This should make approximately 8 cups lamb stock. (The stock can be made in advance and stored in the refrigerator up to 3 days or in the freezer for up to 2 months.)

Heat the oil in a soup pot over medium-low heat. Add the onions, leeks, celery, and carrots and cook, stirring occasionally, until the onions are soft, about 10 minutes. Add 1 cup water, cover, and simmer until the vegetables are very soft, about 30 minutes.

Add the green beans, zucchini, tomatoes, oregano, salt and pepper to taste, and the lamb broth. Bring to a boil over high heat, reduce the heat to low, cover, and simmer for 30 to 40 minutes until the vegetables are very tender and the flavors meld. Add the orzo and continue to simmer until the orzo is tender, about 15 minutes. Taste and season with salt and pepper if necessary.

To serve, ladle the soup into bowls and garnish with the cheese and parsley.

Tomato-Rice Soup with Tiny Meatballs

There is nothing more comforting than tomato-rice soup. Add a few moist, spicy meatballs and it's a meal in itself. I love to serve this with a fruity red wine and whole-grain rolls. Ground beef or pork, or combination of ground meats, can be used in place of veal.

Serves 6

$3/4$ pound ground veal
$1/2$ cup dry bread crumbs
2 garlic cloves, minced
1 tablespoon chopped fresh flat-leaf parsley
1 teaspoon ground coriander
$1/4$ teaspoon freshly grated nutmeg
$1/4$ teaspoon ground cumin
Pinch of cayenne
Coarse salt and freshly ground black pepper
1 tablespoon olive oil
1 large yellow onion, coarsely chopped
1 carrot, coarsely chopped
$1/2$ stalk celery, coarsely chopped
5 cups Chicken Stock (page 78)
5 large ripe red tomatoes, peeled, seeded, and
   chopped, or 6 cups seeded and chopped
   canned tomatoes
$1/4$ cup long-grain white rice

Preheat the oven to 350°F.

In a bowl, combine the veal, bread crumbs, garlic, parsley, coriander, nutmeg, cumin, cayenne, $1/2$ teaspoon salt, and $1/8$ teaspoon pepper. Form into twenty-four $3/4$-inch meatballs, place on a baking sheet, and bake until slightly firm to the touch, 10 to 12 minutes. Remove from the oven and set aside.

Heat the olive oil in a large skillet over medium-low heat. Add the onion, carrot, and celery and cook, stirring occasionally, until the onions are soft, about 10 minutes. Add the chicken stock and tomatoes. Bring to a boil, lower the heat, and simmer, covered, until the tomatoes fall apart, about 20 minutes. Cool for 10 minutes.

Puree the soup in a blender in batches until very smooth, about 3 minutes per batch. Pass through a strainer into a clean pot. Bring the soup to a simmer over medium heat. Add the rice, cover, and cook until the rice is almost tender, 10 minutes. Season to taste with salt and pepper. Add the meatballs and continue to cook until the rice is tender and the meatballs are hot, about 5 minutes.

Ladle into bowls and serve immediately.

Clam Soup with Tomatoes and Pasta Shells

Serve this soup with slices of toasted country-style bread rubbed with garlic and Rouille, the spicy garlic mayonnaise on page 39 if desired.

Serves 6

1 cup small dried semolina pasta shells
1 tablespoon olive oil
3 cups bottled clam juice or Fish Stock (page 80)
1 cup dry white wine
2 large ripe red tomatoes, peeled, seeded, and chopped, or 2½ cups seeded and chopped canned tomatoes
4 garlic cloves, minced
6 parsley stems, tied together with kitchen string
½ teaspoon dried thyme
2 bay leaves
Pinch of cayenne
4 pounds clams, scrubbed
3 tablespoons chopped fresh flat-leaf parsley
Coarse salt and freshly ground black pepper

In a large pot, bring 3 quarts water and 1 tablespoon salt to a boil. Add the pasta shells and cook until al dente, 12 to 15 minutes. Drain the pasta and immediately toss it with the olive oil. Cover and refrigerate.

In a large soup pot, combine the clam juice, wine, 2 cups water, the tomatoes, garlic, parsley stems, thyme, bay leaves, and cayenne and bring to a boil over high heat. Turn the heat down to medium-low, cover, and simmer until the tomatoes soften, 15 min-utes. Remove the parsley and bay leaves and discard.

Discard any open clams that do not close when lightly tapped. Add the clams to the pot, cover, and simmer, shaking the pan periodically, until they open, 3 to 5 minutes. Remove the clams with a slotted spoon and let them cool slightly; discard any unopened clams. Remove the clams from the shell and discard the shells.

Add the pasta, clams, parsley, and salt and pepper to taste to the soup and simmer for 1 minute.

Ladle the soup into individual bowls and serve immediately.

Manhattan Clam Chowder

There has always been rivalry over whose clam chowder is better, New England's or Manhattan's. New England chowder is made with cream; the Manhattan is tomato-based. It is likely that Manhattan clam chowder was inspired by the influx of Neapolitans to New York City, who brought with them their recipes for zuppa di vongole, *tomato soup with clams.*

Serves 6

4 pounds Manila or littleneck clams,
   scrubbed
1 ounce salt pork, finely diced
1 large yellow onion, minced
1 large red potato (about ³/₄ pound), peeled and
   diced
2 bay leaves
3 medium ripe red tomatoes, peeled, seeded,
   and chopped, or 2 cups seeded and chopped
   canned tomatoes
¹/₄ teaspoon chopped fresh thyme
Coarse salt and freshly ground black pepper
Oyster crackers

In a large, deep frying pan, bring 2 cups water to a boil over high heat. Discard any open clams that do not close when lightly tapped. Add the clams to the pan, cover, and simmer, shaking the pan periodically, until they open, 3 to 5 minutes. Remove the clams with a slotted spoon and let them cool slightly; discard any unopened clams.

Remove the clams from the shells and discard the shells. Strain the liquid into a large measuring cup and add enough water to make 4 cups. Set the cooking liquid and the clams aside.

Heat a large heavy soup pot over medium heat. Add the salt pork and cook until it has rendered its fat and is light golden. With a slotted spoon, remove the salt pork and reserve.

Add the onion to the pot and cook, stirring occasionally, until soft, about 7 minutes. Add the potato, the reserved clam liquid, and the bay leaves, cover, and simmer until the potato is soft, about 10 minutes. Add the tomatoes, cover, and simmer for 10 minutes. Add the clams and thyme, cover, and simmer for 5 minutes. Season to taste with salt and pepper. Remove and discard the bay leaves.

Ladle the soup into bowls, garnish with reserved salt pork and oyster crackers, and serve immediately.

Thai Shrimp Soup

Tomatoes are not common in Thai cooking. Yet, paired with coconut milk, red curry paste, and shrimp, they make a simple, can't-eat-just-one-bowl soup. Unsweetened dried coconut is available in health food stores; Thai curry paste is available in cans in Asian markets.

Serves 6

3 cups grated dried unsweetened coconut
$1/2$ cup Fish Stock (page 80) or bottled clam juice
$1/2$ pound medium shrimp, peeled
5 medium ripe red tomatoes, peeled, seeded, and chopped, or $3^3/4$ cups seeded and chopped canned tomatoes
1 tablespoon Thai red curry paste
2 tablespoons fish sauce, preferably nam pla
1 tablespoon fresh lime juice
2 tablespoons chopped fresh cilantro
2 green onions, thinly sliced

Put the coconut in a bowl, pour 3 cups boiling water over it, and let sit, stirring occasionally, for 15 minutes. Strain through a fine strainer and reserve the liquid. Discard the coconut.

Place the fish stock in a medium skillet and bring to a boil over high heat. Add the shrimp and cook, covered, until pink and curled, about 3 minutes. With a slotted spoon, remove one third of the shrimp and reserve; set the shrimp in the broth aside.

Puree the tomatoes in a blender in batches until very smooth, about 3 minutes per batch. Transfer to a soup pot. Puree the shrimp with its poaching liquid and the coconut milk, in batches, until very smooth, 3 minutes. Add to the tomatoes, along with the curry paste, fish sauce, and lime juice, and simmer over low heat for 10 minutes. Add the reserved shrimp.

To serve, ladle the soup into bowls and garnish with the cilantro and green onions.

Chicken Stock

Makes $2^1/2$ to 3 quart

5 pounds chicken parts, backs, necks, and/or wings, excess fat removed
1 onion, coarsely chopped
1 carrot, coarsely chopped
12 sprigs fresh flat-leaf parsley
$1/2$ teaspoon fresh thyme leaves or dried thyme
2 bay leaves

Place all of the ingredients in a stockpot. Add water to cover the bones by 2 inches. Bring to a boil and immediately reduce the heat to a simmer. Simmer slowly until the meat has fallen off the bones and the stock tastes very rich, 5 to 6 hours. As the liquid evaporates, replenish it periodically to maintain its original level.

Strain through a fine strainer into a bowl. Place in the refrigerator and allow the stock to cool completely. When it has cooled, skim the fat from the top with a spoon and discard. Stock may be frozen for 2 months.

Beef, Veal, or Lamb Stock

To make beef stock, use knuckle, neck, shin, and other marrow bones. For veal, use breastbones that have been separated into ribs. For lamb, use shank, shoulder, knuckle, or shin bones. For a lighter broth, mix one part stock to one part water.

Makes 2$\frac{1}{2}$ to 3 quarts

5 pounds beef, veal, or lamb bones
1 large onion, quartered
1 large carrot, coarsely chopped
12 sprigs fresh flat-leaf parsley
Pinch of dried thyme
1 bay leaf

Preheat the oven to 375°F.

Place the bones on a baking sheet, leaving space between them so they will brown evenly. Roast until well browned on all sides, turning occasionally, for 1$\frac{1}{2}$ to 2 hours.

Transfer the bones to a large stockpot. Discard any accumulated fat from the baking sheet. Pour 1 cup water onto the baking sheet and place the baking sheet over two burners of the stove set at high heat. With a spatula, scrape up any cooked bits from the baking sheet. When all of the browned bits have been loosened, pour everything into the stockpot. Add the onion, carrot, parsley, thyme, bay leaf, and enough water to cover the bones by 2 inches. Bring to a boil over high heat. Reduce the heat and simmer, uncovered, for 5 to 6 hours. As the liquid evaporates, replenish with water to the original level.

When the meat has fallen off the bones and the stock is a deep rich brown, strain the stock in a fine strainer. Cool completely in the refrigerator. When the stock is cool, skim the fat from the top and discard. The stock can be frozen for 1 to 2 months.

Vegetable Stock

The best vegetables for stock are onions, leeks, carrots, celery, tomatoes, potatoes, mushrooms, green beans, squash, garlic, fennel, eggplant, cabbage, greens such as spinach, chard, lettuce, and herbs. Avoid cauliflower, Brussels sprouts, artichokes, and beets. Their flavor is too strong and will overpower the other vegetables in the stock.

Makes 2 to 3 quarts

10 cups vegetables and/or trimmings
1 onion, coarsely chopped
1 carrot, coarsely chopped
12 sprigs fresh flat-leaf parsley
4 sprigs fresh thyme or $\frac{1}{4}$ teaspoon dried
   thyme
1 bay leaf

Place all of the ingredients in a stockpot and add cold water to cover by 3 inches. Bring to a boil and immediately reduce to a simmer. Simmer slowly for 45 minutes, until the stock smells aromatic and has a good flavor. As the liquid evaporates, replenish with more water.

Strain through a fine strainer into a bowl. The stock can be frozen for 2 months.

Fish Stock

Bones from nonoily white fish or salmon are the best choice for fish stock. Try those from red snapper, halibut, grouper, cod, perch, sole, trout, and/or pike.

Makes 2 to 3 quarts

4 to 5 pounds fish bones, well washed
1 cup dry white wine
1 yellow onion, chopped
1 carrot, chopped
2 bay leaves
12 sprigs fresh flat-leaf parsley
3 sprigs fresh thyme or ¼ teaspoon dried
    thyme

If necessary, remove the liver, gills, fat, and skin, as well as the tail and any traces of blood, from the fish bones. Place the bones in a stockpot. Fill the pot with water just to cover the bones. Add the white wine, onion, carrot, bay leaves, parsley, and thyme.

Bring to a boil, reduce the heat, and simmer for 35 minutes. While the stock is simmering, periodically pound and smash the bones with a wooden spoon.

Strain through a fine strainer. Skim off any fat. The stock can be frozen for 2 months.

salads

Farmers' Market Summer Tomato Salad

Every Saturday morning throughout the year, we have an exceptional farmers' market at Ferry Plaza in San Francisco. At the crack of dawn, they set up an unbelievable array of local fruits, vegetables, cheeses, fish, and breads. You have to plan to arrive bright and early to get the best. One August Saturday, juicy, sweet ripe red and yellow tomatoes, fresh pungent oregano, and goat's milk yogurt were the inspiration for this salad. If goat's milk yogurt is unavailable, substitute cow's milk yogurt.

Serves 6

1 very small red onion, very thinly sliced
Coarse salt
1/2 cup milk
1/2 cup goat's or cow's milk yogurt
1 to 2 tablespoons fresh lemon juice
1 garlic clove, minced
1 1/2 tablespoons chopped fresh basil, plus a
    handful of basil leaves for garnish
1 tablespoon chopped fresh oregano
2 teaspoons extra virgin olive oil
Freshly ground black pepper
4 ripe red or yellow tomatoes, cut into 1/2-inch
    slices
1 small English cucumber, peeled and sliced

Place the onion in a bowl and salt well. Pour the milk over the onion and let sit for 30 minutes, then drain and pat dry with paper towels.

In the meantime, in a small bowl, whisk together the yogurt, lemon juice, garlic, basil, oregano, olive oil, and salt and pepper to taste. Set aside.

Arrange the tomatoes and cucumber on a plate. Season with salt and pepper. Place the onion on the tomatoes and cucumber, drizzle with dressing, and top with the basil leaves. Serve immediately.

> However it happened, the marriage between olive oil and the tomato was a brilliant unprecedented culinary match, and because of it the world's table, and our own, was forever changed."
>
> From Elisabeth Rozin,
> *Blue Corn and Chocolate*

Tomato-Lemon Salad with Lemon Olive Oil

The choice is up to you—you can prepare your own lemon-scented oil and store it in the refrigerator for one week or you can purchase it at some markets.

Serves 6

2 lemons
1/4 cup extra virgin olive oil
1 tablespoon fresh lemon juice
Coarse salt and freshly ground black pepper
6 large ripe red tomatoes, cut into 1/2-inch slices
1 Preserved Lemon (page 171), peel only, diced
Fresh flat-leaf parsley leaves

With a vegetable peeler, peel the zest from the lemons. Try not to get any of the white pith; if there is any on the back of the colored zest, scrape it off with a small paring knife.

Heat the olive oil in a small saucepan over medium heat. Add the lemon zest and immediately remove from the heat. Stir and let sit for 1 hour.

Strain the oil into a small bowl and discard the lemon zest. Add the lemon juice and whisk together. Season to taste with salt and pepper.

To serve, arrange the tomatoes on a serving plate and season to taste with salt and pepper. Sprinkle the preserved lemons over the top and drizzle with the vinaigrette. Garnish with parsley leaves.

Tomato, Mozzarella, and Basil Salad

The secret of this classic salad, called Caprese, *from the island of Capri, off the coast of Naples, is to buy the very best possible ingredients. Choose vine-ripened tomatoes, fresh mozzarella, sweet tender basil leaves from the herb garden, and fruity virgin olive oil. If buffalo milk mozzarella is unavailable, substitute fresh cow's milk mozzarella.*

Serves 6

6 assorted large tomatoes (red, yellow, gold, zebra-stripe, etc.), cut into 1/4-inch slices
1 pound mozzarella, cut into 1/4-inch slices
3 tablespoons extra virgin olive oil
2 teaspoons balsamic vinegar
Coarse salt and freshly ground black pepper
1/2 cup loosely packed fresh basil leaves

Alternate the tomatoes and slices of mozzarella on a serving plate, overlapping them slightly in rings.

In a small bowl, whisk together the olive oil and vinegar. Season the tomatoes with salt and pepper to taste. Drizzle the vinaigrette over the tomatoes and garnish with the basil leaves. Serve immediately.

Cherry Tomato Salad with Basil Oil

You can make all kinds of herb oils in the same manner as this basil oil. Herbs such as mint, dill, thyme, rosemary, oregano, and savory all pair well with tomatoes. Store oils in the refrigerator for one week.

Serves 6

¹/₄ cup extra virgin olive oil
4 sprigs fresh basil, plus basil leaves for garnish
1 tablespoon red wine vinegar
Coarse salt and freshly ground black pepper
1¹/₂ pounds assorted cherry tomatoes

In a saucepan warm the olive oil over medium heat, then immediately remove it from the heat. With the back of a chef's knife, tap the stems of the basil sprigs to bruise them and release their oil. Chop them very coarsely. Add the basil to the warm oil and let sit for 1 hour.

Strain the oil into a small bowl and discard the basil. Add the red wine vinegar and whisk together. Season to taste with salt and pepper.

To serve, place the cherry tomatoes in a serving bowl and toss with the vinaigrette. Garnish with basil leaves.

Tomato–Roasted Pepper Salad

So many flavorful ingredients in one dish and yet it is even better with feta, ricotta salata, or goat cheese crumbled over the top.

Serves 6

3 tablespoons extra virgin olive oil
1 tablespoon red wine vinegar
1 tablespoon balsamic vinegar
Coarse salt and freshly ground black pepper
2 large red bell peppers, roasted (see page 13), peeled, seeded, and cut into 1-inch strips
2 large yellow bell peppers, roasted (see page 13), peeled, seeded, and cut into 1-inch strips
¹/₂ cup caperberries (about 20) (see Note)
¹/₄ cup cured black olives, such as Kalamata
4 medium ripe red and/or yellow tomatoes, cut into ¹/₂-inch slices
¹/₃ cup loosely packed fresh basil leaves

In a small bowl, whisk together the oil and vinegars. Season with salt and pepper.

In a large bowl, combine the bell peppers, caperberries, olives, and three quarters of the vinaigrette and toss well.

To serve, arrange the tomato slices on a serving platter. Drizzle with the remaining vinaigrette. Top with the pepper mixture and garnish with the basil leaves.

NOTE: *If caperberries are unavailable, substitute half the amount of capers.*

Five-Tomato Salad with Gorgonzola and Chive Toasts

Tomatoes and gorgonzola go so well together. Use the toasts to mop up the juices from the tomatoes and vinaigrette. If an assortment of tomatoes is unavailable, use any flavorful, ripe, juicy red tomatoes.

Serves 6

3 tablespoons pine nuts, toasted
2 tablespoons unsalted butter, at room
   temperature
3 ounces Gorgonzola, at room temperature
3 tablespoons extra virgin olive oil
2 tablespoons balsamic vinegar
Coarse salt and freshly ground black pepper
2 large ripe yellow tomatoes, cut into $1/2$-inch
   slices
2 large ripe red tomatoes, cut into $1/2$-inch slices
2 large ripe orange tomatoes, cut into $1/2$-inch
   slices
3 medium ripe zebra-stripe tomatoes, cut into
   $1/2$-inch slices
$1/2$ pound assorted cherry tomatoes, halved
6 slices country-style bread, toasted
3 tablespoons finely snipped fresh chives

In a bowl, add the pine nuts, butter, and Gorgonzola and mash together with a fork.

In a small bowl, whisk together the olive oil and vinegar. Season to taste with salt and pepper.

Preheat the oven to 400°F.

Alternate the slices of tomato on a serving plate, overlapping them slightly. Scatter the cherry tomatoes over the top. Season to taste with salt and pepper. Drizzle the vinaigrette over the tomatoes.

Spread the cheese mixture on the toasted bread. Place the bread on a baking sheet and bake on the top rack of the oven until golden brown around the edges, 1 to 2 minutes.

Cut the bread on the diagonal into 3-inch-wide pieces. Place the Gorgonzola toasts around the tomatoes. Sprinkle the salad and the toasts with the chives and serve immediately.

Tomato and Truffle Salad

My great-grandmother was a terrific cook. At the turn of the century, she cooked at a Faneuil Hall restaurant in Boston called Pilgrim's Lunch. I found this recipe in one of her cookbooks, *The Good Housekeeping Family Cookbook,* published in 1906. She had it starred.

Skin small tomatoes of uniform size, scoop out a portion of centers, and arrange in nests of lettuce leaves. Fit a thin slice of cucumber in each tomato and arrange a ring of green pepper around each slice of cucumber, then garnish with a small round of truffle.

Plaka Greek Salad

What we know as a Greek salad, curiously enough in Greece, is made with almost-ripe, crisp, green or greenish-red tomatoes, which are surprisingly sweet for how green they are, along with the familiar cucumbers, bell peppers, olives, and feta. Cruets of fruity Greek olive oil and red wine vinegar accompany it and you dress the salad to your own liking. You can assemble the ingredients a few hours in advance and refrigerate, but don't dress the salad until you're ready to serve it.

Serves 6 to 8

3 large ripe red tomatoes, cut into 1- to 1½-inch pieces
1 small red onion, cut into 1-inch chunks
2 red bell peppers, cored, seeded, and cut into 1- to 1½-inch pieces
1 English cucumber, cut into 1-inch chunks
¼ cup plus 2 tablespoons extra virgin olive oil
3 tablespoons red wine vinegar
Coarse salt and freshly ground black pepper
¾ pound feta cheese
1 cup Kalamata olives
1 teaspoon dried oregano, preferably Greek

Arrange the tomatoes, onion, peppers, and cucumber on a serving plate. Drizzle with the olive oil and red wine vinegar. Season with salt and pepper to taste. Crumble the feta over the top. Scatter the olives over the top, sprinkle with the oregano, and serve immediately.

Tomato and Squash Blossom Salad

They say you eat first with your eyes and that is certainly true of this colorful salad. Squash blossoms are sweet, crisp, and floral. Pick them with the tomatoes, put them together, and you have an unusual salad from Mexico City. If yellow tomatoes are unavailable, use all red tomatoes. If you like, garnish the salad with halved cherry tomatoes of different colors.

Serves 6

3 large ripe red tomatoes, cut into ½-inch slices
3 large ripe yellow tomatoes, cut into ½-inch slices
Coarse salt
3 tablespoons corn oil
3 tablespoons olive oil
3½ tablespoons cider vinegar
1 teaspoon sugar
3 tablespoons chopped fresh basil
3 tablespoons chopped fresh cilantro
1 garlic clove, minced
Freshly ground black pepper
18 small tender squash blossoms, washed

Arrange the tomatoes on a serving platter, overlapping them slightly. Season with salt.

In a blender, puree the corn oil, olive oil, vinegar, sugar, basil, cilantro, and garlic until smooth. Season to taste with salt and pepper.

Place the squash blossoms on the tomatoes and drizzle the vinaigrette over the tomatoes and squash blossoms. Serve immediately.

Colombian Marinated Tomatoes

Whole tomatoes marinated overnight in a tart vinaigrette and served cold with crunchy romaine lettuce and whole sprigs of cilantro make an unusual and refreshing salad or first course on a hot day. Thanks to Hilda Barrera of Bogotá for this recipe.

Serves 6

³/₄ cup cider vinegar
1¹/₂ teaspoons sugar
2 teaspoons coarse salt
1¹/₂ teaspoons freshly ground black pepper
¹/₂ cup ketchup
1¹/₂ teaspoons Worcestershire sauce
1¹/₂ tablespoons fresh lemon juice
¹/₂ cup olive oil
4¹/₂ tablespoons coriander seeds, coarsely
　cracked
12 small ripe red tomatoes, peeled
1 head romaine lettuce, cut crosswise into
　¹/₂-inch strips
1 cup fresh cilantro sprigs

In a deep bowl, whisk together the vinegar, sugar, salt, pepper, ketchup, 3 tablespoons water, the Worcestershire sauce, lemon juice, olive oil, and coriander seeds. Prick each tomato with the tines of a fork in three or four places. Submerge the tomatoes in the vinaigrette and marinate overnight in the refrigerator.

To serve, layer half of the lettuce, cilantro, and drained tomatoes in a serving bowl, then repeat the layers.

Tomato and Summer Savory Salad

Summer savory, an annual herb, is intensely aromatic, reminiscent of both mint and thyme. The minced leaves pair well with garlic and tomatoes, while the tiny white or lilac flowers make a colorful and flavorful garnish. If summer savory is unavailable, substitute winter savory, a hardier perennial herb.

Serves 6

3 tablespoons chopped fresh summer savory,
　plus 4 whole sprigs for garnish, preferably
　with flowers
2 garlic cloves, minced
2 green onions, minced
¹/₂ teaspoon grated lemon zest
2 tablespoons fresh lemon juice
¹/₄ cup extra virgin olive oil
Large pinch of crushed red pepper flakes
Coarse salt and freshly ground black pepper
6 large ripe red tomatoes, cut into ¹/₂-inch slices

In a small bowl, whisk together the savory, garlic, green onions, lemon zest, lemon juice, olive oil, and red pepper flakes. Season to taste with salt and pepper.

Arrange the tomatoes on a platter and drizzle with the vinaigrette. Garnish with the sprigs of savory.

Tomato and Herbed Ricotta Salata Salad

Ricotta salata is salted and drained ricotta cheese, with a firmer, drier texture than regular ricotta. Its saltiness complements the acidity of tomatoes very well. Here ricotta salata is mixed with all sorts of fresh herbs from the garden and scattered over a medley of colorful tomatoes. This salad should be prepared just before serving.

Serves 6

1/2 pound ricotta salata
2 tablespoons chopped fresh basil
1 tablespoon chopped fresh mint
1 tablespoon snipped fresh chives
1 teaspoon chopped fresh oregano
1 teaspoon chopped fresh thyme
5 large ripe red tomatoes, cut into 1/4-inch slices
1/2 pound assorted cherry tomatoes, halved
Coarse salt
1/4 cup extra virgin olive oil
3 tablespoons balsamic vinegar
Freshly ground black pepper
Fresh basil, mint, oregano, and/or thyme sprigs

Crumble the ricotta salata into a medium bowl. Add the basil, mint, chives, oregano, and thyme and mix together until the cheese is coated with herbs. Set aside.

Arrange the tomatoes on a serving platter, overlapping them slightly. Scatter the cherry tomatoes on top. Season with salt.

In a small bowl, whisk together the olive oil and vinegar. Season to taste with salt and pepper.

Drizzle the vinaigrette over the tomatoes. Scatter the cheese over the top and garnish with herb sprigs. Serve immediately.

Tostada Salad with Roasted Tomatillo and Avocado Salsa

Each bite of this Southwestern salad offers many different sensations—creamy, crunchy, sour, tart, and fresh. You can also garnish the tostadas with sour cream, chopped green onions, diced avocado, lime wedges, and sprigs of cilantro. Other cheeses can be used in place of the Monterey Jack—try sharp Cheddar or mozzarella. If you use freshly made tortillas, they can be folded in half and eaten as soft tacos.

Serves 6

1 cup black beans, picked over and rinsed
1 cup corn oil
6 corn tortillas
3 cups coarsely grated Monterey Jack (about 3/4 pound)
3/4 pound (2 medium) ripe zebra-stripe or red tomatoes, diced
3 cups romaine lettuce cut into thin strips
1 recipe Roasted Tomatillo and Avocado Salsa (page 36)

Place the beans in a bowl, add plenty of water to cover, and soak for about 3 hours.

Drain the beans and place in a saucepan with water to cover by 2 inches. Bring to a boil, reduce the heat to low, and simmer, uncovered, until tender, about 45 minutes. Drain.

Heat the oil in a skillet over medium-high heat. Add the tortillas, one at a time, and cook until golden and almost crisp, 1 to 2 minutes. Drain on paper towels.

To serve, place a tortilla on each plate. Scatter the beans, cheese, tomatoes, and lettuce over the top and then spoon on the salsa.

"...bad news: Sweet corn, melons, and tomatoes, which are subtropical crops and need heat, are advancing slowly due to cool nights and days.

"Advancing slowly isn't the half of it. By this time of year, when the Independence Day oratory has finally died away, Shelter Island is usually awash in tomatoes. But no. Instead of a glut, we have a shortage. Even old George Blados's superdependable farm stand has run dry. On Saturday it displayed a sign reading NO TOMATOES. On Sunday it had been amended to include the word SORRY. And on Monday a further addition read MAYBE WEDNESDAY. Even with this summer's odd-even rationing, it's easier to get gasoline than tomatoes, and gas isn't nearly as tasty."

From Vladimir Estragon,
Waiting for Dessert

Latino Tomato, Avocado, and Red Onion Salad

Tart lime juice, creamy avocados, and biting red onions have an affinity for fragrant ripe, red tomatoes. Serve this Central American salad as a first course followed by paella or Arroz con Pollo (page 203).

Serves 6 to 8

4 large ripe red tomatoes, cut into $\frac{1}{4}$-inch slices
2 medium avocados, halved, peeled, seeded, and cut into $\frac{1}{4}$-inch slices
$\frac{1}{2}$ medium red onion, cut into $\frac{1}{4}$-inch slices
3 tablespoons fresh lime juice
3 tablespoons olive oil
2 tablespoons chopped fresh cilantro, plus $\frac{1}{2}$ cup whole leaves
Coarse salt and freshly ground black pepper

Alternate the tomato, avocado, and red onion slices in overlapping rows on a serving plate.

In a small bowl, whisk together the lime juice, olive oil, and chopped cilantro. Season to taste with salt and pepper.

Drizzle the vinaigrette over the tomatoes, avocados, and red onions. Garnish with the cilantro leaves and serve immediately.

Grilled Vegetable Salad

Grilled vegetable salads are best made in the late summer or early autumn, when the vegetables are at their peak and full of flavor. This one is drizzled with olive oil and sprinkled with parsley, garlic, and black olives; you can also garnish it with a few slices of toasted bread, rubbed with garlic and olive oil. If you don't have a grill, char the vegetables under the broiler or directly over a gas burner.

Serves 6

3 long thin eggplants (about ³/₄ pound)
3 small ripe red tomatoes
3 small ripe yellow tomatoes
1 large red bell pepper
1 large green bell pepper
2 small yellow onions
Coarse salt and freshly ground black pepper
3¹/₂ tablespoons extra virgin olive oil
3 tablespoons chopped fresh flat-leaf parsley
2 garlic cloves, minced, plus 1 whole garlic
    clove
12 cured black olives, such as Niçoise or
    Kalamata
6 slices coarse-textured bread

Preheat an outdoor grill. Preheat the oven to 350°F.

Grill the eggplant, tomatoes, bell peppers, and onions over a very hot fire, turning occasionally, until they are black on all sides, about 10 minutes.

Remove the vegetables from the grill and place on a baking sheet. Place in the oven and bake until soft; the eggplant, tomatoes, and peppers will cook in about 20 minutes, the onions will take about 1 hour. As the vegetables are done, place them in a plastic bag and let cool enough to handle.

Core, seed, and peel the peppers and slice into thin strips. Peel the eggplant and tear the flesh into thin strips. Peel and thinly slice the onions. Slip the tomatoes out of their skins and cut them into quarters.

Arrange the vegetables on a large serving platter, alternating the colors. Season with salt and pepper and drizzle with 2 tablespoons of the olive oil. (The vegetables can be prepared several hours in advance.)

Combine the parsley and minced garlic and sprinkle over the vegetables. Garnish with the olives.

Toast the bread until golden. Rub one side of each toast with the whole garlic clove. Brush with the remaining 1¹/₂ tablespoons olive oil. Tuck the toasts around the vegetables and serve immediately.

Grilled Corn Salad with Tomato Vinaigrette

Corn on the cob has far too short a season. But when it's fresh and sweet, I like to roast it with bell peppers on the outdoor grill to make this salad, inspired by gifted chef Gary Danko. I use the peppers and tomatoes to make a zippy, slightly smoky vinaigrette to toss with peppery arugula, the corn kernels, Parmigiano, olives, and cherry tomatoes. (Alternatively, the corn can be boiled or steamed until tender and the peppers roasted in a 350°F oven for thirty minutes.) If you want, roast the corn and peppers and make the dressing a few hours ahead, so when you are ready to serve the salad, all you have to do is assemble it.

Serves 6 to 8

3 ears fresh corn in the husk
2 red bell peppers
1 ripe red tomato, diced
1/2 garlic clove, chopped
1 tablespoon tarragon vinegar
1/4 cup extra virgin olive oil
Coarse salt and freshly ground black pepper
3 bunches arugula, tough stems removed
   (about 10 cups)
1/4 cup plus 2 tablespoons freshly grated aged
   Pecorino or Parmigiano-Reggiano
3/4 cup cured black or green olives
1 1/2 cups red and yellow cherry tomatoes,
   halved

Preheat an outdoor grill.

Grill the corn and peppers 4 inches from the flame, turning occasionally, until the skins of the peppers and the corn husks are black and when the husk is pulled back, a few of the corn kernels are light golden, 7 to 8 minutes. Remove from the grill and place the peppers in a paper or plastic bag for 10 minutes. Let the corn cool.

Cut the kernels from the cob. Remove the skin and seeds from the peppers.

In a blender or food processor, puree the peppers, tomato, garlic, vinegar, and olive oil. Season to taste with salt and pepper. Strain the vinaigrette through a fine strainer and spoon it evenly onto individual serving plates.

In a large bowl, toss together the corn, arugula, and cheese. Place the salad on the plates and garnish with the olives and cherry tomatoes. Serve immediately.

Tomato-Lentil Salad

During the summer, when red, green, and yellow peppers are plentiful in the garden, and cherry tomatoes hang in clusters from the vines, make this salad. Use a variety of cherry tomatoes: yellow pear, green grape, orange and red Sweet 100s. Garnished with mint, the salad is colorful and full of vibrant flavors. Substitute black or white beans for the lentils and basil for the mint if you like.

Serves 8

1 cup lentils, preferably French le Puy, picked
   over and rinsed
$1/4$ cup extra virgin olive oil
$1/4$ cup plus 2 tablespoons red wine vinegar, or
   more to taste
2 garlic cloves, minced
$1/2$ teaspoon ground cumin
Coarse salt and freshly ground black pepper
1 small red onion, diced
$1/2$ medium red bell pepper, diced
$1/2$ medium yellow bell pepper, diced
$1/4$ cup chopped fresh mint
$1/2$ pound (about $1 1/2$ cups), cherry or pear
   tomatoes, halved
6 ounces goat cheese, crumbled
18 cured black olives, such as Kalamata or
   Niçoise

Place the lentils in a large saucepan and add water to cover by 2 inches. Bring to a boil, turn down the heat, and simmer, uncovered, for 20 to 30 minutes, until tender. Drain and cool. (The lentils can be cooked 1 day in advance and refrigerated.)

In a small bowl, whisk together the olive oil, vinegar, garlic, and cumin. Season to taste with salt and pepper. Combine the lentils, onion, bell peppers, $1/2$ teaspoon salt, and pepper to taste in a large bowl. Toss with the vinaigrette and let sit for 20 minutes. Taste and season as needed with additional salt, pepper, and vinegar. (This salad can be prepared and refrigerated up to this point 6 hours in advance.) Bring to room temperature before serving.

To serve, toss the salad with the mint and tomatoes and place on a platter. Garnish with the crumbled goat cheese and olives.

And by good tomatoes, everyone means tomatoes so red-flavored, so sharply sweet, that they need no more than olive oil as a dressing and plenty of pepper, tomatoes that need no vinegar or lemon juice since they carry their own acidity, just as good radishes carry their own pepper."

From Jane Grigson,
The Best of Jane Grigson

Couscous Salad with Tomatoes and Hot Green Peppers

This method of cooking couscous takes a little longer than the no-brainer technique described on the side of the box, but the results are far superior. It can be steamed a few days in advance. If time is of the essence, however, simply bring three cups of water to a boil, add the couscous, remove from the heat, cover, and let sit until the water is absorbed, about ten minutes, then fluff with a fork.

Serves 6

1 1/4 cups couscous
Coarse salt
1 yellow bell pepper, roasted (see page 13), peeled, seeded, and diced
1 red bell pepper, roasted (see page 13), peeled, seeded, and diced
1/2 pound assorted cherry tomatoes, halved
1 small cucumber, peeled, seeded, and diced
1 to 2 green or red jalapeños, seeded and minced
1/4 cup chopped fresh flat-leaf parsley
1/4 cup chopped fresh cilantro
1/4 cup extra virgin olive oil
1/4 cup plus 2 tablespoons fresh lemon juice
1 1/2 teaspoons ground cumin
1/2 teaspoon sweet paprika
3 garlic cloves, minced
Freshly ground black pepper

Rinse the couscous in cold water and drain immediately. Lift and rake the grains with your fingertips to separate them. Let sit for 10 minutes.

Heat about 6 cups of water in the bottom of a soup pot fitted with a steamer basket. Line the steamer with a layer of cheesecloth so it comes over the top. Make certain that the steamer fits snugly into the soup pot and that the bottom of the steamer doesn't touch the water. Add the couscous to the steamer and steam for 30 minutes, uncovered, fluffing the grains with a fork halfway through the cooking.

Dump the couscous into a baking pan. Combine 1/2 cup cold water and 1/2 teaspoon salt and stir until the salt dissolves. Sprinkle the couscous with the saltwater. Lift and rake the grains with your fingertips for 10 minutes to separate them. Let cool completely.

Place the couscous in a large bowl and add the bell peppers, tomatoes, cucumber, jalapeños, parsley, and cilantro.

In a small bowl, whisk together the olive oil, lemon juice, cumin, paprika, and garlic. Season with salt and pepper.

Toss the couscous and vegetables with the vinaigrette, season with salt and pepper, and serve.

Green Pepper and Tomato Salad

At the height of summer, tomatoes and peppers ripen at the same time. Roasted peppers tossed together with tomatoes, green and black olives, garlic, and spicy-hot harissa make a great addition to any al fresco dinner table. You can substitute one pound assorted or all red cherry tomatoes, halved, for the large tomatoes.

Serves 6

1/4 cup extra virgin olive oil
2 tablespoons white wine vinegar or fresh lemon juice
1/2 teaspoon ground cumin
3 tablespoons chopped fresh flat-leaf parsley
2 garlic cloves, minced
1/4 to 1/2 teaspoon harissa
Coarse salt and freshly ground black pepper
3 large green bell peppers, roasted (see page 13), peeled, seeded, and diced
3 large ripe red tomatoes, peeled and diced
1/4 cup cured black olives, such as Kalamata or Niçoise
1/4 cup cured green olives

In a small bowl, whisk together the olive oil, vinegar, cumin, parsley, and garlic. Season to taste with the harissa and salt and pepper.

Combine the peppers, tomatoes, and vinaigrette in a large bowl and toss together.

Mound the salad in the center of a serving platter, garnish with the olives, and serve.

Fattoush

Throughout the Mediterranean, bread salads have been made for centuries. They are part of a culture that knows how to make a feast from the humblest of foods. Fattoush, the Middle Eastern bread salad, is no exception. Succulent flavorful tomatoes are combined with stale or toasted pita bread, the crisp, succulent green purslane, cucumbers, and plenty of mint and cilantro. Sumac, a slightly acidic, astringent spice from the dried crushed berries of a decorative bush, is sprinkled over the top. Sumac is available in Middle Eastern markets, purslane at farmers' markets or some specialty produce markets. If they are unavailable, the salad will still be delicious.

Serves 6

1 medium cucumber, peeled, seeded, and diced
Coarse salt
2 large loaves pita breads, 3 to 4 days old
3 medium ripe red tomatoes, seeded and diced
6 green onions (white and green parts), cut into 1/4-inch slices
1 green bell pepper, cored, seeded, and diced
1 bunch purslane, tough stems removed (about 1 cup) (optional)
1/4 cup coarsely chopped fresh flat-leaf parsley
1/3 cup coarsely chopped fresh mint
1/4 cup coarsely chopped fresh cilantro
Freshly ground black pepper
2 large garlic cloves, minced
1/4 cup fresh lemon juice
1/3 cup extra virgin olive oil
2 teaspoons ground sumac berries (optional)

Preheat the oven to 375°F.

Spread the cucumbers in a single layer on paper towels. Sprinkle with salt and let drain for 20 minutes.

Trim the edges off the outside of the pita bread and tear each loaf of pita into two circles. Then tear into 1-inch pieces and spread them out on a baking sheet. Bake until light golden and dry, 10 to 15 minutes.

Place the cucumbers in a colander, run cold water over them for a moment, drain them well, and dry on clean paper towels.

In a large bowl, combine the cucumbers, tomatoes, green onions, bell pepper, purslane, if using, the parsley, mint, and cilantro. Season with salt and pepper and toss gently.

In a small bowl, whisk together the garlic, lemon juice, and olive oil. Season with salt and pepper.

Toss the vegetables and bread with the vinaigrette. Place on a platter, sprinkle with the sumac, if using, and serve immediately.

Tomato Soup Dressing

In the fifties, canned tomato soup was so much the rage that The White Drum, a restaurant in Orange, Massachusetts, made a salad dressing using the stuff. Here is their recipe:

1 can Campbell's tomato soup
3/4 cup vinegar
1/2 cup oil
1/4 cup sugar
1 tablespoon Worcestershire sauce

1 small onion, minced
1 green pepper, chopped
1 teaspoon salt
1 teaspoon paprika

Combine the ingredients and whisk together. Makes 1 quart to serve with iceberg lettuce, sliced Chinese cabbage, sliced cucumbers, wedges of tomato, sliced radishes, cauliflower florets, sliced celery, and watercress.

Panzanella: Tuscan Bread Salad

Imagine a sandwich of ripe, juicy tomatoes, crisp cucumbers, thin slices of sweet red onion, and sprigs of fresh herbs tucked between two thick slices of crusty European-style bread. Now imagine tearing that sandwich into pieces, dousing it with vinegar and fruity olive oil, and tossing it all together in a bowl. You'd have all the makings for the Italian bread salad called panzanella.

Serves 6

1/2 pound coarse-textured bread, 3 to 4 days
    old, cut into 1-inch slices
1 medium cucumber, peeled, seeded, and diced
Coarse salt
3 medium ripe red tomatoes, seeded and diced
2 medium ripe yellow tomatoes, seeded and
    diced
1 medium red onion, diced
1/2 cup lightly packed fresh basil leaves
1/4 cup plus 1 tablespoon red wine vinegar
2 garlic cloves, minced
1/3 cup extra virgin olive oil
Freshly ground black pepper

Sprinkle the bread with 1/2 cup water and let sit for about 2 minutes. Carefully squeeze the bread dry. Tear it into rough 1-inch pieces and let drain on paper towels for 20 minutes.

In the meantime, spread the cucumber in a single layer on paper towels. Sprinkle with salt and let drain for 20 minutes.

Place the cucumbers in a colander, run cold water over them for a moment, drain them, and dry on clean paper towels.

In a large bowl, combine the cucumber, tomatoes, and onion. Tear the basil into 1/2-inch pieces and add to the vegetables. Add the bread and toss carefully.

In a small bowl, whisk together the vinegar, garlic, and olive oil. Season with salt and pepper.

Carefully toss the vegetables and bread with the vinaigrette and let sit for 20 minutes. Place on a platter and serve.

When Tasting Tomatoes

There are three things to note when tasting tomatoes—fragrance, taste, and texture. Is the aroma sweet, earthy, or sharp, musty or fresh? Is the taste sweet and/or sour? What is the aftertaste like? Is the texture firm or soft, mealy or juicy, or gelatinous? Is the skin thick or thin?

Istanbul Bread Salad with Tomatoes and Olives

This zippy, pungent, aromatic salad was inspired by my Turkish friend Angel Stoyanof. For other bread salads, such as fattoush and panzanella (see pages 94 and 96), the tomatoes are seeded. Not with this one—it uses the whole tomato. Be sure to add the ripe tomatoes and all the juices and seeds to the salad.

Serves 6

3 medium ripe red tomatoes, diced
1 small red onion, diced
1 cup pitted dry-cured black olives, coarsely
    chopped
$1/4$ cup fresh lemon juice
$1/3$ cup extra virgin olive oil
Coarse salt and freshly ground black pepper
$1/2$ pound coarse-textured sourdough bread, 3
    to 4 days old
$1/4$ cup coarsely chopped fresh mint

In a large serving bowl, combine the tomatoes, red onion, olives, lemon juice, olive oil, and salt and pepper to taste. Mix well.

Tear the bread into $3/4$- to 1-inch pieces. (This salad can be made up to this point 1 to 3 hours before serving.)

Just before serving, add the bread to the tomato and olive mixture and toss well. Sprinkle the mint on top and serve immediately.

Warm BLT Salad

Here's a new way to satisfy the urge for a good old BLT sandwich. For a change, crumble goat cheese on top of the salad and serve with crusty whole grain rolls as a light lunch main course.

Serves 6

6 thick slices bacon, preferably apple-smoked,
    cut into $1/2$-inch pieces
2 tablespoons extra virgin olive oil
3 tablespoons red wine vinegar
Coarse salt and freshly ground black pepper
1 large head curly escarole or 2 heads frisée,
    torn into 2-inch pieces, washed, and spun
    dry
4 large ripe red tomatoes, cut into $1/2$-inch
    wedges
4 green onions, thinly sliced

Cook the bacon in a large frying pan over medium heat, turning occasionally, until golden and crisp, 4 to 5 minutes. With a slotted spoon, remove the bacon and drain on paper towels.

Drain off all but 2 tablespoons of the bacon fat from the pan. Add the olive oil and stir together. Return the bacon to the pan and warm gently over low heat. Remove from the heat and whisk in the vinegar. Season to taste with salt and pepper.

Place the escarole, tomatoes, and green onions in a salad bowl. Toss with the vinaigrette and serve immediately.

Warm Salad of Grilled Tuna, Beans, and Cherry Tomatoes

To celebrate the height of summer, pick fresh flageolets, black-eyed peas, cranberry beans, limas, or cannellini beans and combine them with grilled fresh tuna, green and yellow beans, and cherry tomatoes. If fresh shell beans are unavailable, substitute half a cup of dried flageolet, cranberry, lima, or cannellini beans. Soak them for several hours in cold water, then drain and cook in plenty of water until tender. In place of garlic mayonnaise in the salad, the Tomato Mayonnaise with a Kick (page 40) is a killer.

Serves 6

2 pounds fresh shell beans, shelled
1/4 cup plus 1 tablespoon red wine vinegar
1/4 cup plus 1 tablespoon extra virgin olive oil
Coarse salt and freshly ground black pepper
1/2 pound green beans, trimmed
1/2 pound yellow beans, trimmed
3/4 pound assorted cherry tomatoes (red, yellow, and/or pear-shaped), halved
1 pound fresh tuna steak, 3/4 inch thick
1 recipe Aïoli (page 38)
About 20 fresh basil leaves

Bring a large saucepan of water to a boil over medium-high heat. Add the shell beans and cook until they are very soft, about 20 to 30 minutes.

Preheat an outdoor grill.

Drain the beans and toss with 1/4 cup of the vinegar, 1/4 cup of the olive oil, and salt and pepper to taste.

Place in a bowl and cover with foil to keep warm.

Blanch the green beans and yellow beans in boiling salted water until they are tender but still slightly crisp, 5 to 8 minutes. Drain. Add to the shell beans and toss together. Cover to keep warm.

In a medium bowl, toss the cherry tomatoes with salt and pepper to taste and the remaining 1 tablespoon vinegar.

Brush the tuna with the remaining 1 tablespoon oil. Grill 4 inches from the flame until golden on one side, about 3 minutes. Turn the tuna, season with salt and pepper, and cook until the tuna is done but still slightly pink in the center, about 4 more minutes. Remove from the grill.

In the meantime, whisk the aïoli with 2 tablespoons water to make a barely fluid paste. Cut the basil into thin strips.

To serve, flake the tuna into 1-inch pieces. Place the beans on a platter and top with the tomatoes, tuna, and a spoonful of the aïoli. Garnish with the basil. Pass the remaining mayonnaise in a bowl on the side.

Smoked Chicken Salad with Tomato Vinaigrette

For added smoky flavor, the smoked chicken and greens in this salad are tossed with a vinaigrette made with a grilled tomato. If an outdoor grill is unavailable, grill the tomato on the stovetop in a hot cast-iron pan or on a cast-iron ridged grill, turning occasionally, until it begins to ooze its juices and the skin is black, ten to twelve minutes. The vinaigrette can be made several hours in advance and tossed with the chicken and salad greens just before serving.

Serves 6

1 medium ripe red or yellow tomato
3 tablespoons extra virgin olive oil
2 tablespoons red wine vinegar
Coarse salt and freshly ground black pepper
One 2½-pound smoked chicken, skin removed, meat removed from bones and torn into thin strips
8 cups mixed baby salad greens (mesclun), washed and spun dry
½ pound assorted or all red cherry tomatoes, halved

Preheat an outdoor grill.

Grill the tomato, turning occasionally, until black on all sides, about 15 minutes. Remove from the grill and cool for 10 minutes.

Core the tomato and cut into ½-inch dice. Place in a skillet over medium-high heat and cook until most of the liquid has evaporated, about 5 minutes.

Place the tomato in a blender, add the olive oil and red wine vinegar, and process until smooth, 1 minute. Strain through a fine strainer into a bowl. Season to taste with salt and pepper.

In a large bowl, toss the chicken, salad greens, cherry tomatoes, and vinaigrette together. Place in a serving bowl and serve immediately.

About Catalonia

At Vendrell lunch began every day with these fruits cut in half across, scored with the point of a knife on the exposed surfaces, some slices of peeled garlic inserted, then sprinkled with salt and *orenga*, wild marjoram. Some very fine slices of raw sweet white onion were laid on top of each half, and sometimes one or two desalted anchovy fillets. Always prepared at the last moment for the sake of freshness. Everyone helped themselves to olive oil from the *setrill*, a little glass bottle with a spout."

From Patience Gray, *Honey from a Weed*

Salt Cod, Tomato, and Cured Olive Salad

The saltiness of salt cod pairs very well with tomatoes, as you'll see from this Catalonian dish from Spain. It is called esqueixada, *from the word to tear or shred, because the salt cod is torn into strips. Make this several hours in advance to give the flavors time to marry.*

Serves 6

10 ounces salt cod
1 small red onion, thinly sliced
Coarse salt
3 medium ripe red tomatoes, peeled, seeded, and chopped
1 red bell pepper, cored, seeded, and diced
2 garlic cloves, minced
1/4 cup plus 1 tablespoon extra virgin olive oil
3 tablespoons red wine vinegar
24 cured black olives, such as Kalamata or Niçoise
Freshly ground black pepper
12 slices country-style bread, toasted

Soak the salt cod in cold water for 2 or 3 days, changing the water a few times per day.

Drain the salt cod and squeeze with your hands to get rid of the excess water. Remove the skin and bones and discard. Tear the cod into thin strips and place in a bowl.

Soak the onion in salted water for 30 minutes. Drain and pat dry.

Place the onion in the bowl with the cod, along with the tomatoes, bell pepper, garlic, oil, vinegar, and olives. Season with salt and pepper. Let marinate for 2 hours at room temperature.

To serve, place the cod salad on a serving plate and surround with the toasted bread.

savory pies, tarts, pizzas, and flatbreads

Tomato Galette

Some people think pastry making is impossible, but the cornmeal crust for this galette, or thin flat pie, is a breeze to prepare. Just make sure to keep the dough ice-cold at all times while you are working with it; if it warms up as you assemble the galette, put it back in the refrigerator and chill until cold.

Serves 6

1 cup all-purpose flour, placed in the freezer
  for 1 hour
¼ cup yellow cornmeal or polenta, placed in
  the freezer for 1 hour
Coarse salt
8 tablespoons unsalted butter (1 stick), cut into
  ½-inch pieces and placed in the freezer for 1
  hour
3 tablespoons sour cream
1 teaspoon fresh lemon juice
¾ cup coarsely grated mozzarella (about 3
  ounces)
¾ cup coarsely grated Fontina (about 3 ounces)
¼ cup fresh basil leaves, cut into thin strips
3 ripe but firm medium red tomatoes, thinly
  sliced
Freshly ground black pepper

Mound the flour, cornmeal, and ½ teaspoon salt on a work surface or in a bowl. Add the butter to the flour and with a pastry scraper, cut in the butter until it looks like oatmeal. Alternatively, this can be done in a food processor, pulsing several times.

Whisk together the sour cream, lemon juice, and ⅓ cup ice water. Add a tablespoon at a time to the flour mixture, using a fork to toss and distribute the liquid. Add just enough water so the dough holds together. Wrap well and let rest for at least 30 minutes, or overnight, in the refrigerator.

Preheat the oven to 400°F.

Roll out the dough on a floured surface to a 12-inch circle. Trim the edges to make a rough circular shape. Place on a baking sheet. (This can be done several hours in advance and refrigerated.)

In a bowl, combine the mozzarella, Fontina, and basil and toss well. Spread the cheeses over the dough, leaving a 2-inch border. Place the tomatoes over the cheese overlapping them slightly in rings. Season with salt and pepper. Fold the uncovered edge of the pastry over the cheese, pleating it to make it fit and leaving the center uncovered.

Bake until the pastry is golden brown, 35 to 45 minutes. Let cool for 5 minutes, then slide the galette onto a serving plate. Cut into wedges and serve hot, warm, or at room temperature.

Tomato and Green Onion Tart

Making traditional puff pastry is a whole-day affair. Here is a short-cut puff pastry that takes only ten minutes to make, and the results are astounding for so little effort. Freezing the flour and butter first and using ice water keeps the pastry very, very cold and keeps the layers of butter and flour separate. Filled with sliced tomatoes and mozzarella and Parmesan cheese, this is an ideal first course or light vegetarian main course. You can substitute store-bought puff pastry.

Serves 6 to 8

3 medium ripe red tomatoes, cut into ¹/₄-inch
    slices
1 cup all-purpose flour, placed in the freezer
    for 1 hour
¹/₃ cup cake flour, placed in the freezer for 1
    hour
¹/₄ teaspoon salt
12 tablespoons unsalted butter (1¹/₂ sticks),
    diced into ¹/₄-inch cubes and placed in the
    freezer for 1 hour
2 teaspoons fresh lemon juice
³/₄ cup coarsely grated fresh mozzarella (about 3
    ounces)
¹/₂ cup freshly grated Parmigiano-Reggiano
2 tablespoons chopped fresh oregano
6 green onions, thinly sliced

Place the tomato slices on paper towels and let drain for 1 hour.

Place the all-purpose flour, cake flour, salt, and butter in a food processor and pulse until the butter is cut into ¹/₄-inch and cornmeal-size pieces. Transfer to a mixing bowl. Combine the lemon juice and ¹/₄ cup ice water, add to the bowl, and mix until the dough just holds together.

Turn the dough out onto a lightly floured board and press it together to form a rough rectangular shape. There will be chunks of butter showing. With a rolling pin, roll the dough into a ¹/₂-inch-thick rectangle approximately 8 × 10 inches. Fold the narrow ends over to meet in the center. Fold in half again so that there are four layers. (This is your first turn.)

Turn the dough so the fold is on your left. Roll again to form an 8 × 10-inch rectangle. Repeat the folding process. (This is your second turn.) Turn the dough again so the fold is on your left. Roll again to form an 8 × 10-inch rectangle. Repeat the folding process. Wrap the dough in plastic wrap and chill in the refrigerator for 1 hour or up to 2 days.

Preheat the oven to 400°F.

Using a floured rolling pin, on a floured surface, roll the pastry into approximately a 12-inch square and trim it to make a 12-inch circle. Crimp the edges to form a decorative edge. Place on a baking sheet.

Sprinkle the mozzarella, ¹/₄ cup of the Parmigiano, and the oregano evenly over the pastry. Sprinkle the green onions over the cheese. Arrange the tomato slices in concentric circles, overlapping them slightly on top, and sprinkle with the remaining ¹/₄ cup Parmigiano. Bake in the top third of the oven until the crust is golden, 25 to 35 minutes.

Cut the tart into wedges and serve immediately, or serve warm.

Ratatouille Torta

R*atatouille, the quintessential Provençal vegetable stew of tomatoes, eggplant, onions, bell peppers, zucchini, and garlic, uses the bounty of the summer harvest. Layering it with creamy Fontina cheese in a pastry shell creates a savory torte that is perfect for summer entertaining al fresco. You can make the pastry and ratatouille the day before and bake the torta just before serving, or you can bake it ahead and serve it at room temperature.*

Serves 8

3 tablespoons olive oil
1 red bell pepper, cored, seeded, and diced
1 large red onion, chopped
1 small eggplant (about 1$^1/_4$ pounds), cut into
    $^1/_2$-inch cubes
2 small zucchini, cut into $^1/_4$-inch slices
3 garlic cloves, minced
1 teaspoon chopped fresh thyme
2 large ripe red or yellow tomatoes, peeled,
    seeded, and chopped
$^1/_4$ cup minced fresh flat-leaf parsley
$^1/_2$ cup pitted cured black olives, such as
    Kalamata or Niçoise, coarsely chopped
Coarse salt and freshly ground black pepper
2 cups all-purpose flour
10 tablespoons (1$^1/_4$ sticks) unsalted butter, cut
    into 12 pieces and chilled
$^1/_4$ cup vegetable shortening, chilled
2 cups coarsely grated Fontina (about 8 ounces)
$^3/_4$ cup freshly grated Parmigiano-Reggiano
1 large egg
1 tablespoon milk

Heat the olive oil in a large skillet over medium heat. Add the bell pepper and onion and cook, stirring occasionally, until soft, 10 minutes. Add the eggplant, zucchini, garlic, and thyme and cook, stirring occasionally, until the zucchini is soft, about 10 minutes. Add the tomatoes and parsley and simmer over medium-low heat until the eggplant is soft and the liquid has evaporated, about 40 minutes.

Add the olives and season to taste with salt and pepper. Let cool completely. (This can be made up to 1 day in advance and stored in the refrigerator. Bring to room temperature when ready to use.)

In the meantime, in a food processor, pulse the flour and $^1/_2$ teaspoon salt together. Add the butter and shortening and pulse until the mixture resembles cornmeal. Transfer to a bowl. Add just enough ice water (about $^1/_4$ cup) so the dough holds together as you stir with a fork. Wrap in plastic wrap and place in the refrigerator for at least 1 hour, or overnight.

Preheat the oven to 375°F.

> "... but the truly remarkable side to the world's tomatomania is that it was able to develop and spread in an atmosphere of almost universal tomatophobia. Out of initial ignorance and disgust grew ultimate passion."
>
> From Raymond Sokolov,
> *Why We Eat What We Eat*

Divide the pastry in half and, using a floured rolling pin, on a floured surface, roll out half of the dough to a 12-inch circle. Line a 9-inch pie plate with the pastry, letting the excess hang over the sides.

In a bowl, combine the Fontina and Parmigiano-Reggiano. Spread half of the vegetable mixture in the pie shell. Sprinkle with half of the cheese. Repeat with the remaining vegetable mixture and cheese. Brush the edges of the pastry lightly with water. Roll out the remaining dough to a 10-inch circle and place on top of the pie. Trim and crimp the edges to make a decorative pattern. Cut a 1-inch hole in the center for the steam to escape.

In a small bowl, whisk together the egg and milk. Brush the top of the pastry lightly with the mixture and bake until golden, 25 to 30 minutes. Serve hot, warm, or at room temperature.

One of the major surprises of my early womanhood was a remark my father made as we drove hell-for-leather from Whittier to San Francisco on some bit of family derring-do. We stopped at King City for a salad or a sandwich, in the blistering heat. And it was there, in a café I could draw today, or go to if it still stood and if ever again I went to King City, which I shall try not to, that Rex said mildly about a bit of garnish on his plate, 'Anyone who serves tomatoes without peeling them should be shot at dawn.' I believe we walked out: It was too hot for eating, anyway, but what astounded me was that my father, who seldom made any comment about flavor or texture at the table or indeed in our presence, could have felt thus strongly all the time I was growing up under his eye, and was probably expressing myself firmly on a great many aspects of our daily meals . . . *politely* but firmly, and not at the table. Many years later, when I went to keep house for him in his old age, I was careful never to serve tomatoes unless they had been meticulously flayed."

From M. F. K. Fisher,
With Bold Knife and Fork

Lamb and Tomato Pie

Maria and Dimitri Likouressis are two of the best cooks in Greece. He bakes crusty wholesome breads in his bee-hive oven while Maria cooks rustic pies, pastries, and stews. She loves to garden, growing some of the tastiest tomatoes I've ever had, which she mixes with lamb, feta, green onions, and garlic for this savory pie. Make the dough a day in advance and let it rise overnight in the refrigerator.

Serves 8

■ pastry
1 tablespoon dry yeast
³/₄ cup warm milk
3³/₄ cups all-purpose or unbleached bread flour
¹/₂ cup plus 1 tablespoon olive oil
1 teaspoon salt
1 large egg, lightly beaten

■ filling
1¹/₂ pounds lamb cut from the leg or shoulder, trimmed of fat
2 tablespoons olive oil
8 green onions, thinly sliced
4 garlic cloves, minced
2¹/₂ cups peeled, seeded, chopped, and drained canned or fresh tomatoes
2 bay leaves, very finely crumbled
Coarse salt and freshly ground black pepper

■ assembly
1 tablespoon olive oil
1 cup crumbled feta cheese (about 5 ounces)
1 tablespoon unsalted butter, melted

For the pastry, combine the yeast and milk in a large bowl and stir well to dissolve the yeast. Let sit for 10 minutes, or until frothy. Add the flour, ¹/₂ cup of the olive oil, ¹/₄ cup water, the salt, and egg and mix until the dough comes together. Remove from the bowl and knead on a floured surface until smooth and elastic, 6 to 7 minutes. (Alternatively, this can be made in an electric mixer using a dough hook.) Oil a large bowl with the remaining 1 tablespoon olive oil. Place the dough in the bowl and turn over to coat. Cover with plastic wrap and let sit in the refrigerator overnight or for up to 2 days.

For the filling, cut the lamb into thin ¹/₄ × 1¹/₂-inch strips. Heat the olive oil in a large skillet over medium-high heat. Add the lamb and sauté until browned, about 5 minutes. Reduce the heat to medium-low, add the green onions and garlic, and cook until the green onions are wilted, 3 minutes. Add the tomatoes and bay leaves and cook, uncov-ered, until the liquid has evaporated, 15 to 20 min-utes. Season to taste with salt and pepper. Cool. (This filling can be made up to 3 days in advance and refrigerated.)

Preheat the oven to 375°F. Brush a 10-inch round springform pan lightly with olive oil.

> **W**hen you no longer care about fresh toma-toes and sweet corn, then death is near. . . ."
>
> Garrison Keillor

 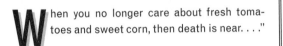

To assemble the pie, divide the dough into 2 pieces. On a floured surface, roll one piece of dough into a 14-inch circle, 1/8 inch thick. Place the dough in the cake pan, stretching slightly so it comes up over the edges. Brush with the olive oil. Spread the cooled filling evenly over the dough. Sprinkle the feta on top of the filling.

Roll the other piece of dough into an 11-inch cir-cle. Place on top of the filling, press the edges of the dough together, and trim the excess to 1/2 inch. Roll the crust inward to form a rim. Brush the top with the melted butter. Bake for 15 minutes. Re-duce the heat to 325°F and continue to bake until golden, 45 to 55 minutes. If the top gets too dark, cover with foil and continue to bake. Remove from the oven and let rest for 20 minutes before serving.

Release the springform. Cut into wedges and serve hot or at room temperature.

Cheddar-Crusted Tomato and Roasted Pepper Flan

The Cheddar cheese gives the crust a crisp texture, but if you serve this flan warm, it will literally melt in your mouth. The filling is sweet from the tomatoes and red bell peppers; if you like the tanginess of fresh goat cheese, add five ounces, crumbled, to the filling.

Serves 8

■ pastry
1¼ cups all-purpose flour
5 tablespoons unsalted butter, cut into 12 pieces and frozen
1 cup coarsely grated Cheddar cheese (about 4 ounces)
¼ cup vegetable shortening, frozen
⅛ teaspoon salt

■ filling
2 cups peeled, seeded, chopped, and drained fresh or canned tomatoes
Coarse salt and freshly ground black pepper
2 large eggs
1 large egg yolk
1 cup half-and-half
3 red bell peppers, roasted (see page 13), peeled, seeded, and diced

For the pastry, in a food processor, pulse the flour, butter, and Cheddar together until the mixture resembles coarse meal. Add the shortening and pulse only until the pieces of shortening are a little larger than the butter pieces. Transfer to a bowl. Mix the salt and ¼ cup ice water together and add just enough of the liquid to the flour mixture, stirring with a fork, so the dough comes together. Wrap the dough in plastic and let rest in the refrigerator for at least 30 minutes, or overnight.

With a floured rolling pin, on a floured surface, roll out the pastry to a 12-inch circle. Place in a 9-inch pie plate. Crimp the edges and prick the bottom of the pastry. Place in the freezer for 30 minutes.

Preheat the oven to 400°F.

Line the pastry with parchment or aluminum foil. Fill with dried beans or metal pie weights and bake until the edges of the crust are golden brown, 15 to 20 minutes. Remove the beans or pie weights and lining. Return to the oven and bake until light golden, 5 to 7 minutes. (The pastry shell can be baked several hours in advance.)

For the filling, in a saucepan, bring the tomatoes to a boil over high heat. Reduce the heat to low and simmer until the tomatoes break down and are reduced to ½ cup, 15 to 20 minutes. Season to taste with salt and pepper. Let cool.

In a bowl, whisk together the eggs, egg yolk, and half-and-half. Add the tomato sauce and the bell peppers. Season to taste with salt and pepper. Pour into the pastry shell and bake until set, 30 to 40 minutes.

To serve, cut into wedges.

Pizza Dough

This dough is made in two simple steps. First you make a sponge, then you add the remaining ingredients and knead seven to eight minutes. You can also use an electric mixer.

Makes enough for two 9-inch pizzas

2 teaspoons active dry yeast
2 cups all-purpose flour
2 tablespoons olive oil
1 tablespoon milk
$^1/_2$ teaspoon salt

In a small bowl, combine $^1/_4$ cup lukewarm (110°F) water, the yeast, and $^1/_4$ cup of the flour. Let stand for 20 minutes.

Add the remaining $1^3/_4$ cups flour, $^1/_2$ cup lukewarm water, the olive oil, milk, and salt and mix thoroughly. Turn the dough out onto a floured surface and knead until smooth, elastic, and a bit tacky to the touch, 7 to 8 minutes.

Place the dough in an oiled bowl and turn to cover with oil. Cover with plastic wrap and let rise in a warm place (75°F) until doubled in volume, about 1 hour. Proceed as directed in individual recipes.

Alternatively, you can let this dough rise in the refrigerator overnight. The next day, bring the dough to room temperature and proceed.

The Pompeiians also ate pizza. It was pizza without tomatoes, of course, for 1,500 years had to elapse before the first tomato would be seen in Europe—according to local legend, when Neapolitan sailors brought the first seeds back from Peru. There is no evidence to support this belief, except that Naples makes lavish use of the tomato; but in any case the antiquity of pizza as a Neapolitan dish is firmly established. It is probably the single food most firmly associated with Naples."

From Waverley Root,
The Food of Italy

Pizza Margherita

So often, cooks pile too many ingredients onto a pizza. The secret of this classic one is to keep it simple. The crust isn't drowned in tomato sauce and cheese; instead, fresh plum tomatoes are stewed until they are thick and spread onto the dough. Thin slices of fresh mozzarella are layered on top and then, when it comes from the oven, all crispy and golden, the pizza is sprinkled with torn fresh basil.

Makes two 10-inch pizzas

10 ripe plum tomatoes, peeled, seeded, and
   chopped
2 tablespoons thinly sliced fresh basil, plus 6
   leaves, torn into small pieces
Coarse salt and freshly ground black pepper
1 recipe Pizza Dough (page 109)
1 tablespoon extra virgin olive oil
5 ounces fresh mozzarella, thinly sliced

Thirty minutes before baking, place a pizza stone or unglazed quarry tiles on the bottom rack of the oven and preheat the oven to 500°F.

In a saucepan, bring the tomatoes and thinly sliced basil to a boil over high heat. Reduce the heat to low and simmer until the tomatoes are reduced to $1/2$ cup, 15 to 20 minutes. Season to taste with salt and pepper. Cool.

Punch down the dough. On a floured surface, divide the dough into 2 pieces and form each into a ball. Roll one piece into a 10-inch circle, about $1/4$ inch thick. Transfer it to a well-floured pizza peel or paddle. Brush the dough to within $1/2$ inch of the edge with half of the oil. Spread half of the tomato sauce to within $1/2$ inch of the edge. Place half of the cheese over the sauce, distributing evenly. Slide the pizza onto the pizza stone and bake until golden and crisp, 8 to 12 minutes. Remove from the oven and serve immediately, topped with half of the torn basil. Repeat with the remaining dough and topping ingredients.

Pizza with Tomatoes, Shrimp, and Aïoli

Take a traditional tomato pizza, top it with shrimp and a sprinkling of hot red pepper flakes, and bake until crispy and golden. Serve immediately drizzled with garlic mayonnaise and watch it melt into the spicy shrimp. In place of shrimp, thin slices of calamari or shelled clams or mussels may be used.

Makes two 10-inch pizzas

3 garlic cloves, minced
2 tablespoons extra virgin olive oil
10 ripe plum tomatoes, peeled, seeded, and
 chopped
Pinch of crushed red pepper flakes
Coarse salt and freshly ground black pepper
$1/4$ cup Aïoli (page 38)
$1/2$ pound medium shrimp, shelled
1 recipe Pizza Dough (page 109)
1 tablespoon snipped fresh chives

Thirty minutes before baking, place a pizza stone or unglazed quarry tiles on the bottom rack of the oven and preheat the oven to 500°F.

In a small bowl, combine the garlic and olive oil and let stand for 30 minutes.

In the meantime, in a large saucepan, bring the tomatoes and crushed red pepper flakes to a boil over high heat. Reduce the heat to low and simmer until the tomatoes are reduced to $1/2$ cup, 15 to 20 minutes. Season to taste with salt and pepper. Cool.

In a bowl, whisk together the aïoli and 1 to $1 1/2$ tablespoons warm water to make a barely fluid paste. Set aside or refrigerate. Slice the shrimp in half down the back. Put in a bowl, season with salt and pepper, and refrigerate.

Punch down the dough. On a floured surface, divide the dough into 2 pieces and form each into a ball. Roll one piece into a 10-inch circle, about $1/4$ inch thick. Transfer it to a well-floured pizza peel or paddle. Brush the dough to within $1/2$ inch of the edge with half of the garlic-infused oil. Spread half of the tomato sauce to within $1/2$ inch of the edge. Slide the pizza onto the pizza stone and bake until it just starts to turn golden, 4 to 5 minutes. Remove from the oven and quickly distribute half the shrimp on top. Return to the oven and bake until golden, 4 to 7 more minutes. Drizzle with half the aïoli and sprinkle with half the chives. Serve immediately. Repeat with the remaining dough and topping ingredients.

Pizza with Tomatoes, Fontina, and Gorgonzola

Three different cheeses might seem like overkill, but, used in small amounts, each one provides its own taste and texture. Italian Fontina is a creamy cow's milk cheese with a mild, nutty flavor that combines well with melting mozzarella and savory, pungent Gorgonzola.

Makes two 10-inch pizzas

3 garlic cloves, minced
2 tablespoons extra virgin olive oil
1/2 cup coarsely grated Italian Fontina (about 2 ounces)
1/2 cup coarsely grated mozzarella (about 2 ounces)
4 ounces Gorgonzola
10 ripe plum tomatoes, peeled, seeded, and chopped
Coarse salt and freshly ground black pepper
1 recipe Pizza Dough (page 109), made with 2 teaspoons chopped fresh rosemary

Thirty minutes before baking, place a pizza stone or unglazed quarry tiles on the bottom rack of the oven and preheat the oven to 500°F.

In a small bowl, combine the garlic and olive oil and let stand for 30 minutes. In another bowl, combine the Fontina, mozzarella, and Gorgonzola cheeses.

In the meantime, in a saucepan, bring the tomatoes to a boil over high heat. Reduce the heat to low and simmer until the tomatoes are reduced to 1/2 cup, 15 to 20 minutes. Season to taste with salt and pepper. Cool.

Punch down the dough. On a floured surface, divide the dough into 2 pieces and form each into a ball. Roll one piece into a 10-inch circle, about 1/4 inch thick. Transfer it to a well-floured pizza peel or paddle. Brush the dough to within 1/2 inch of the edge with half the garlic-infused oil. Spread half of the tomato sauce to within 1/2 inch of the edge. Sprinkle with half of the cheese. Slide the pizza onto the pizza stone and bake until golden and crisp, 8 to 12 minutes. Remove from the oven and serve immediately. Repeat with the remaining dough and topping ingredients.

All-in-One Pizza and Salad

A *green salad often accompanies a pizza, so why not combine the two? When your herb garden is at its peak, pick lots of sweet basil, cilantro, flat-leaf parsley, and mint. Add a big handful of peppery arugula and toss with a lemony dressing. Pile the salad and some feta on top of a fresh tomato pizza after it comes out of the oven.*

Makes two 10-inch pizzas

10 ripe plum tomatoes, peeled, seeded, and
   chopped
Coarse salt and freshly ground black pepper
2 1/2 tablespoons extra virgin olive oil
1 tablespoon fresh lemon juice
1 garlic clove, minced
1 recipe Pizza Dough (page 109)
1/4 cup fresh flat-leaf parsley leaves
1/4 cup fresh cilantro leaves
1/4 cup small fresh basil leaves
1/4 cup fresh mint leaves
1 cup arugula, tough stems removed
3 green onions, thinly sliced
1 cup crumbled feta cheese (about 5 ounces)

Thirty minutes before baking, place a pizza stone or unglazed quarry tiles on the bottom rack of the oven and preheat the oven to 500°F.

In a large saucepan, bring the tomatoes to a boil over high heat. Reduce the heat to low and simmer until the tomatoes are reduced to 1/2 cup, 15 to 20 minutes. Season to taste with salt and pepper. Cool.

In a large bowl, whisk together 1 1/2 tablespoons of the olive oil, the lemon juice, and garlic. Season to taste with salt and pepper. Set aside.

Punch down the dough. On a floured surface, divide the dough into 2 pieces and form each into a ball. Roll one piece into a 10-inch circle, about 1/4 inch thick. Transfer it to a well-floured pizza peel or paddle. Brush the dough to within 1/2 inch of the edge with 1 1/2 teaspoons of the oil. Spread half of the tomato sauce to within 1/2 inch of the edge. Slide the pizza onto the pizza stone and bake until golden and crisp, 8 to 12 minutes.

Add the parsley, cilantro, basil, mint, arugula, and green onions to the vinaigrette and toss together.

Remove the pizza from the oven. Top with half of the salad. Scatter half the feta on top and serve immediately. Repeat with the remaining dough and topping ingredients.

Pizza with Arugula and Tomato Salad

There is nothing like a tomato and arugula salad tossed with lemon juice, garlic, and olive oil and placed on top of a hot, crisp pizza crust. It's sweet, hot, crunchy, crispy, tart, and sour, all in one bite. You can also place a few thin slices of prosciutto on each pizza as it comes from the oven.

Makes two 10-inch pizzas

4 garlic cloves, minced
$1/4$ cup plus 1 tablespoon extra virgin olive oil
$3/4$ cup coarsely grated Fontina (about 3 ounces)
$3/4$ cup coarsely grated mozzarella (about 3 ounces)
2 tablespoons fresh lemon juice
Coarse salt and freshly ground pepper
1 recipe Pizza Dough (page 109)
4 cups very, very coarsely chopped arugula
3 small ripe red tomatoes, cut into $1/2$-inch dice

Thirty minutes before baking, place a pizza stone or unglazed quarry tiles on the bottom rack of the oven and preheat the oven to 500°F.

In the meantime, in a small bowl, combine three quarters of the garlic and 2 tablespoons of the olive oil and let stand for 30 minutes.

In another small bowl, combine the Fontina and mozzarella and set aside. In a large bowl, whisk together the remaining 3 tablespoons olive oil, the lemon juice, the remaining garlic, and salt and pepper to taste. Set aside.

Punch down the dough. On a floured surface, divide the dough into 2 pieces and form each into a ball. Roll one piece into a 10-inch circle, about $1/4$ inch thick. Transfer it to a well-floured pizza peel or paddle. Brush the dough to within $1/2$ inch of the edge with the garlic-infused oil. Spread half of the cheese to within $1/2$ inch of the edge. Slide the pizza onto the pizza stone and bake until golden and crisp, 8 to 12 minutes.

In the meantime, toss the arugula and tomatoes with the vinaigrette.

Remove the pizza from the oven, top with half of the arugula and tomato salad, distributing it evenly, and serve immediately. Repeat with the remaining dough and topping ingredients.

Crispy Cracker Pizza with Tomatoes and Anchovies

Made with a paper-thin, crisp crust, this cracker pizza can be cut into thin wedges and served with drinks. Or accompany it with a bowl of soup or a salad for a simple lunch. The dough can be made ahead and allowed to rise overnight in the refrigerator. When you are ready to bake it, bring it to room temperature and roll it out.

Makes two 12-inch pizzas

■ dough
2 teaspoons dry yeast
2 cups all-purpose or unbleached bread flour
3 tablespoons extra virgin olive oil
$1/2$ teaspoon salt

■ topping
2 tablespoons extra virgin olive oil
5 medium red onions, cut into $1/2$-inch slices
3 medium ripe red tomatoes, peeled, seeded, chopped, and drained, or 2 cups canned tomatoes
$1/3$ cup pitted black olives, chopped
Coarse salt and freshly ground black pepper
4 anchovy fillets, soaked in water for 10 minutes, drained, patted dry, and chopped
$1/3$ cup freshly grated Parmigiano-Reggiano

For the dough, in a large bowl, combine $1/4$ cup lukewarm (110°F) water, the yeast, and $1/4$ cup of the flour. Let stand until it bubbles and rises slightly, 20 minutes.

Add $1/2$ cup lukewarm (110°F) water, the remaining $1^3/4$ cups flour, the olive oil, and salt. Mix thoroughly and turn the dough out onto a well-floured surface. Knead until smooth and elastic but still a bit tacky to the touch, 7 to 8 minutes. Place the dough in an oiled bowl and turn to coat with oil. Cover with plastic wrap and let rise in a warm place (75°F) until doubled in volume, about 1 hour.

In the meantime, for the topping, heat the olive oil in a large skillet over medium heat. Add the onions and cook until very soft, about 40 minutes. Add the tomatoes and cook until the vegetables are dry, 10 to 15 minutes. Add the olives and season to taste with salt and pepper. Remove from the heat and let cool, then add the anchovies and stir to combine. (This can be made up to 1 day in advance and stored in the refrigerator until ready to use.)

Thirty minutes before baking, place a pizza stone or unglazed quarry tiles on the bottom rack of the oven and preheat the oven to 500°F.

Punch down the dough. On a floured surface, divide the dough into 2 pieces and shape each into a smooth ball. Roll one piece of dough into a 13- to 14-inch circle, about $1/8$ inch thick. Place on a well-floured pizza peel or paddle. Spread half the tomatoes and onions evenly over the dough, leaving a $1/2$-inch border around the edge. Transfer the dough to the pizza stone and bake until crisp and light golden, 6 to 9 minutes.

Remove the pizza from the oven, sprinkle with half the Parmesan, and serve immediately. Repeat with the remaining dough and topping ingredients.

Turkish Spiced Lamb and Tomato Pizza

On many a corner in Istanbul, you'll find small stands brightly painted yellow, orange, and red, where cooks make paper-thin pizzas, called lahmacun, topped with an aromatic paste of tomatoes, spices, and minced lamb. After it's baked, the soft, pliable dough is rolled up in a tube and handed to you still warm.

Serves 8

■ dough
2½ teaspoons dry yeast
2 tablespoons unsalted butter, melted
2 tablespoons olive oil
1 teaspoon coarse salt
3 cups all-purpose or unbleached bread flour

■ filling
2 tablespoons olive oil
1 large yellow onion, finely chopped
1 pound ground lamb
1 cup peeled, seeded, chopped, and drained
   fresh or canned tomatoes
2 tablespoons tomato paste
⅓ cup chopped fresh flat-leaf parsley
¼ cup pine nuts, toasted
¼ teaspoon ground cinnamon
¼ teaspoon ground allspice
⅛ teaspoon ground cloves
¼ teaspoon crushed red pepper flakes
½ teaspoon coarse salt
½ teaspoon freshly ground black pepper
1 tablespoon fresh lemon juice
3 tablespoons unsalted butter, melted

For the dough, combine the yeast and ¼ cup lukewarm (110°F) water in a large bowl and mix well. Let stand for 10 minutes, or until the yeast is dissolved and frothy. Add ¾ cup lukewarm (110°F) water, the butter, olive oil, salt, and flour. Mix well until a dough forms.

Turn the dough out onto a floured surface and knead until smooth and elastic, 7 to 10 minutes. Place in an oiled bowl and turn over to coat with oil. Cover with plastic wrap and let rise in a warm place (75°F) until doubled in volume, about 1 hour. (Alternatively, this can be left to rise in the refrigerator overnight. The next day, bring to room temperature and proceed.)

For the filling, heat the olive oil in a large frying pan over medium-high heat and cook the onion, stirring occasionally, until soft, about 7 minutes. Add the lamb, tomatoes, tomato paste, parsley, pine nuts, cinnamon, allspice, cloves, crushed red pepper flakes, salt, and black pepper. Lower the heat and cook slowly, uncovered, breaking up the lamb into small pieces with a spoon, until the mixture is almost dry, 8 minutes. Add the lemon juice and mix well. Remove from the heat and cool.

Preheat the oven to 450°F.

On a floured work surface, divide the dough into 16 egg-size pieces. With a rolling pin, roll each piece of dough into a very thin 7- to 8-inch circle, about 1/16 inch thick. Place in a single layer on 3 to 4 oiled baking sheets and let rest for 10 minutes.

Divide the cooled filling evenly among the circles and spread the filling to the edges of the dough; although the filling may not completely cover the dough. Drizzle with the butter. Bake the pizzas in batches until light golden around the edges but still soft enough to roll up, 6 to 7 minutes.

Remove from the oven, roll up each pizza, and serve immediately.

Rosemary Flatbread with Oven-Dried Tomatoes

This flatbread is basically a thick pizza or focaccia, flavored with fresh rosemary and topped with big chunky pieces of oven-dried tomatoes. Serve cut into wedges alongside a bowl of Tomato-Basil Soup (page 60). This dough can be allowed to rise overnight in the refrigerator. When you are ready to bake it, bring the dough to room temperature and shape the bread.

Serves 6 to 8

$1/4$ cup extra virgin olive oil
4 sprigs fresh rosemary, plus 2 teaspoons
    chopped
$2^1/2$ teaspoons dry yeast
$2^1/2$ cups all-purpose or unbleached bread flour
Coarse salt
$3/4$ cup Oven-Dried Tomatoes (page 14), halved

In a small saucepan, warm the olive oil and rosemary over medium heat. As soon as the rosemary sizzles, remove from the heat. Let sit for 1 hour, then discard the rosemary sprigs.

In a large bowl, mix together the yeast, $1/2$ cup of the flour, and $1/2$ cup warm (110°F) water. Let stand until the mixture bubbles up and rises slightly, about 20 minutes.

Add the remaining 2 cups flour, the rosemary oil, chopped rosemary, $1/2$ cup warm (110°F) water, and 1 teaspoon salt. Mix thoroughly and turn the dough out onto a well-floured surface. Knead until smooth and elastic but still a bit tacky to the touch, 7 to 8 minutes. Place the dough in an oiled bowl and turn to coat with oil. Cover with plastic wrap and let rise in a warm place (75°F) until doubled in volume, about 1 hour.

Place a pizza stone or unglazed quarry tiles on a rack in the lower third of the oven and preheat the oven to 500°F.

Remove the dough from the bowl and punch down on a floured surface. Form the dough into a ball and let rest for 5 minutes. Roll the dough into a 10 × 12-inch oval, about $1/2$ inch thick. Place on a well-floured pizza peel or paddle. Distribute the tomatoes evenly on the flatbread, leaving a $1/2$-inch border around the edge. Press the tomatoes slightly into the dough. Sprinkle with salt.

Transfer the flatbread to the pizza stone and bake until golden brown and crispy, 12 to 15 minutes. Cut into wedges and serve.

Calzone with Oven-Dried Tomatoes and Herbed Goat Cheese

You can fill a calzone with a variety of meats, cheeses, and vegetables. This one features herbed goat cheese and sweet oven-dried plum tomatoes. The dough is a breeze to prepare and can be made a day in advance and allowed to rise overnight in the refrigerator. You can also make the filling a day in advance. Several hours before serving, form the calzone and store in the refrigerator until you are ready to bake them.

Makes 2 large or 4 individual-size calzone; serves 4

1 cup Oven-Dried Tomatoes (page 14), thinly
  sliced
2 tablespoons coarsely chopped pitted Niçoise
  or Kalamata olives
1 tablespoon capers
¹/₂ cup grated Fontina (about 2 ounces)
¹/₂ cup grated mozzarella (about 2 ounces)
1 cup crumbled goat cheese (about 5 ounces)
2 tablespoons chopped fresh basil
1 tablespoon chopped fresh mint, plus a few
  whole sprigs for garnish
2 teaspoons chopped fresh oregano, plus a few
  whole sprigs for garnish
1 recipe Calzone Dough (recipe follows)

Thirty minutes before baking, place a pizza stone or unglazed quarry tiles on the bottom rack of the oven and preheat the oven to 500°F.

In a large bowl, combine the tomatoes, olives, capers, Fontina, mozzarella, goat cheese, basil, mint, and oregano.

Punch down the dough. On a floured surface, divide the dough into 2 pieces and form each into a ball. (If you are making 4 small calzone, divide the dough into 4 pieces and proceed.) Roll one piece of the dough into a 12-inch circle, approximately ¹/₄ inch thick, and place it on a well-floured pizza peel or paddle. Spread half of the tomato and cheese mixture over half of the dough, leaving a 1¹/₂-inch border around the edge. With a pastry brush, moisten the bottom edge of the dough lightly with water and fold the dough over the filling, pressing the edges together well to seal completely. Roll the edges of the dough over and press to make a tight seal.

Slide the calzone onto the pizza stone and bake until golden and crisp, 10 to 12 minutes. Remove from the oven and place on a wooden cutting board. Let rest for 10 minutes, then garnish with herb sprigs and serve.

Repeat with the remaining dough and filling ingredients.

Calzone Dough

2 teaspoons dry yeast
3 cups all-purpose or unbleached bread flour
3/4 teaspoon coarse salt
3 tablespoons extra virgin olive oil

Combine the yeast, 1/4 cup lukewarm (110°F) water, and 1/4 cup of the flour in a large bowl. Let sit until the mixture bubbles up, about 20 minutes.

Add the remaining 2 3/4 cups flour, the salt, olive oil, and 3/4 cup lukewarm (110°F) water. Mix thoroughly. Turn the dough out onto a floured surface and knead until smooth and elastic but still a bit tacky to the touch, 7 to 8 minutes. Place in an oiled bowl and turn to coat with oil. Cover with plastic wrap and let rise in a warm place (75°F) until doubled in volume, about 1 hour.

Tomato and Zucchini Coca

*C*ontrary *to popular belief, not all pizzas come from Italy.* Coca, *traditional fare of Catalonia, Spain, is made from a thin pizza-like dough, formed into an oval and baked in a wood-fired oven. No cheese topping on this one, however—*cocas *feature the harvest's bounty of fresh produce. This version uses sliced tomatoes, zucchini, garlic, and toasted pine nuts.*

Serves 6

■ dough
2 teaspoons dry yeast
2^1/$_4$ cups all-purpose or unbleached bread flour
^{3}/$_4$ teaspoon salt
3 tablespoons olive oil

■ topping
1 tablespoon extra virgin olive oil
1 small red onion, thinly sliced
5 garlic cloves, minced
1 small zucchini, unpeeled, sliced paper-thin
1^1/$_2$ tablespoons white wine vinegar
Coarse salt and freshly ground black pepper
2 medium ripe red tomatoes, thinly sliced
^{1}/$_4$ cup pine nuts, toasted

For the dough, in a large bowl, dissolve the yeast in 1^1/$_2$ tablespoons warm (110°F) water. Let stand for 10 minutes, or until frothy. Add the flour, salt, ^{3}/$_4$ cup warm (110°F) water, and the olive oil and mix until a dough forms.

Turn the dough out onto a floured surface (or transfer to an electric mixer fitted with a dough hook)

and knead until smooth and elastic but still slightly tacky to the touch, about 7 minutes. Place the dough in an oiled bowl and turn it to coat with oil. Cover with plastic wrap and place in a warm place (75°F) until doubled in volume, 1 hour. (Alternatively, let the dough rise in the refrigerator overnight. The next day, bring to room temperature and proceed.)

In the meantime, for the topping, heat the olive oil in a large skillet over medium heat. Add the onion and cook, stirring occasionally, until almost soft, 5 minutes. Add the garlic and zucchini and cook until the zucchini is almost soft, 4 minutes. Sprinkle the vinegar over the top and season with salt and pepper. Set aside.

Thirty minutes before baking, place a pizza stone or unglazed quarry tiles on the bottom rack of the oven and preheat the oven to 400°F.

Punch down the dough. On a floured work surface, roll and shape the dough into an 8 × 10-inch oval, about ^{3}/$_8$ inch thick. Build up the edges slightly to form a rim. Place the dough on a floured pizza peel or paddle.

Distribute the onions and zucchini evenly on the dough, leaving a ^{1}/$_2$-inch border around the edge. Place the tomatoes in a single layer over the vegetables. Sprinkle the pine nuts on top and season with salt and pepper. Transfer the coca to the pizza stone and bake until golden and crisp, 20 to 25 minutes.

Remove the coca from the pan and cut into wedges. Serve immediately, or at room temperature.

pasta and grains

Egg Pasta

Pasta dough is easier to prepare than you think. With the addition of eggs, the end results are tender and delicate.

Makes ¹/₂ pound (or twelve to fourteen 5-inch squares pasta)

1¹/₄ cups all-purpose flour, plus more if needed
¹/₄ teaspoon coarse salt
1 large egg
1 large egg yolk

Combine the flour and salt on a work surface and make a well in the center. In a small bowl, beat together the egg, egg yolk, and 2 tablespoons water. Add the liquid to the well. Using a fork or your thumb and first finger, bring the flour in from the sides until the mixture thickens. Add 1 to 2 additional tablespoons water as needed until the dough holds together in a ball. Then use a pastry scraper to incorporate the remaining flour. The dough should be fairly dry but still hold together. Turn the dough out onto a well-floured work surface and knead the dough for 2 to 3 minutes by forming it into a ball. Knead until it is smooth, kneading in additional flour if it sticks to your fingers or to the work surface. Wrap the dough in plastic wrap and let it rest for 30 minutes.

Alternatively, this can be made in a food processor. If using this method, add 1 to 2 tablespoons less of the combined egg and water mixture to the flour and process until it looks crumbly in texture.

The dough can be refrigerated for 1 day or frozen for up to 1 month.

Orecchiette with Balsamic Cherry Tomatoes

This is the essence of simplicity, in terms of both the few pristine flavors and the minimal effort it takes to make such a fresh-tasting dish. Choose all different colors and varieties of cherry tomatoes and make the vinaigrette several hours ahead if possible so the tomatoes give off some of their sweet juices and the flavors meld together.

Serves 6

¹/₄ cup extra virgin olive oil
¹/₄ cup balsamic vinegar
2 garlic cloves, minced
1 teaspoon chopped fresh oregano
1¹/₄ pounds assorted cherry tomatoes, halved
Coarse salt and freshly ground black pepper

1 pound dried orecchiette
20 large fresh basil leaves

In a large bowl, whisk together the olive oil, vinegar, garlic, and oregano. Add the tomatoes and stir together. Season to taste with salt and pepper.

Bring a large pot of salted water to a boil. Add the orecchiette and cook until al dente, 12 to 15 minutes.

In the meantime, cut the basil leaves into strips.

Drain the pasta and toss with the tomatoes and vinaigrette. Season to taste with salt and pepper. Place on a platter, sprinkle with the basil, and serve immediately.

Farfalle with Baked Green Tomatoes

During the fall, when there isn't enough sunshine to ripen the tomatoes in your garden, pick them green and bake them with olive oil, garlic, and basil. When they're soft, mash them into a tart, garlicky-flavored sauce and toss them with hot farfalle, or another shaped pasta, and Parmigiano-Reggiano.

Serves 6

$^1/_4$ cup extra virgin olive oil
6 medium green tomatoes (about $2^1/_2$ pounds),
  cut into $^1/_4$-inch slices
Coarse salt and freshly ground black pepper
3 garlic cloves, minced

12 large fresh basil leaves
12 ounces dried farfalle (bowties)
$^2/_3$ cup freshly grated Parmigiano-Reggiano

Preheat the oven to 300°F.

Oil a large shallow baking dish with 1 tablespoon of the oil. Arrange the tomatoes in the dish in a single layer. Season with salt and pepper and drizzle with the remaining 3 tablespoons olive oil. Bake until the tomatoes soften slightly, about 20 minutes.

In the meantime, chop the garlic and basil together. Sprinkle the garlic and basil on top of the tomatoes. Cover with foil and bake until soft and lightly caramelized, 15 to 20 minutes. Remove from the oven and place the tomatoes in a bowl. Mash with a fork or potato masher to form a creamy sauce. Season to taste with salt and pepper. Cover to keep warm.

In the meantime, bring a large pot of water to a boil. Add salt and the pasta and cook until al dente, 10 to 12 minutes.

Drain the pasta and toss with the sauce, half the Parmigiano-Reggiano, and pepper to taste. Place on a platter, sprinkle with the remaining Parmigiano-Reggiano, and serve immediately.

Fettuccine with Wild Mushrooms and Tomatoes

Fresh porcini mushrooms are worth almost their weight in gold, so instead, use dried porcini mushrooms. The earthy flavors of the mushrooms stewed with lots of garlic and tomatoes make a very satisfying sauce for pasta.

Serves 6

3 cups Chicken Stock (page 78)
2 ounces dried porcini mushrooms
3 tablespoons extra virgin olive oil
4 garlic cloves, minced
3 cups peeled, seeded, and chopped fresh or
   canned tomatoes
Coarse salt and freshly ground black pepper
12 ounces dried fettuccine
1¹/₂ cups freshly grated Parmigiano-Reggiano

Bring the chicken stock to a boil. Place the porcini mushrooms in a bowl and cover them with the boiling stock. Let sit until the chicken stock is cold.

Strain the mushrooms and coarsely chop them. Strain the mushroom soaking liquid through a paper towel–lined sieve and reserve.

Heat the olive oil in a large heavy frying pan over medium heat. Add the garlic and mushrooms and cook, stirring occasionally, for 3 minutes. Increase the heat to high, add the tomatoes and the reserved mushroom soaking liquid, and bring to a boil. Reduce the heat to medium-low and simmer until the sauce thickens, 10 to 15 minutes. Season with salt and pepper. (The sauce can be made a day in advance and refrigerated; reheat just before serving.)

In the meantime, bring a large pot of water to a boil. Add salt and the pasta and cook until al dente, 7 to 10 minutes.

Drain the pasta and toss with the sauce and half of the Parmigiano-Reggiano. Place on a platter, sprinkle with the remaining Parmigiano-Reggiano, and serve immediately.

Spaghetti alla Norma

A *Sicilian classic, spaghetti alla Norma is best made at the height of summer, when growers bring baby eggplants, fresh-picked garlic, sweet basil, and vine-ripened tomatoes to your local farmers' market. The fresh flavors of the vegetables come alive when ricotta salata, a dried and salted sheep's milk cheese, is grated over the top. If ricotta salata is unavailable, substitute Pecorino, a grating cheese also made from sheep's milk.*

Serves 6

3 small eggplants (about 1½ pounds), cut into ¼-inch slices
Coarse salt
5 tablespoons extra virgin olive oil
3 garlic cloves, crushed
4 cups peeled, seeded, and chopped fresh or canned plum tomatoes
3 sprigs fresh basil, plus 10 basil leaves, torn into small pieces
Freshly ground black pepper
1 pound dried spaghetti, linguine, or fettuccine
4 ounces ricotta salata, coarsely grated

Toss the eggplant slices with salt and place in a colander. Let drain for 30 minutes.

Preheat the oven to 375°F.

Rinse the eggplant and dry with paper towels. Toss the eggplant with 3 tablespoons of the olive oil and place on a well-oiled baking sheet in a single layer. Bake, turning occasionally, until the eggplant is light golden and tender, 15 to 20 minutes.

Meanwhile, heat the remaining 2 tablespoons olive oil in a large frying pan over medium heat. Add the garlic and cook until golden. Increase the heat to high, add the tomatoes and basil sprigs, and cook until the liquid evaporates, about 10 minutes. Remove and discard the garlic and basil. Season to taste with salt and pepper. (This sauce can be made a day in advance and refrigerated. Reheat when ready to serve.)

Bring a large pot of water to a boil. Add salt and the spaghetti and cook until al dente, 7 to 10 minutes.

Drain the pasta and toss with the eggplant and tomato sauce. Place on a platter, sprinkle with the ricotta salata and basil leaves, and serve immediately.

Penne with Tomatoes, Sausage, and Cream

This is a dish not to be missed! My thanks goes to Giovanna Fenati, a terrific cook and restaurateur from Colorado Springs, who gave me this family recipe. The sauce lends itself to being prepared a day in advance and reheated just before serving.

Serves 6

1 tablespoon extra virgin olive oil
1½ pounds sweet Italian sausage, crumbled
1 small red onion, chopped
2 garlic cloves, minced
2 bay leaves
1 teaspoon chopped fresh sage
1 teaspoon chopped fresh rosemary
Pinch of crushed red pepper flakes
1 cup dry red wine
3 cups peeled, seeded, and chopped fresh or
    canned tomatoes
1 cup heavy cream
1 cup freshly grated Parmigiano-Reggiano
Coarse salt and freshly ground black pepper
1 pound dried penne or rigatoni

Heat the olive oil in a large frying pan over medium heat. Add the sausage and cook until the fat is rendered and the juices have evaporated, 8 to 10 minutes. Add the onion, garlic, bay leaves, sage, rosemary, and crushed red pepper flakes and cook, stirring occasionally, until the onion is golden brown, 20 to 25 minutes.

Drain off all but 2 tablespoons of fat from the pan.

Turn the heat to high, add the wine, and boil until it evaporates, 3 to 5 minutes. Add the tomatoes and bring to a boil. Reduce the heat to low and simmer until the sauce thickens, 30 to 40 minutes. Remove the bay leaves and discard.

Add the cream and half of the Parmigiano-Reggiano to the sauce and stir together. Season to taste with salt and pepper.

In the meantime, bring a large pot of water to a boil. Add salt and the penne and cook until al dente, 10 to 12 minutes.

Drain the pasta, put it back in the pot, and toss with the tomato sauce. Place on a platter, sprinkle with the remaining Parmigiano-Reggiano, and serve immediately.

Feta and Goat Cheese Ravioli with Tomatoes and Mint

Ravioli with a tangy filling of feta and goat cheese served with a simple sauce that is really the essence of tomatoes and garnished with chopped fresh mint makes an extraordinary combination. The ravioli can be made up to a week ahead of time and stored in the freezer. When you are ready, boil the pasta still frozen, and serve with the hot sauce.

Serves 6

12 ounces feta cheese, at room temperature
6 ounces fresh goat cheese, at room
    temperature
2 garlic cloves, minced
Pinch of cayenne
1 teaspoon dried oregano
1/2 cup fresh bread crumbs
2 teaspoons fresh lemon juice
Coarse salt and freshly ground black pepper
Double recipe Egg Pasta (page 122)
3 tablespoons extra virgin olive oil
3 cups peeled, seeded, and chopped fresh or
    canned tomatoes
3 tablespoons chopped fresh mint

Place the feta cheese, goat cheese, and garlic in a food processor and pulse a few times to form a paste. Transfer to a bowl. Add the cayenne, oregano, bread crumbs, and lemon juice. Mix well and season to taste with salt and pepper. (Alternatively, this can be made by hand by mashing all the ingredients together with a fork.) Refrigerate until ready to use. (The filling can be made up to 1 day in advance.)

Divide the pasta dough into 4 pieces. With a pasta machine, roll each piece of pasta out 1/16 inch thick, or so you can almost see your hand through it. Cut the pasta into 5-inch squares.

Place 1 tablespoon of the filling in the center of each square. Spray a light mist of water around the edges or use a pastry brush to brush lightly with water. Fold over to form a triangle. Seal and trim the edges for a more attractive shape. Place on a heavily floured baking sheet. You should have approximately 28 triangles.

Heat the olive oil in a large frying pan over medium-high heat. Add the tomatoes, reduce the heat to medium, and cook until the tomatoes are hot, 2 minutes. Season to taste with salt and pepper.

In the meantime, bring a large pot of salted water to a boil. Add the ravioli and boil until al dente, 3 to 4 minutes.

Drain the ravioli and toss with the hot tomatoes. Place on a serving platter and garnish with the mint. Serve immediately.

Pasta with Scallops

Tomatoes, red wine vinegar, garlic, fresh herbs, capers, and olives make a zesty sauce perfect for tossing with scallops and hot pasta or spooning over grilled chicken. It can be prepared several hours in advance and reheated just before serving.

Serves 6

3 tablespoons extra virgin olive oil
1 small yellow onion, chopped
3 garlic cloves, chopped
3 cups peeled, seeded, chopped, and drained
   fresh or canned tomatoes
1 1/2 cups dry red wine
2 tablespoons chopped fresh flat-leaf parsley,
   plus whole leaves for garnish
1/2 teaspoon chopped fresh rosemary
1/2 teaspoon chopped fresh thyme
1/2 teaspoon chopped fresh oregano
2 bay leaves
2 whole cloves
1 tablespoon red wine vinegar
Coarse salt and freshly ground black pepper
1 pound bay or sea scallops, side muscle
   removed
1/2 cup cured black olives, such as Kalamata or
   Niçoise, pitted and chopped
1/4 cup capers
1 pound dried linguine or fettuccine

Heat 2 tablespoons of the oil in a large frying pan over medium heat. Add the onion and cook until soft, about 7 minutes. Add the garlic and cook for 1 minute. Add the tomatoes, 2 cups water, the wine, parsley, rosemary, thyme, oregano, bay leaves, and cloves. Reduce the heat to medium-low and cook, uncovered, until the sauce is thick, 45 to 55 minutes. Remove the cloves and bay leaves and discard.

Pass the sauce through a food mill or puree in a blender until smooth. Strain through a fine strainer into a saucepan. Add the red wine vinegar and season to taste with salt and pepper. Set aside.

If you are using sea scallops, cut them into 1/4-inch slices. Heat the remaining 1 tablespoon olive oil in a large frying pan over medium heat. Add the scallops and cook until almost firm to the touch, 2 to 3 minutes. Add the scallops to the tomato sauce. Add the olives and capers to the frying pan and cook, stirring, until hot, 1 minute. Set aside in the pan.

Meanwhile, bring a large pot of salted water to a boil. Add the pasta and cook until al dente, 7 to 10 minutes.

In the meantime, heat the sauce over medium-low heat until hot.

Drain the pasta, toss with the sauce, and place on a serving platter. Garnish with the olives and capers and the parsley, and serve immediately.

Caponata Lasagne

Caponata is a Sicilian summer vegetable stew made with eggplant, tomatoes, peppers, celery, capers, and green olives. Layered with egg noodles and ricotta and drizzled with a creamy sauce, it makes an unforgettable lasagne. Assemble the lasagne the day before serving.

Serves 8 to 10

8 ounces dried lasagne noodles
1 tablespoon olive oil
One 15-ounce container ricotta
³/4 cup freshly grated Parmigiano-Reggiano
Coarse salt and freshly ground black pepper
3 tablespoons unsalted butter
4¹/2 tablespoons all-purpose flour
3 cups whole milk
Freshly grated nutmeg
¹/2 recipe Caponata (page 226)
10 ounces whole-milk mozzarella, coarsely
    grated

Bring a large pot of salted water to a boil. Add the lasagne noodles and cook until al dente, 8 to 12 minutes.

While the pasta is cooking, fill a large bowl with cold water and add the olive oil. When the pasta is done, drain the pasta and place in the water to cool for 5 minutes. Drain the pasta and place in a single layer on a baking sheet. Cover with plastic wrap and set aside.

In a small bowl, mix together the ricotta, Parmigiano-Reggiano, and salt and pepper to taste. Set aside.

Melt the butter in a medium saucepan over medium-high heat. Stir in the flour and cook, stirring constantly, for 2 minutes. Add the milk and whisk constantly until the sauce comes to a boil and thickens, 3 to 4 minutes. Season with salt and pepper and nutmeg to taste.

Preheat the oven to 375°F.

Grease a 13 × 9-inch baking dish with olive oil. Cover the bottom of the baking dish with a single layer of pasta. Cover the pasta with one third of the ricotta mixture, spread one third of the caponata over the ricotta, and spread one third of the sauce over the caponata. Repeat with the remaining ingredients to make two more layers. Sprinkle the mozzarella evenly over the top. (This can be made 1 day in advance and stored in the refrigerator. It can also be frozen; bake it still frozen, increasing the baking time by 20 to 30 minutes.)

Bake the lasagne on the top rack of the oven until the top is golden and the sauce is bubbling around the edges, 40 to 50 minutes. Let stand for 15 minutes before serving.

Ricotta Cannelloni with Herbed Tomatoes

Cannelloni making is perfect for a rainy autumn day. Buy luscious, juicy, end-of-season ripe red tomatoes, sturdy greens for wilting, plenty of herbs, and freshly made ricotta, which is available in Italian markets. The ricotta must be drained overnight to rid it of excess moisture. The cannelloni can be prepared completely a day in advance and baked just before serving.

Serves 6

1 large bunch sturdy greens (about 1 pound),
    such as Swiss chard, escarole, or turnip,
    beet, or mustard greens
1 pound fresh ricotta, drained overnight in a
    paper towel–lined sieve
2 large eggs
$\frac{1}{2}$ teaspoon chopped fresh mint
$\frac{1}{2}$ teaspoon chopped fresh oregano
$\frac{1}{2}$ teaspoon chopped fresh thyme
$\frac{1}{4}$ teaspoon chopped fresh rosemary
$\frac{3}{4}$ teaspoon coarse salt
Freshly ground black pepper
$\frac{1}{4}$ cup freshly grated Parmigiano-Reggiano
1 recipe Egg Pasta (page 122)
2 tablespoons olive oil
1 recipe Tomato-Herb Sauce (page 22)
Fresh flat-leaf parsley leaves

Wash the greens and cut them into 1-inch-wide strips. Heat a large skillet over medium-high heat. Add the greens, cover, and cook just until they begin to wilt, about 1 minute. Remove the cover and with tongs, toss the greens until wilted. Transfer to paper towels and squeeze out the excess moisture.

In a large bowl, combine the greens with the ricotta, eggs, mint, oregano, thyme, rosemary, salt, pepper to taste, and the Parmigiano-Reggiano.

Divide the dough into 4 pieces. With a pasta machine, roll 1 piece at a time to approximately $\frac{1}{16}$ inch thick, or so you can almost see your hand through it. Cut the pasta into 5-inch squares; you should have 12 to 14 squares.

Bring a large pot of salted water to a boil. Fill a large bowl with ice water and add the oil. A few at a time, add the pasta squares to the boiling water and cook for 30 seconds. Transfer them to the bowl of ice water. When all of the pasta squares have been cooked, lay them in a single layer on slightly dampened cotton dish towels. Cover with plastic wrap.

Preheat the oven to 350°F. Oil a 13 × 9-inch baking dish.

Put 2 heaping tablespoons of the filling in the center of each square of pasta and roll the pasta square up into a tube. Place a small ladle of the sauce on the bottom of the baking dish. Place the cannelloni next to each other in a single layer in the dish. Pour the remaining sauce on top. Bake until the cannelloni are hot and bubbling around the edges, 20 to 30 minutes.

To serve, place the cannelloni on serving plates and garnish with parsley leaves.

Ricotta-Spinach Gnocchi with Stewed Tomatoes

Unfortunately, the word gnocchi *sometimes conjures up the image of heavy potato dumplings that seem to sit in the bottom of your stomach. However,* gnocchi *is the generic term for small dumplings, and in Italy, there are all kinds—spinach, polenta, semolina, in addition to the potato version—which, when made correctly, can be featherlight too. These gnocchi, made with ricotta and spinach and finished with fresh tomatoes simply warmed in virgin olive oil, are melt-in-your-mouth sumptuous—and foolproof besides. Instead of the tomato sauce, try serving them with Sicilian Tomato Pesto (page 25). If desired, you can assemble the dish several hours in advance, but bake it just before serving.*

Serves 6

1 1/2 teaspoons extra virgin olive oil
2 pounds greens, such as spinach, Swiss chard, or dandelion, turnip, or mustard greens, stems removed, washed, well dried, and chopped
1 cup freshly grated Parmigiano-Reggiano
1/2 cup plus 1 tablespoon all-purpose flour, or more if needed
1 cup ricotta cheese, drained in a paper towel–lined sieve for 2 hours
2 large eggs
Coarse salt and freshly ground black pepper
2 tablespoons unsalted butter
4 medium ripe red tomatoes, peeled, seeded, and chopped
2 tablespoons chopped fresh flat-leaf parsley

Heat the olive oil in a large frying pan over medium-high heat. Add the greens, cover, and cook, tossing occasionally with tongs, until the greens are wilted, 1 to 4 minutes, depending upon the greens. Remove the greens from the pan, place in a clean kitchen towel, and wring out all of the excess moisture.

Place the greens in a bowl. Add 1/2 cup of the grated Parmigiano-Reggiano, 1/4 cup plus 1 tablespoon of the flour, the ricotta, eggs, and salt and pepper to taste and mix thoroughly. If the dough sticks to your hands, add more flour, a tablespoon at a time, until it is no longer sticky.

Preheat the oven to 375°F. Oil a 2-quart baking dish.

Bring a large pot of salted water to a boil. With the aid of a spoon, shape the dough into large oval walnut-size balls and roll them in the remaining 1/4 cup flour. Add the gnocchi to the water a few at a time and as soon as they rise to the surface, remove them with a slotted spoon and place in the baking dish. Roll the gnocchi in the baking dish to coat them with oil.

Melt the butter in a large frying pan over high heat. Add the tomatoes and cook until they are hot and some of the liquid has evaporated, 3 to 4 minutes. Season to taste with salt and pepper.

Pour the tomato sauce over the gnocchi and bake until hot, 10 to 15 minutes. Garnish with the parsley, sprinkle with the remaining 1/2 cup Parmigiano-Reggiano, and serve immediately.

Pasta with Red Wine-Stewed Duck

When you taste something as good as duck stewed with red wine and tomatoes, you might think it would take hours of work in the kitchen for such results. Instead it is really quite simple! This is a perfect winter dish, so by all means feel free to use canned tomatoes. Make the sauce up to two days in advance. At the last minute, cook the pasta and toss with the sauce.

Serves 6

1 tablespoon olive oil
1 duck, about 5 pounds, cut into 8 pieces,
    excess fat and skin removed
1 large yellow onion, diced
1 large carrot, diced
4 ounces pancetta, diced
3 cups tomatoes, peeled, seeded and chopped,
    fresh or canned
1 1/2 cups plus 1 cup dry red wine
1 tablespoon chopped fresh rosemary
Coarse salt and freshly ground black pepper
1 pound dry pappardelle
1 cup finely grated Parmigiano-Reggiano

Heat the olive oil in a large, heavy casserole over medium-high heat. Add the duck in a single layer and cook until golden on all sides, 10 to 12 minutes. Add the onions, carrots, and pancetta and continue to cook until the onions are soft, 10 minutes. Add the tomatoes, 1 1/2 cups red wine, and rosemary and bring to a boil. Reduce the heat to low, cover, and simmer 1 hour. Remove the cover, add the remaining red wine, stir well, and continue to cook until the meat falls off the bones, about 1 1/4 hours.

Remove the duck from the pan with tongs, place in a bowl, and let cool enough to handle. Remove the meat from the bones and discard the bones. Return the meat to the sauce and bring to a boil over medium heat. Simmer until the sauce has thickened slightly, 5 to 10 minutes. Season to taste with salt and pepper.

Bring a large pot three-quarters full of salted water to a boil. Cook the pappardelle until al dente, 7 to 10 minutes. Drain the pappardelle and toss with the duck and sauce.

To serve, place the pappardelle and sauce in a large serving bowl and garnish with Parmigiano-Reggiano.

Spicy Thai Noodles with Pork and Tomato Curry

Tomatoes appeared late on the scene in Thailand, so at most you'll find one or two, or on a rare occasion, three, tomatoes in any one dish. In this dish of fiery-hot noodles and pork, tomatoes pair well with Thai red curry paste, a hot red chile condiment, miso (soybean paste), and fresh egg noodles available in any well-stocked Asian market.

Serves 6

2 tablespoons vegetable oil
1 tablespoon Thai red curry paste
1¼ pounds pork tenderloin, cut into ¾-inch cubes
3 tablespoons miso (soybean paste)
2 medium ripe red tomatoes, chopped
8 ounces green beans, trimmed and cut on the diagonal into 1-inch pieces
⅓ cup fish sauce (nam pla)
2 tablespoons fresh lime juice
6 ounces fresh egg noodles
4 green onions, thinly sliced on the diagonal
1½ cups bean sprouts (about 3 ounces)
⅓ cup pickled ginger

Heat the oil in a large saucepan over medium heat. Add the curry paste and cook, stirring continuously, for 2 minutes. Add the pork and miso and cook, stirring continuously, for 3 minutes. Add the tomatoes, green beans, fish sauce, lime juice, and 2 cups water. Increase the heat to high and bring to a boil. Reduce the heat to medium-low and simmer until the pork is tender and the liquid is reduced by half, 15 to 20 minutes. (You can make the dish up to this point 1 day in advance, store in the refrigerator, and reheat over low heat.)

In the meantime, bring a large pot of water to a boil. Add the noodles and cook until tender, about 30 seconds. Drain.

To serve, place the noodles on a large platter and spoon the pork curry over them. Garnish with some of the green onions, bean sprouts, and pickled ginger and pass the remainder in separate bowls so guests can help themselves.

Vietnamese Rice Noodles with Pork and Shrimp

In Vietnam, tomatoes are not at all a centerpiece of the cuisine as they are in America or the Mediterranean, but they are used in a few noodle and soup dishes. The Vietnamese believe that tomatoes offer a perfect balance of acid/sweet. In each bite of a Vietnamese dish, the cook strives for many different flavors, textures, and sensations—sweet, salty, and sour, crunchy and creamy, hot and spicy, and refreshingly cool. This zippy noodle dish with pork and shrimp is a sublime example.

Serves 6

$^1/_4$ cup dried shrimp (optional)
$^1/_4$ cup peanut oil
3 garlic cloves, crushed
1 pound medium shrimp, peeled and deveined
$^1/_2$ pound pork tenderloin, cut into $^1/_4$-inch-thick slices
2 teaspoons brown sugar
Pinch of freshly ground black pepper
3 large eggs, lightly beaten
1 cup Chicken Stock (page 78)
$^1/_4$ cup Vietnamese fish sauce
1 teaspoon shrimp paste
1 jalapeño or serrano pepper, halved
4 small ripe red tomatoes, each cut into 8 wedges
12 ounces Chinese rice noodles or rice vermicelli
$^1/_4$ cup fresh mint leaves
$^1/_4$ cup fresh cilantro leaves, plus a few sprigs for garnish
$^1/_4$ cup fresh basil leaves
12 green onions, thinly sliced on the diagonal
2 tablespoons fresh lime juice

If using the dried shrimp, place in a bowl and cover with cold water. Let sit for 15 minutes, then drain.

Heat 2 tablespoons of the peanut oil in a wok or a large nonstick frying pan over high heat. Add the garlic and stir-fry for 30 seconds. Add the dried shrimp if using, the fresh shrimp, pork, sugar, and pepper and stir-fry until the pork is cooked, 3 minutes. Add the eggs, quickly mix well, and tilt the pan to spread the mixture evenly over the bottom of the pan. Cook until the eggs are set, about 2 minutes. Slide the omelette onto a work surface and cut it into $^1/_4$-inch strips.

In a medium saucepan, bring the chicken stock to a boil. Add the fish sauce, shrimp paste, chile, and tomatoes and stir together. Cover, remove from the heat, and set aside.

Bring a large pot of water to a boil. Add the noodles and cook until al dente, 3 to 4 minutes. Drain.

Wipe out the pan with a paper towel. Heat the remaining 2 tablespoons peanut oil in the wok or frying pan over high heat. Add the noodles and chicken stock mixture and cook until the liquid has reduced by half, about 1 minute. Discard the chile. Add the omelette strips, mint, cilantro, basil, green onions, and lime juice and toss together until hot, about 2 minutes.

To serve, place on a serving platter and garnish with cilantro sprigs.

Indian Tomato Rice

This tomato rice inspired by accomplished chef and friend, Brett Frechette, is flavored with garam masala, an Indian spice blend consisting of cardamom, cumin, cloves, coriander, and cinnamon. You can either mix up your own or buy it at an Indian or specialty market or any well-stocked health food store. The natural sweetness of the tomatoes tempers the spiciness of the rice.

Serves 6 to 8

2 cups basmati rice
1$^3/_4$ cups peeled, seeded, and chopped fresh or canned tomatoes
2 tablespoons peanut oil
1 medium yellow onion, diced
1 stalk celery, diced
2 garlic cloves, minced
3$^1/_2$ cups Vegetable Stock (page 79) or Chicken Stock (page 78)
2 teaspoons garam masala (recipe follows)
1 teaspoon coarse salt
$^1/_4$ teaspoon freshly ground black pepper

Rinse the rice under cold water until the water runs clear. Drain well and set aside. Puree the tomatoes in a blender or food processor until smooth. Set aside.

Heat the oil in a large saucepan over medium heat. Add the onion, celery, and garlic and cook until soft, about 7 minutes. Add the rice and cook, stirring, until the rice smells nutty, 2 minutes.

In the meantime, in another large saucepan, combine the stock, tomato puree, garam masala, salt, and pepper and bring to a boil over high heat.

Add to the rice, stirring once to prevent sticking. When the mixture reaches a boil, reduce the heat to low, cover, and cook until the rice is tender and the liquid has evaporated, about 15 minutes. Remove from the heat and let sit for 5 minutes before serving.

Garam Masala

Makes about 3 tablespoons and keeps 3 to 4 months

1 tablespoon cardamom seeds
2 teaspoons cumin seeds
1 teaspoon whole cloves
1 teaspoon coriander seeds
1 teaspoon black peppercorns
1 cinnamon stick, broken into pieces
1 bay leaf, crumbled
$^1/_2$ teaspoon ground mace
$^1/_2$ teaspoon grated nutmeg

Place the cardamom seeds, cumin seeds, whole cloves, coriander seeds, black peppercorns, cinnamon stick, and bay leaf in a dry skillet over medium heat. Stir until the color of the spices deepens slightly, 2 minutes. Remove from the pan and cool. Grind in a spice grinder until the mixture is a fine powder. Add the mace and nutmeg and stir together.

Tabouleh

Bulgur and tomatoes are the main components of this healthy Middle Eastern summer salad made with heaps of parsley and mint, green onions, lemon juice, and crunchy cucumbers. Instead of forks, serve with crisp romaine leaves or triangles of pita bread to use as scoops. Tabouleh is best made at least one day in advance.

Serves 6 to 8

1 cup medium-fine bulgur or cracked wheat
$^1/_2$ cup extra virgin olive oil
5 garlic cloves, minced
1 cup fresh lemon juice, or more to taste
1 large bunch green onions, diced
1 cup chopped fresh flat-leaf parsley
$^1/_3$ cup chopped fresh mint
5 large ripe red tomatoes, diced
1 large English cucumber, peeled, seeded, and diced
Coarse salt and freshly ground black pepper
Romaine leaves or warm pita bread cut into wedges

Place the bulgur in a large salad bowl. In a small bowl, whisk together the olive oil, garlic, and lemon juice and drizzle over the bulgur. Layer the green onions, parsley, mint, tomatoes, and cucumber, in that order, on top of the bulgur. Sprinkle with $1^1/_2$ teaspoons salt and $^1/_4$ teaspoon pepper and cover with plastic wrap. Refrigerate for at least 1 and up to 2 days.

Bring the tabouleh to room temperature. Taste and season with salt and more lemon juice if needed. Serve with romaine leaves or pita bread.

A world devoid of tomato soup, tomato sauce, tomato ketchup, and tomato paste is hard to visualize. Could the tin and processed food industries have got where they have without the benefit of the tomato compounds which color, flavor, thicken, and conceal so many deficiencies? How did the Italians eat spaghetti before the advent of the tomato? Was there such a thing as a tomato-less Neapolitan pizza? What were English salads like before there were tomatoes to mix with lettuce? Did Provençal cooking exist without *tomates provençal, salade niçoise,* and *ratatouille*? Then there is that warmed red billiard ball with its skin slit round the middle, so oddly known as a grilled tomato. Without it could the British landlady's and railway dining-car breakfast ever have become what it is? How many of us still remember that among the food shortages of the war years and after, the scarcity of fresh tomatoes was a privation on the same level as the lack of lemons, onions, and butter."

From Elizabeth David, Jill Norman, and Robert Hale,
An Omelette and a Glass of Wine

Indian Shrimp and Tomato Pilaf

In the southern tip of India, shrimp pilaf has been made for a very long time by the fishermen of Kerala, who have a penchant for combining their favorite ingredients, shrimp, rice, and tomatoes, in a variety of ways. This elegant pilaf can be assembled well in advance, making it perfect for entertaining. The recipe was inspired by Madhur Jaffrey, the incomparable Indian cooking teacher and author.

Serves 6

2 cups long-grain white or basmati rice
1 tablespoon coriander seeds
6 cardamom pods
8 whole cloves
1/4 cup vegetable oil
1 small yellow onion, thinly sliced
6 garlic cloves, sliced
One 2-inch piece fresh ginger, peeled and
    coarsely chopped
2 jalapeño or serrano peppers, halved and
    seeded
1 1/2 teaspoons ground cumin
2 cups peeled, seeded, and chopped fresh or
    canned tomatoes
1/2 cup plain yogurt
1/2 cup grated fresh or dried unsweetened
    coconut
1/2 cup coconut milk
1 1/4 pounds medium shrimp, peeled and
    deveined
1/2 cup raw cashews, toasted
3/4 teaspoon coarse salt
2 cinnamon sticks

Place the rice in a fine sieve and rinse with cold water until the water runs clear. Set aside.

In a dry skillet, toast the coriander seeds, cardamom pods, and cloves until fragrant, 1 to 3 minutes. Set aside.

Preheat the oven to 325°F.

Heat 1 tablespoon of the oil in a large frying pan over medium heat. Add the onion and cook until soft and golden brown, about 10 minutes.

In the meantime, in a food processor, process the garlic, ginger, chiles, cumin, and the remaining 3 tablespoons oil to make a smooth paste.

Remove the onion from the pan. Add the spice paste to the pan and cook, stirring, for 2 to 3 minutes. Add the tomatoes and cook until they are soft and some of the liquid has evaporated, 5 to 7 minutes. Add the yogurt and cook over low heat, stirring constantly, until the yogurt curdles, 2 to 3 minutes. Add the coconut and coconut milk and cook for 1 minute. Transfer to a 2-quart baking dish.

Add the shrimp, onion, and cashews and mix together. Set aside.

In a medium saucepan, bring 4 cups water to a boil. Add the rice, salt, cinnamon sticks, and the coriander seeds, cardamom, and cloves and boil for 8 minutes. Remove from the heat and pour evenly over the shrimp. Cover with foil. (The pilaf can be made several hours in advance up to this point and store in the refrigerator.)

Bake the rice until the rice is tender and the liquid is absorbed, 20 minutes. Fluff the rice and serve.

Spanish Saffron Rice

Three things grow in harmony along the east coast of Spain: big, juicy red tomatoes, white rice, and lovely beds of purple crocuses. The threadlike stamens from these crocuses are removed by hand, dried, and sold as saffron, the most expensive spice in the world. The trinity of saffron, tomatoes, and rice is a natural one.

Serves 4

3 tablespoons extra virgin olive oil
1 medium yellow onion, minced
1½ cups long-grain white rice
1 cup Chicken Stock (page 78)
2 cups peeled, seeded, and chopped fresh or
    canned tomatoes
1 teaspoon saffron threads
Coarse salt
Freshly ground black pepper
1 large red bell pepper, roasted (see page 13),
    peeled, seeded, and diced
¼ cup Spanish green olives, pitted and cut into
    thin strips
1 tablespoon chopped fresh flat-leaf parsley

Heat the olive oil in a large saucepan over medium heat. Add the onion and cook until soft, about 7 minutes. Add the rice and cook, stirring to coat the rice with oil, for 1 minute. Increase the heat to high and add the chicken stock, 1 cup water, the tomatoes, saffron, and 1 teaspoon salt. Bring to a boil, reduce the heat to low, and simmer, covered, until the rice is tender and the liquid is absorbed, about 20 minutes. Remove the cover and season to taste with pepper.

Add the red pepper, olives, and parsley to the rice and fluff and mix with a fork. Season to taste with pepper and serve.

The World Record

The current world record for the largest tomato grown, held by Gordon Graham of Oklahoma, is 7 pounds and 12 ounces.

Portuguese Tomato Pilaf

When it's summer in Portugal, the outdoor markets are amass with impeccably fresh vegetables: colorful peppers stacked in rows, wooden crates chock-full of wild greens, mounds of rose-colored garlic, and big baskets of juicy tomatoes. Especially in the central province of Alentejo, tomatoes flourish in the intense summer sunshine. But no matter where you are in Portugal, tomatoes are used to make tomato rice, or arroz de tomate, a household favorite. If you don't have any bacon drippings, use all olive oil.

Serves 6

2 tablespoons bacon drippings
2 tablespoons olive oil
1 large yellow onion, chopped
1 garlic clove, minced
2^1/$_2$ cups peeled, seeded, and chopped fresh or
    canned tomatoes
3 cups Chicken Stock (page 78)
2 cups long-grain white rice
Coarse salt and freshly ground black pepper

Heat the bacon drippings and olive oil in a large saucepan over medium heat. Add the onion and garlic and cook, stirring, until lightly golden, 12 to 15 minutes.

Add the tomatoes and stock and bring to a boil over high heat. Add the rice and salt and pepper to taste, reduce the heat to low, and simmer, covered, until the rice is tender and the liquid is absorbed, 20 minutes.

Fluff the rice with a fork and serve.

Four-Grain and Tomato Pilaf

You can combine hearty grains, such as barley, couscous, and bulgur, and lighten them up with freshly grated tomatoes to make an easy, welcome alternative to potatoes or rice.

Serves 6

3 medium ripe red tomatoes
1 tablespoon canola or vegetable oil
^{3}/$_4$ cup basmati rice
^{1}/$_4$ cup amaranth
^{1}/$_4$ cup quinoa
^{1}/$_4$ cup millet
^{1}/$_2$ teaspoon chopped fresh thyme
1 cup Chicken Stock (page 78)
Coarse salt and freshly ground black pepper
^{1}/$_2$ cup pine nuts, toasted

Cut the tomatoes in half. Cup each tomato half in your hand, cut side out, and, using the large holes of a grater, grate the tomato into a bowl. Discard the skins.

Heat the oil in a large saucepan over medium heat. Add the rice, amaranth, quinoa, millet, and thyme and stir until the grains are coated and hot, 1 to 2 minutes. Increase the heat to high and add the stock, 1^1/$_2$ cups water, the tomato juices and pulp, ^{3}/$_4$ teaspoon salt, and pepper to taste. Bring to a boil, reduce the heat to low, and simmer, covered, until the grains are tender and the liquid is absorbed, about 25 minutes.

Add the pine nuts and fluff with a fork to mix. Season to taste with salt and pepper if necessary. Serve.

Red Beans and Rice, Southern Style

Red beans and rice have long been a staple in the southern United States, especially in Louisiana, where red bean and tomato plants grow in harmony. Steamed white rice makes a nutritious partner to beans. The beans can be made a day or two in advance; steam the rice just before serving.

Serves 6

1¼ cups pinto or red kidney beans, picked over and rinsed
1 small smoked ham hock (about ½ pound)
2 tablespoons olive oil
1 medium yellow onion, chopped
3 garlic cloves, minced
1 small green bell pepper, cored, seeded, and diced
¼ cup chopped fresh flat-leaf parsley
3 cups peeled, seeded, and chopped fresh or canned tomatoes
1 tablespoon tomato paste
2 to 3 teaspoons hot pepper sauce, such as Tabasco sauce
Coarse salt and freshly ground black pepper
1 cup long-grain white rice

Cover the beans with plenty of cold water and soak for at least 4 hours, or overnight. Drain.

Place the beans and ham hock in a saucepan with enough water to cover by 2 inches. Simmer, uncovered, until the skins begin to crack and the beans are tender, about 45 minutes.

In the meantime, heat the oil in a large frying pan over medium heat. Add the onion, garlic, and bell pepper and cook, stirring, until soft, 10 minutes.

Add the onion mixture to the beans, along with the parsley, tomatoes, tomato paste, and hot pepper sauce. Season to taste with salt and pepper. Reduce the heat to low and simmer slowly until the mixture thickens, about 2 hours. Remove the ham hock and discard. (The beans can be cooked up to 2 days ahead. Cool, cover, and refrigerate; reheat over low heat.)

About 30 minutes before serving, in a heavy saucepan, bring 2 cups water and ½ teaspoon salt to a boil. Slowly add the rice, cover, and simmer slowly, without stirring, until the rice is tender and the liquid is absorbed, about 20 minutes.

To serve, spoon the rice into bowls and top with the beans.

breads, sandwiches,

and eggs

Red Bread

No matter what way you serve it, hot from the oven or toasted for the perfect BLT, this bread can't be beat. If by chance you do have an extra loaf, wrap it in plastic and then foil and freeze for later use.

Makes 2 loaves

5 cups all-purpose flour
1 (¹/₄-ounce) package dry yeast
1 cup buttermilk
1 tablespoon unsalted butter
2 tablespoons sugar
1¹/₂ teaspoons coarse salt
¹/₄ cup tomato juice
³/₄ cup peeled, seeded, and diced fresh or
    canned tomatoes
Melted unsalted butter for brushing

In a large mixing bowl, combine 2¹/₂ cups of the flour and the yeast and set aside. In a medium saucepan over low heat, heat the buttermilk, butter, sugar, and salt just until the butter melts and the mixture is warm. In another medium saucepan over low heat, warm the tomato juice and tomatoes just until warm (110°F). Add the warm buttermilk mixture to the flour and beat at low speed for 30 seconds. Add tomatoes and beat for an additional 30 seconds. Scrape the sides of the bowl and beat until well mixed, 3 minutes.

With a wooden spoon, stir in 2 cups of the flour until well mixed. Turn the dough onto a lightly floured surface and knead in enough of the remaining ¹/₂ cup flour until the dough is smooth and elastic, 7 to 10 minutes.

Shape the dough into a ball, place it in a well-oiled bowl, and turn to coat with oil. Cover with plastic and let rise in a warm place (75°F) until doubled in volume, about 1¹/₂ hours.

Preheat the oven to 375°F.

Divide the dough into 2 pieces and form into round balls. Let rest for 10 minutes. Lightly grease 2 8¹/₂ × 4¹/₂ × 2¹/₂-inch loaf pans. Shape the dough into 2 sausage-like rolls. Place in the loaf pans, cover lightly with a kitchen towel, and let rise until nearly doubled in size, about 1 hour.

Bake the bread until it is golden and sounds hollow when it is tapped on the bottom, 35 to 40 minutes. Remove from the oven and cool on a wire rack. After 15 minutes, brush the top with the melted butter.

Tomato-Olive Bread

There is nothing like the smell of freshly baked bread, especially when it's studded with oven-dried tomatoes and cured black olives. This bread has a crisp crust with a soft, fine center, perfect for making a good old BLT.

Makes 1 loaf

1 1/2 teaspoons dry yeast
1/4 cup whole wheat flour
1/4 cup rye flour
2 1/2 cups all-purpose or unbleached bread flour
1 teaspoon coarse salt
6 Oven-Dried Tomatoes (page 14), finely
   chopped
1/4 cup cured black olives, such as Kalamata or
   Niçoise, pitted and chopped

In a large bowl, stir the yeast, whole wheat flour, rye flour, and 1/2 cup warm (110°F) water together. Cover with plastic wrap and let rest until the mixture bubbles up and begins to rise, about 1 hour.

Add the all-purpose flour, salt, 3/4 cup water, the tomatoes, and olives to the yeast mixture and mix until the dough forms a rough mass. Turn the dough out onto a floured surface and knead, dusting with flour as needed, until it is soft and supple, about 8 minutes. Place the dough in an oiled bowl and turn once to coat with oil. Cover with plastic and let rise in a warm place (75°F) until slightly more than doubled in volume, about 2 hours. (Alternatively, place the dough in the refrigerator and let rise overnight. The next day, bring to room temperature and proceed.)

Remove the dough from the bowl and deflate the dough with your fist to distribute the air bubbles. Roll or shape the dough into a log shape, 8 inches long. Place in a 9 × 5-inch loaf pan and let rise in a warm place (75°F) until it is doubled in volume, 50 to 60 minutes.

Preheat the oven to 375°F.

Bake the bread until it is golden brown on top and sounds hollow when tapped on the bottom, 40 to 45 minutes. Place on a cooling rack and cool for at least 20 minutes before slicing.

For the BLT Lover

The great all-American bacon, lettuce, and tomato sandwich is a panacea for just about anything that ails you, right up there with chicken soup. Make sure you wait until the season is right and make it with the best-quality ingredients: apple-smoked bacon, ripe red tomatoes fresh off the vine, crisp romaine or oak leaf lettuce, toasted coarse-textured French or Italian bread, and, of course, homemade mayonnaise. It can't be beat.

Pecorino and Dried Tomato Scones

There are good scones and there are great scones. The secret to a great scone is to incorporate air when you mix the butter and flour. These cheesey scones are flecked with sun-dried tomatoes and spiced with cayenne. If Pecorino is unavailable, substitute Parmigiano-Reggiano.

Makes 9 large scones

2$^1/_2$ cups all-purpose flour
1 tablespoon baking powder
$^1/_4$ teaspoon cayenne
1 teaspoon sweet paprika
1 teaspoon coarse salt
6 tablespoons unsalted butter, at room
   temperature
1$^3/_4$ cups grated Pecorino (about 7 ounces)
$^1/_2$ cup sun-dried oil-packed tomatoes, finely
   chopped
1$^1/_4$ cups buttermilk, at room temperature

Preheat the oven to 400°F.

Sift the flour, baking powder, cayenne, paprika, and salt together into a large bowl. Rub the butter into the flour with your fingertips, picking up clumps of the mixture as you work and dropping it from far above the bowl to incorporate air, until it resembles coarse meal. Add the Pecorino and sun-dried tomatoes and stir to combine. Start adding the buttermilk, stirring until the mixture holds together.

Form the dough into a mass and turn it out onto a well-floured surface. Quickly roll it into a 9-inch square, about $^3/_4$ inch thick. Fold it in half and roll again to form a 9-inch square. Repeat once more. Cut into nine 3-inch square scones, and place on an ungreased baking sheet.

Bake until golden, 22 to 25 minutes. Serve warm.

Spoonbread with Corn and Green Tomatoes

Spoonbread is an old-timey, colonial American half-pudding, half-soufflé bread traditionally served as a side dish to crispy fried clams or soft-shell crabs. You can substitute red tomatoes here if green are unavailable.

Serves 8

3 ears fresh corn, husked
3 slices bacon, preferably apple-smoked
2 large green tomatoes, diced
1$^1/_2$ cups half-and-half
1$^1/_2$ cups milk
1 cup cornmeal
4 tablespoons unsalted butter, at room
   temperature
3 large eggs, separated, at room temperature
Coarse salt and freshly ground black pepper

Preheat the oven to 375°F. Butter a 2-quart baking dish.

Cook the corn in boiling salted water until tender, about 3 minutes. Cool. Remove the corn from the cob; you should have about 2 cups.

Cook the bacon in a large skillet over medium heat

until light golden, 4 minutes. Remove from the pan, cool, and crumble into a bowl. Set aside.

Add the tomatoes and corn to the skillet with the bacon fat and cook until hot, 3 minutes. Add to the bacon.

In a large saucepan, bring the half-and-half and milk to a boil over medium heat. Immediately sprinkle the cornmeal into the pan, whisking constantly. Once the mixture has thickened slightly, change to a wooden spoon and stir until thick, 2 to 3 minutes. Remove from the heat and stir in the butter until melted. Add the egg yolks one at a time, beating well after each addition. Add the bacon mixture and mix well. Season to taste with salt and pepper.

In a bowl, whip the egg whites to stiff peaks. Fold the egg whites into the cornmeal mixture. Place the mixture in the prepared baking dish and bake until golden and puffed considerably, 35 to 40 minutes.

Immediately spoon onto serving plates and serve.

Grilled Cheddar and Tomato Sandwiches with Grainy Mustard

Grilled cheese with tomato is an all-American favorite, especially when served with a bowl of Creamy Tomato Bisque.

Serves 4

2 tablespoons unsalted butter, melted
8 slices coarse-textured Italian or French bread
4 ounces sharp Cheddar cheese, thinly sliced
3 to 4 medium ripe red tomatoes, cut into
    1/4-inch slices
2 tablespoons Pommery or other grainy
    mustard

Brush half the butter over one side of 4 slices of the bread. Place the slices butter side down on a work surface. Top the bread with half of the Cheddar, then top with the tomato slices and the remaining cheese. Spread the mustard on the remaining bread. Top the sandwiches with the bread, mustard side down, and brush the remaining butter over the bread.

Heat a large frying pan over medium heat. Place the sandwiches in the pan and cook until golden on the bottom and the cheese is beginning to melt, 2 to 3 minutes. Turn the sandwiches and continue to cook until golden on both sides and the cheese is melted, another 2 to 3 minutes. Slice the sandwiches in half on the diagonal and serve immediately.

Tomato-Cucumber Sandwiches with Dill Mayonnaise

Sandwiches can be so bland and boring. But when you use crunchy cucumbers, juicy ripe tomatoes, tart dill, and good old-fashioned homemade mayonnaise, a sandwich is elevated to another level. Pick fresh cucumbers and ripe tomatoes from your garden, slather the bread with mayonnaise, and put it all together. The best part is the first bite.

Serves 4

4 medium ripe red tomatoes, cut into $1/4$-inch slices
2 small cucumbers, peeled and cut into $1/4$-inch slices
Coarse salt
$1/4$ cup Mayonnaise (page 38)
1 tablespoon chopped fresh dill
8 slices coarse-textured white bread

Season the tomatoes and cucumbers with salt.

In a small bowl, whisk together the mayonnaise and dill.

Place the bread on the work surface and spread the mayonnaise evenly on the slices. Top 4 slices of the bread with the tomatoes and cucumbers. Place the remaining slices of bread on top, cut in half on the diagonal, and serve immediately.

Roasted Tomato and Herbed Goat Cheese Sandwiches

Warm roasted tomatoes and fresh creamy herbed goat cheese make a simple irresistible sandwich that packs a punch of tartness and sweetness. When your garden is full of ripe tomatoes, make several batches of these dried tomatoes and keep them on hand as a garnish for grilled rib-eye steaks or to use in salsa.

Serves 4

4 small ripe red or yellow tomatoes
Coarse salt
1 large baguette, ends removed, cut into 2 pieces on the diagonal, and split open
5 ounces fresh goat cheese
1 tablespoon chopped fresh flat-leaf parsley
2 tablespoons finely snipped fresh chives
1 teaspoon chopped fresh oregano
1 teaspoon chopped fresh thyme
Freshly ground black pepper

Preheat the oven to 325°F.

Cut the tomatoes crosswise in half. Place them cut side up in a baking pan and sprinkle with salt. Let sit for 20 minutes.

Bake the tomatoes, removing the excess liquid from the pan every 20 minutes, until soft and beginning to dry out, about 1 hour and 15 minutes. Remove from the oven, cover, and keep warm.

In the meantime, wrap the baguettes in foil and heat in the oven until warm, about 10 minutes.

In a bowl, mash together the goat cheese, parsley, chives, oregano, and thyme. Season to taste with salt and pepper. (You can make the herbed goat cheese several days ahead and store in the refrigerator. Bring to room temperature before using.)

Spread the goat cheese evenly over the inside of the warmed baguettes. Cut the warm tomatoes in half and place in the sandwiches. Serve immediately.

Grilled Chicken Sandwiches with Tomato Tapenade and Fontina

Have you ever wondered what the first sandwich was? It may well be one of the all-time best culinary creations. Take this one, for example, grilled chicken and sun-dried tomato paste, with Fontina cheese—the flavors just melt together.

Serves 4

4 skinless, boneless chicken breasts (6 to 8
    ounces each)
1 tablespoon olive oil
Coarse salt and freshly ground black pepper
2 tablespoons unsalted butter, melted
8 slices coarse-textured Italian or French bread
4 ounces Italian Fontina cheese, thinly sliced
1/2 cup Sun-Dried Tomato Tapenade (page 244)

Preheat an outdoor grill.

Brush the chicken breasts with the oil. Place them on the grill and grill until golden on one side, about 5 minutes. Turn, season with salt and pepper, and continue to grill until cooked through, about 5 more minutes. (Alternatively, these can be cooked on the stovetop or a cast-iron ridged grill.) Cut the chicken on the diagonal into 1/2-inch slices.

Brush the butter over one side of 4 slices of the bread. Place buttered side down on a work surface. Top the bread with half of the Fontina and spread the tapenade on the cheese. Top with the sliced chicken and then the remaining cheese. Top with the remaining bread and brush the remaining butter over the bread.

Heat a large frying pan over medium heat. Place the sandwiches in the pan and cook until golden on the bottom and the cheese is beginning to melt, 2 to 3 minutes. Turn the sandwiches and continue to cook until the bread is golden on both sides and the cheese is melted, another 2 to 3 minutes. Slice the sandwiches in half on the diagonal and serve immediately.

Spanish-Style Gypsy Omelette

Called huevos flamenco, *or "flamenco eggs," this dish is usually served as a tapa or main course in Spain, but, of course, it can also be served for breakfast or brunch. Because of the vibrant red, green, white, and yellow of the spiced vegetables and eggs and the zesty flavor of cayenne, it's meant to conjure up the image of the colorful flamenco dancers, gypsies, and robust guitar music of Spain.*

Serves 6

1 tablespoon olive oil
1 medium yellow onion, finely chopped
2 garlic cloves, minced
2 medium ripe red tomatoes, peeled, seeded, chopped, and drained, or 1¹/₂ cups seeded, chopped, and drained canned tomatoes
1 teaspoon sweet paprika
Coarse salt and freshly ground black pepper
¹/₃ cup Chicken Stock (page 78)
6 large eggs
¹/₄ teaspoon cayenne
8 asparagus spears, cut into 1¹/₂-inch lengths and blanched for 1 minute in boiling water
¹/₂ cup fresh or frozen peas, blanched for 10 seconds in boiling water
1 medium red bell pepper, roasted, (see page 13), peeled, seeded, and cut into thin strips
2 tablespoons chopped fresh flat-leaf parsley

Preheat the oven to 400°F.

Heat the oil in a large frying pan over medium heat. Cook the onion until soft, about 7 minutes.

Add the garlic and stir constantly for 1 minute. Add the tomatoes, paprika, and salt and pepper to taste and simmer until the tomatoes soften, about 3 minutes. Increase the heat to high, add the chicken stock, and bring to a boil. Reduce the heat to a simmer, cover, and simmer for 5 minutes. (This sauce can be made 1 day in advance and stored in the refrigerator.)

Pour the sauce into a 2-quart baking dish. Break the eggs one at a time into a small bowl, keeping them separate, and slip them into the sauce, distributing them evenly. Season the eggs with the cayenne and salt and pepper. Arrange the asparagus, peas, and roasted pepper strips decoratively around and between the eggs. Season well with salt and pepper. Bake until the whites of the eggs are lightly set but the yolks are still runny, about 10 minutes.

Sprinkle with the parsley and serve immediately.

Mexican Ranch-Style Eggs

This is a traditional midmorning snack in Mexico, crispy corn tortillas topped with two fried eggs and a peppery hot tomato sauce. That's enough to wake you up! Now you find huevos rancheros *eaten at all times of the day, served with fried beans and extra tortillas.*

Serves 8

1/4 cup plus 3 tablespoons corn oil
2 small yellow onions, minced
4 garlic cloves, minced
10 medium ripe red tomatoes, peeled, seeded,
   and chopped, or 8 cups canned tomatoes
1 teaspoon ground cumin
4 serrano peppers, seeded and minced
Coarse salt and freshly ground black pepper
8 corn tortillas
16 large eggs

Heat 3 tablespoons of the oil in a large frying pan over medium heat. Add the onions and garlic and cook until soft, about 7 minutes. Add the tomatoes, cumin, and chiles cook until the sauce starts to thicken, 3 to 4 minutes. Season to taste with salt and pepper. Keep warm. (The sauce can be made a day ahead and refrigerated. Reheat when ready to serve.)

Heat the remaining 1/4 cup corn oil in another large frying pan over medium-high heat. Add the tortillas, one at a time, and cook until golden and crispy, about 30 seconds. Turn and cook for another 30 seconds. Drain on paper towels.

Drain off all but 1 tablespoon oil from the pan. Cook the eggs sunny-side up until set, about 1 minute. Season with salt and pepper.

To serve, place the hot tortillas on individual plates, top each tortilla with 2 eggs, and spoon the tomato sauce over the top.

Tomato Sandwiches

Think of tomatoes and sandwiches, and the BLT immediately comes to mind. Or is your favorite a grilled cheddar with tomato? For some, a hamburger without a thick slab of tomato is unthinkable. For others, a tomato sandwich is nothing more than a sliced tomato with some mayonnaise on great bread.

But if you're game for something new, try these: A BAT, crisp apple-smoked bacon, arugula, and tomato on sourdough bread. Grilled fontina, roasted red peppers, and tomato on rye. Tomato with dill mayonnaise or red onion and tomato with garlic mayonnaise. Goat cheese and tomatoes dusted with fresh herbs on toasted rustic bread. Thinly sliced prosciutto and tomatoes on toasted Italian bread that has been rubbed with garlic and brushed with olive oil.

There are few rules for tomato sandwiches. Use tomatoes when they're in season. Buy the best bread you can find. Tomato sandwiches can be eaten at any time of the day. Finally, remember that tomatoes are juicy, so eat the sandwiches before they become soggy.

Scrambled Eggs Cartagena

This is Colombian comfort food, scrambled eggs with lots of tomatoes, parsley, and onions. Serve with golden-fried potatoes and sausages. Ariana Kumpis, who grew up in Cartagena, Colombia, gave me this family favorite.

Serves 6

2 tablespoons unsalted butter
2 medium yellow onions, diced
4 small ripe red tomatoes, diced
12 large eggs
$^{1}/_{4}$ cup plus 1 tablespoon chopped flat-leaf parsley
Coarse salt and freshly ground black pepper

Melt the butter in a large nonstick frying pan over medium heat. Add the onions and cook until almost soft, about 5 minutes. Add the tomatoes and cook until almost soft, about 2 minutes.

In a bowl, whisk together the eggs, 2 tablespoons water, $^{1}/_{4}$ cup of the parsley, and salt and pepper to taste. Add the eggs slowly to the pan and stir very slowly until the eggs are set, 3 to 4 minutes. Fold the eggs over as you would an omelette and place on a plate. Sprinkle with the remaining 1 tablespoon parsley and serve immediately.

One-Slice Wonder

Now more deeply imprinted by my native soil, I have joined the legions of Southerners who know that tomatoes alone justify the sweaty travails of gardening in the South. In fact I'll go one further: The highest calling of any vegetable is that special tomato, that one-slice-makes-a-sandwich tomato, seamless, huge, and perfectly colored. Few Southern gardeners willingly settle for less, nor should they. This may be our sole divine compensation for the heat and humidity of July and August.

"By the time that these high-summer, tomato-harvest months arrive, Southerners are more than ready. For long weeks we have suffered the insult of the tomato-labeled objects in grocery stores, the ones genetically predisposed for shelf life, not sandwiches, at least not the kind we crave. Every Southerner knows that only a home-grown tomato can provide a cross section large enough to cover an entire piece of bread. Only a home-grown tomato can bring to the table the caliber of flavor and texture that, mingled with mayonnaise and soft white bread, will yield an unforgettable three-napkin lunch. . . .

"Sometime in September I will assemble my final one-slice tomato sandwich. It will represent the symbolic end of my tomato vine and that's the day I plan to hang up my hoe and bid tomato sandwiches—*real* tomato sandwiches—farewell for another season.

"No self-respecting Southerner would do otherwise."

From Glenn Morris, *Southern Living* magazine, July 1995

Greek Fishermen's Stew

Known as kakavia, *this tomato-seafood stew is made by Greek fishermen with some of their daily catch, either on the boat or back on shore. It is really a cinch to make but the results taste and look impressive. Thanks to Angel Stoyanof for his inspiration. You can make the tomato sauce several hours in advance, then finish the stew in the oven just before serving.*

Serves 6

¹/₄ cup olive oil
4 garlic cloves, chopped
2 large yellow onions, chopped
3 cups peeled, seeded, and chopped fresh or
    canned tomatoes
2 bay leaves
1 tablespoon dried oregano
Coarse salt and freshly ground black pepper
3 tablespoons tomato paste
¹/₂ cup dry white wine
¹/₂ cup Fish Stock (page 80) or bottled clam
    juice
1 pound mussels, scrubbed and beards
    removed
1 pound Manila or littleneck clams, scrubbed
³/₄ pound medium shrimp, peeled and deveined
1 pound rock cod, snapper, or halibut fillets,
    skinned, boned, and cut into large chunks

Heat the oil in a large frying pan over medium heat. Add the garlic and cook until soft, about 1 minute. Add the onions and cook, stirring occasionally, until soft, about 7 minutes. Add the tomatoes, bay leaves, oregano, and salt and pepper to taste and simmer until the tomatoes are soft, about 10 minutes. Add the tomato paste, white wine, and fish stock and cook until the sauce thickens, 10 to 12 minutes. Season to taste with salt and pepper. (You can prepare this several hours in advance and refrigerate.)

Preheat the oven to 375°F.

Place the mussels, clams, shrimp, and fish in a large deep casserole. Pour the tomato sauce over the fish and bake, covered, until the mussels open, about 20 minutes. Stir well and continue to bake until the clams open, about 10 minutes.

To serve, distribute the shellfish and fish among individual bowls, discarding any unopened clams or mussels. Season the tomato sauce to taste with salt and pepper, spoon over the fish and shellfish, and serve immediately.

Shellfish Gumbo with Okra

Gumbo *got its name from the African word for okra, gombo. Shellfish gumbo with tomatoes and okra is a staple of Louisiana's Cajun country, where it's served with hot cooked rice. Pass a bottle of red pepper sauce so your guests can make it as hot and spicy as they like. Make this gumbo a day in advance and reheat it just before serving.*

Serves 6

1/4 cup plus 2 tablespoons vegetable oil
1/4 cup all-purpose flour
3 medium yellow onions, chopped
4 garlic cloves, minced
1 stalk celery, chopped
1 green bell pepper, cored, seeded, and
　chopped
1 pound fresh or frozen okra, cut into 1/2-inch
　slices
3 medium tomatoes, peeled, seeded, and
　chopped, or 2 cups seeded and chopped
　canned tomatoes
3 cups Fish Stock (page 80) or bottled clam
　juice
1 teaspoon chopped fresh thyme
1/4 teaspoon crushed red pepper flakes
2 bay leaves
1 pound medium shrimp, shelled and deveined
1/2 pound crabmeat, picked over and shells
　removed
1/2 pound bay or sea scallops, side muscle
　removed
6 green onions, thinly sliced
3 tablespoons chopped fresh flat-leaf parsley
Coarse salt and freshly ground black pepper

In a large soup pot, heat the oil over medium-low heat. Add the flour and cook, stirring, until the mixture, or roux, is golden brown, about 15 minutes. Add the onions, garlic, celery, and bell pepper and cook until the vegetables wilt, about 10 minutes. Add the okra and tomatoes, cover, and simmer slowly, stirring occasionally, for 10 minutes.

Combine the fish stock and 2 cups water. Slowly add this liquid, a ladle at a time, stirring constantly, to the pot. Add the thyme, crushed red pepper, and bay leaves and simmer slowly, uncovered, for 30 minutes.

Add the shrimp, crabmeat, scallops, green onions, parsley, and salt and pepper to taste. Simmer for 10 minutes until the shrimp and scallops are cooked. Discard the bay leaves.

Ladle into bowls and serve immediately.

Marseillaise Fish Stew with Garlic Mayonnaise

This Provençal fish medley of all kinds of fish, tomatoes, and saffron is the classic dish called bouillabaisse, and the garlicky sauce that melts into it is rouille. This recipe is the closest you can get to the real thing without putting on a pair of espadrilles and buying a ticket to Marseilles.

Serves 6

3 pounds assorted fish fillets, such as sea bass, flounder, red snapper, grouper, perch, sole, pike, haddock, and/or cod, cut into 1-inch chunks

■ marinade
1/4 cup extra virgin olive oil
1 garlic clove, minced
1/2 teaspoon saffron threads

2 large yellow onions, coarsely chopped
4 garlic cloves, minced, plus 2 whole garlic cloves

3 pounds fish bones
5 cups peeled, seeded, and chopped fresh or canned tomatoes
6 sprigs fresh flat-leaf parsley
1 sprig fresh basil
1/2 teaspoon chopped fresh thyme
2 bay leaves
1/4 teaspoon ground fennel seed
One 2-inch strip orange zest, removed with a vegetable peeler
2 carrots, coarsely chopped
2 leeks (white and 1 inch of green part), coarsely chopped and rinsed
Coarse salt and freshly ground black pepper
1 1/4 cups dry white wine
2 pounds clams, scrubbed
1 teaspoon saffron threads
1 tablespoon Pernod (optional)
2 baguettes, sliced on a sharp diagonal
1 recipe Rouille (page 39)

Displayed in enormous round shallow pans, these tomatoes, together with pimentos and small marrows [squash] cooked in the same way, are a feature of every Athenian taverna, where one goes into the kitchen and chooses one's meal from the pans arrayed on the stove. It is impossible to describe the effect of the marvelous smells which assail one's nose and the sight of all those bright-colored concoctions is overwhelming. Peering into every stewpan, trying a spoonful of this, a morsel of that, it is easy to lose one's head and order a dish of everything on the menu."

From Elizabeth David, *A Book of Mediterranean Food*

In a bowl, combine the fish with 2 tablespoons olive oil, chopped garlic, and saffron. Set aside to marinate.

In a large soup pot, heat 2 remaining tablespoons olive oil over medium heat. Add the onions and minced garlic and cook, stirring occasionally, until soft, 7 minutes. Add the fish bones, tomatoes, parsley, basil, thyme, bay leaves, fennel, orange zest, carrots, leeks, $1/2$ teaspoon salt, and pepper and cook, covered, for 10 minutes. Add 6 cups water and 1 cup of the wine and bring to a boil over high heat. Reduce the heat to low and simmer, uncovered, crushing the bones from time to time with a wooden spoon, until the bones fall apart and the broth smells sweet, about 30 minutes. Let cool for 20 minutes.

In a blender, blend the mixture for a few seconds and then strain the broth through a fine strainer lined with cheesecloth into a large clean pot; discard the residue in the strainer. Season to taste with salt and pepper. (The broth can be made up to 1 day in advance and refrigerated.)

Bring the broth to a boil over medium-high heat. Add the clams and simmer until they just begin to open, 3 minutes. Add the fish, all of the marinade, and the remaining $1/4$ cup wine and cook at a low rolling boil for 10 minutes. Add the saffron threads and cook for another 5 minutes. Add the Pernod if using and season to taste with salt and pepper.

In the meantime, toast the bread on both sides until light golden. Rub the bread lightly with the whole garlic cloves.

Ladle the soup into bowls. Spread the rouille onto the toasted bread and float a few slices in each bowl of soup. Serve immediately.

> ". . . but I hardly got any. They dropped a lot of blossoms in the heat, then most of what fruit there was got eaten—I thought by Mamselle but just yesterday saw a porcupine suspiciously close to the patch. Very discouraging to see those bites out, I'll tell you."
>
> From Leslie Land and Roger Phillips,
> *The 3,000 Mile Garden*

Cioppino with Clams, Shrimp, and Crab

This is the real San Francisco treat! Cioppino is a simple shellfish, fish, and tomato stew that pairs well with sourdough bread and a good bottle of sauvignon blanc. The shellfish is always left in the shell, so I recommend that you serve this stew with bibs, finger bowls, and plenty of napkins.

Serves 6

Coarse salt
2 Dungeness crabs or 4 blue crabs, cooked
1/4 cup olive oil
1 large yellow onion, chopped
1 small green bell pepper, cored, seeded, and
    diced
4 garlic cloves, minced
1 pound snapper or rock cod fillets, cut into
    1-inch chunks
1 cup dry white wine
2 cups Fish Stock (page 80) or 1 cup bottled
    clam juice plus 1 cup water
2 1/2 cups peeled, seeded, and chopped fresh or
    canned tomatoes
1 tablespoon tomato paste
2 bay leaves
1/2 teaspoon dried basil
Pinch of crushed red pepper flakes
1 pound clams, scrubbed
1 pound large shrimp
Freshly ground black pepper
3 tablespoons chopped fresh flat-leaf parsley

Bring a large pot of water to the boil. Add salt and the crabs. Cook until the crabs turn bright red, 8 to 10 minutes for Dungeness crabs, 6 to 8 minutes for blue crabs. Pull off the top shell and apron from the crabs and discard. Remove the spongy white gills and intestines and wash out the inside of the crabs. Working over a bowl, break the crabs lengthwise in half. Cut each half into 3 pieces so that each piece of the body is attached to a leg or claw. Crack the legs and claws with a large mallet or hammer.

In a large soup pot, heat the olive oil over medium heat. Add the onion, green pepper, and garlic and cook, stirring, until soft, about 7 minutes. Add the crab, crab juices, and snapper and cook, stirring occasionally, for 10 minutes. Increase the heat to high, add the wine, and simmer until reduced by half, about 2 minutes. Decrease the heat to low, add the fish stock, 2 cups water, the tomatoes, tomato paste, bay leaves, basil, and red pepper flakes, and simmer for 10 minutes.

Add the clams and simmer until they open, 3 to 5 minutes. Discard any that do not open. Add the shrimp and cook until the shrimp are firm to the touch, 3 to 4 minutes. Season to taste with salt and pepper.

To serve, ladle into bowls and garnish with the parsley.

Menorcan Lobster Stew

Spain's "bouillabaisse," this stew from the island of Menorca is called caldereta, *from the word* caldero, *or cauldron, the cooking vessel used to make this shellfish masterpiece. Its main component is* langosta, *the spiny lobster with five pairs of legs, no claws, and a tail full of meat. You can substitute our American lobster without compromising the finished dish.*

Serves 6

1/4 cup extra virgin olive oil
3 medium yellow onions, minced
4 garlic cloves, chopped
3 cups peeled, seeded, and chopped fresh or
    canned tomatoes
1 large green bell pepper, cored, seeded, and
    chopped
6 sprigs fresh flat-leaf parsley, plus
    2 tablespoons chopped parsley
Coarse salt and freshly ground black pepper
2 lobsters or spiny lobsters (1 1/4 pounds each)
5 cups Fish Stock (page 80) or 2 1/2 cups bottled
    clam juice plus 2 1/2 cups water
1 baguette, sliced diagonally into twelve
    1/2-inch slices, toasted

In a large frying pan, heat 2 tablespoons of the olive oil over medium heat. Add the onions, garlic, tomatoes, green pepper, parsley sprigs, 1 cup water, and salt and pepper to taste. After it comes to a boil, reduce the heat to low and simmer for 30 minutes. Remove from the heat.

In the meantime, in a large soup pot, bring 2 cups lightly salted water to a boil. Add the lobsters one at a time, cover, and cook for 4 minutes. Remove the lobsters and reserve the cooking water in the pot. Cut off the lobster tails and slice the tails. Remove the claws and crush slightly. Split the bodies down the middle. Cut off the heads and discard. Remove and reserve the green tomalley and coral; discard the gill tissues and digestive tracts.

Heat the remaining 2 tablespoons oil in a large pot over medium-high heat. Add the lobster pieces in the shells, a few at a time, and toss and cook for 1 minute. Place the lobster pieces in a bowl and set aside.

Transfer the tomato mixture to a blender or food processor and blend until smooth. Add to the reserved lobster water in the soup pot, along with the fish stock. In a small bowl, mix together the tomalley and coral and add to the pot. Bring to a boil. Simmer, uncovered, for 20 minutes.

Add the lobster pieces and simmer for 6 minutes until just cooked. Season to taste with salt and pepper.

To serve, place 2 slices of toasted bread in the bottom of each bowl. Ladle the soup and lobster over the bread. Garnish with the chopped parsley and serve immediately.

Trapanese Couscous Stew with Shellfish

There is only one little pocket of Italy where couscous is cooked with any seriousness, and that's in western Sicily. Just ninety miles of blue water separates this part of Sicily from Tunisia, and couscous, the North African semolina pasta, was brought here hundreds of years ago by Tunisian soldiers recruited to fight in Sicily. From Trapani to Marsala, this shellfish and tomato stew is called cuscusu.

Serves 6

3/4 cup couscous
2 1/2 cups Fish Stock (page 80) or bottled clam
   juice
Coarse salt
1 pound clams, scrubbed
3/4 pound mussels, scrubbed and beards
   removed
3 tablespoons olive oil
1 small yellow onion, minced
3 garlic cloves, minced
Small pinch of crushed red pepper flakes
1 cup dry red wine
1 1/2 cups peeled, seeded, and chopped fresh or
   canned tomatoes
1 teaspoon red wine vinegar
2 bay leaves
Freshly ground black pepper
3 tablespoons chopped fresh flat-leaf parsley,
   plus extra for garnish
1/2 teaspoon saffron threads

1/2 pound medium shrimp, peeled and deveined
1/4 pound scallops, preferably sea scallops, side
   muscle removed

Place the couscous in a fine strainer and rinse with cold water. Drain and dump the couscous into a large baking dish. Periodically lift and rake the grains with your fingertips for about 10 minutes to separate them.

Bring the fish stock to a simmer in a large soup pot fitted with a steamer. Line the steamer or top of a couscoussiere with cheesecloth or paper towels. Add the couscous to the steamer and steam, uncovered, for 20 minutes, fluffing the grains halfway through the cooking. Remove from the steamer and dump the couscous back into the baking pan. Combine 1/3 cup water and 1/4 teaspoon salt and sprinkle the couscous with the salt water. Periodically lift and rake the grains for about 10 minutes.

Heat the fish stock to a simmer over medium heat. Add the clams and mussels to the pot and cook until they open, 3 to 5 minutes. Remove the clams and mussels, discarding any that do not open. Transfer the broth to a bowl and reserve.

Heat the olive oil in the soup pot over medium heat. Add the onion and cook, stirring occasionally, until soft, about 7 minutes. Add the garlic and red pepper flakes and stir for 1 minute. Turn the heat to high and immediately add the wine. Boil until reduced by one half, about 2 minutes. Add the tomatoes, vinegar, bay leaves, the reserved shellfish broth, and pepper to taste. Bring to a boil, then reduce the heat to low to maintain a slow simmer.

Place the cheesecloth-lined steamer back on the top of the soup pot and place the couscous in the steamer. Steam slowly, uncovered, until the couscous on top is hot to the touch, about 15 minutes. Remove the steamer and cover to keep warm.

Add the parsley, saffron, and all the shellfish to the pot and simmer slowly for 2 minutes. Turn off the heat and let sit for 3 minutes. Season to taste with salt and pepper.

Divide the couscous among individual bowls, ladle the soup over the couscous, garnish with parsley, and serve immediately.

The first cookbook published in America containing a recipe using tomatoes appear[ed] in 1792. The recipe, 'To Dress Haddock in the Spanish Way,' is found in Richard Brigg's 'New Art of Cookery' (Philadelphia, from the London edition of 1788). This book was very popular among the Quakers of Philadelphia and influential through its use in Mrs. Goodfellow's Cooking School, which flourished in that city in the early nineteenth century."

From Jan Langone, "From the Kitchen,"
*The American Magazine and
Historical Chronicle,* Winter 1987–88

Portuguese Shellfish and Linguiça Stew

Rosa Gabao spends half of her year cooking along the northern coast of Portugal and the other half in the North End of Boston, cooking at a little restaurant on Hanover Street called Omero. She loves using linguiça, the dry Portuguese sausage made from pork shoulder, plenty of garlic, and paprika in her fish soup. She says the sausage brings out the sweetness of the shellfish, onions, and tomatoes. If linguiça is unavailable, substitute another spicy pork, garlic, and paprika sausage. You can make this several hours in advance; reheat gently and garnish with parsley just before serving.

Serves 6 to 8

3 tablespoons extra virgin olive oil
1/2 pound linguiça, cut into 1/8-inch slices
3 medium yellow onions, thinly sliced
4 carrots, cut into 1/4-inch slices
5 garlic cloves, thinly sliced
6 bay leaves
2 teaspoons sweet paprika
1/4 teaspoon crushed red pepper flakes
1/4 teaspoon freshly ground black pepper
2 1/2 cups peeled, seeded, and chopped fresh or canned tomatoes
1 1/2 cups dry white wine
1 1/2 cups Fish Stock (page 80) or bottled clam juice
2 pounds clams, scrubbed
1 1/2 pounds mussels, scrubbed and beards removed
1 pound monkfish or other firm white fish fillets, cut into 1-inch cubes
1/2 pound medium shrimp, peeled and deveined
1/4 cup green Spanish olives, pitted and thinly sliced
1 pound Yukon Gold or other waxy potatoes, peeled, cubed, and boiled just until tender
Coarse salt
2 tablespoons chopped fresh flat-leaf parsley

Heat the olive oil in a large soup pot over medium heat. Add the linguiça, onions, carrots, garlic, and bay leaves and cook, stirring occasionally, until the onions are soft, 7 minutes. Add the paprika, red pepper flakes, and black pepper and stir for 2 minutes. Add the tomatoes, white wine, and fish stock and simmer over low heat for 8 to 10 minutes.

Increase the heat to high, add the clams and mussels, and stir together. Reduce the heat to medium, cover, and simmer until the clams and mussels open, 5 to 8 minutes. Discard any unopened clams or mussels. Add the fish, shrimp, olives, potatoes, and stir together. Simmer, covered, for 3 to 4 minutes until the shrimp and fish are cooked. Season to taste with salt.

Ladle the stew into bowls, sprinkle with the parsley, and serve immediately.

Red Snapper Roasted with Tomatoes, Olives, and Capers

When I see freshly caught whole fish such as red snapper, I immediately think of roasting it this way. When it emerges hot from the oven, the flesh of the fish falls from the bone, and the zesty sauce is a great foil for steamed rice flavored with lemon zest. You can make the sauce early in the day and place it with the fish in a baking dish in the refrigerator until you're ready to bake the fish. Fillets can be substituted for whole fish. Reduce the baking time to fifteen to twenty minutes.

Serves 6

3 tablespoons olive oil
1 large yellow onion, minced
3 garlic cloves, thinly sliced
1½ cups dry white wine
4 cups peeled, seeded, and chopped fresh or
  canned tomatoes
¼ cup capers
Coarse salt and freshly ground black pepper
2 whole red snapper, striped bass, gulf
  snapper, or other firm white fish (1½ to 1¾
  pounds each), gutted and scaled, washed,
  and dried, or 6 fillets (6 to 8 ounces each)
¾ cup cured black olives, such as Kalamata or
  Niçoise

Preheat the oven to 400°F.

Heat the olive oil in a large frying pan over medium heat. Add the onion and garlic and cook, stirring, until soft, about 7 minutes. Increase the heat to high, add the wine, and simmer until re-duced by half, 3 to 4 minutes. With a food mill, puree the tomatoes directly into the pan. Add the capers and cook over low heat until the sauce is thick, about 10 minutes. Season to taste with salt and pepper.

Place half of the sauce in a large baking dish. Place the whole fish on top of the tomato sauce. Sprinkle the olives around the fish. Pour the remaining sauce over the fish, spreading it evenly. Cover with foil and bake until the fish is just cooked through and registers an internal temperature of 140°F, 30 to 35 minutes.

Remove the foil and serve immediately, directly from the baking dish.

Red Snapper with Picadillo

La Carihuela, a little fishing village in the south of Spain near Torremolinos, has managed to hold its own against the onslaught of tourists seeking the Mediterranean sunshine and beaches. At a little fish house on a quiet back alley, you can taste this dish, a perfect fillet of freshly caught snapper stewed in a sweet-and-sour tomato sauce and topped with the colorful vegetable relish called picadillo. *You can make the picadillo an hour before serving.*

Serves 6

■ picadillo
5 medium ripe red tomatoes, peeled and
    seeded, plus 1 small ripe red tomato, diced
3 tablespoons tomato paste
2 garlic cloves, minced
2 tablespoons extra virgin olive oil
1 teaspoon sugar
1 tablespoon sherry vinegar, or more to taste
Coarse salt and freshly ground black pepper

■ vegetables and fish
1 carrot, diced
1 small zucchini, diced
1 tablespoon extra virgin olive oil
1/4 cup cured green Spanish olives, diced
1/4 red bell pepper, diced
1/4 cup minced red onion
1 1/2 tablespoons minced fresh flat-leaf parsley
1 tablespoon fresh lemon juice
2 1/2 to 3 pounds red snapper fillet, skin and
    bones removed and cut into 6 pieces
    (6 to 8 ounces each)
Lemon wedges

In a blender or food processor, puree the 5 medium tomatoes, the tomato paste, garlic, 2 tablespoons of the olive oil, the sugar, and sherry vinegar until smooth, about 1 minute. Place the mixture in a frying pan and bring to a boil over medium-high heat. Reduce the heat to low and simmer until the sauce thickens slightly, 5 minutes. Season to taste with salt and pepper and additional vinegar if needed. Remove from the heat and set aside.

Bring a medium saucepan of salted water to a boil. Add the carrot and simmer for 3 minutes. Add the zucchini and simmer for 1 minute, until crisp and tender. Drain and place the carrot and zucchini in a bowl. Add 1 tablespoon olive oil, the olives, red pepper, onion, parsley, the diced tomato, and the lemon juice. Season to taste with salt and pepper. Set aside.

Heat the tomato sauce over medium heat until simmering. Season the fish fillets with salt and pepper and place in the tomato sauce. Simmer until the fish is opaque, 7 to 8 minutes.

Spoon the tomato sauce onto individual serving plates. Place the fillets in the center of the sauce. Distribute the vegetables on the top of the fish. Garnish with lemon wedges and serve immediately.

Tuna Mediterraneo

When I thought about writing a book about tomatoes, I never imagined the tremendous variety of recipes I would want to include. At one point, I had six tuna and tomato recipes that I had to whittle down to the best two. Make sure to buy the freshest ingredients for this flavorful Mediterranean dish.

Serves 6

12 ripe plum tomatoes, peeled, seeded, and
   chopped
3 tablespoons chopped fresh flat-leaf parsley
20 fresh basil leaves, torn into small pieces,
   plus 6 whole sprigs for garnish
$1/4$ teaspoon crushed red pepper flakes
$1/2$ cup minced yellow onions
2 tablespoons capers
2 tablespoons extra virgin olive oil
3 garlic cloves, crushed
2 anchovy fillets, soaked in water for 10
   minutes, drained, and patted dry
6 tuna steaks (6 to 8 ounces each)
Coarse salt and freshly ground black pepper
1 cup dry white wine

In a medium bowl, combine the tomatoes, parsley, basil, red pepper flakes, onions, and capers. Set aside.

Heat the olive oil in a large frying pan over medium heat. Add the garlic and anchovies and cook until the garlic is light golden and the anchovies have fallen apart, 1 to 2 minutes. Add the tuna steaks and cook for 3 minutes per side. Season with salt and pepper. Transfer to a plate and set aside, covered with foil.

Increase the heat to high, add the wine, and cook until most of the wine is evaporated, 1 to 2 minutes. Add the tomato mixture, reduce the heat to low, and simmer until the sauce is thickened, about 12 minutes.

Return the tuna steaks to the pan and simmer for 3 minutes until warm. Remove the garlic cloves and discard. Season to taste with salt and pepper.

To serve, place a tuna steak on each plate. Spoon the tomatoes over the tuna, garnish with the sprigs of basil, and serve immediately.

Salmon in the Garden

Wrap a whole side of salmon with garden herbs and vine-ripened tomatoes in foil and bake in the oven for a simple yet festive main course that celebrates fresh summer flavors. Serve it al fresco; in fact, if it is too hot in the kitchen, cook the salmon on the outdoor grill, with the cover closed. The salmon will stay warm, wrapped in foil for up to an hour once it is taken from the oven. It can be served warm, at room temperature, or cold.

Serves 8

1/4 cup chopped fresh basil
1 tablespoon chopped fresh oregano
1 tablespoon chopped fresh mint
2 teaspoons chopped fresh sage
1/3 cup capers, chopped
Coarse salt and freshly ground white pepper
1 whole salmon fillet (about 4 pounds), skin
    and any bones removed
8 small ripe red tomatoes, 4 cut into 1/4-inch
    slices and 4 peeled and cut into 1/2-inch dice
1/4 cup extra virgin olive oil
1 tablespoon red wine vinegar
1 tablespoon white wine vinegar
2 tablespoons chopped fresh flat-leaf parsley

Preheat the oven to 325°F.

In a small bowl, combine the basil, oregano, mint, sage, capers, 1 teaspoon salt, and 1/2 teaspoon pepper and mix well. Rub both sides of the fish with the mixture.

On a baking sheet large enough to hold the fish, lay a 2 1/2 × 1 1/2-foot piece of heavy-duty foil. Place the sliced tomatoes in the center of the foil. Season with salt and pepper. Lay the fish on top of the tomatoes and cover with a matching piece of foil. Fold and crimp the edges to make an airtight package. Bake the fish until an instant-read thermometer registers 140°F, 40 to 50 minutes.

In the meantime, in a small bowl, whisk together the olive oil, red wine vinegar, and white wine vinegar. Season to taste with salt and pepper.

Remove the salmon from the oven. Cut a corner off the foil and empty the liquid from the foil into a frying pan. Set the salmon aside. Reduce the liquid over high heat to 2 to 3 tablespoons, 2 to 3 minutes. Add the reduced liquid to the vinaigrette and whisk together. Toss the diced tomatoes with the vinaigrette and season to taste with salt and pepper.

Tear open the foil and place the salmon on a serving platter. Distribute the tomatoes on the top of the salmon. Sprinkle with the parsley and serve.

Almond-Crusted Trout with Tomato and Pepper Salad

A *crunchy tart salad of sweet bell peppers, red onions, and tomatoes sets off the flavors of these small whole trout in their crisp, nutty crust. The trout can be breaded several hours ahead of time and refrigerated until ready to cook.*

Serves 6

1/4 cup extra virgin olive oil
1 tablespoon sherry vinegar
1 tablespoon white wine vinegar
Coarse salt and freshly ground black pepper
2 green bell peppers, cored, seeds removed,
   and diced
1 small red onion, thinly sliced
2 cups almonds, whole, unblanched
1/2 cup all-purpose flour
3 large eggs, whisked together
6 whole trout (10 ounces each), gutted and
   scaled, washed, and dried
1 tablespoon unsalted butter
1 tablespoon olive oil
3 medium ripe red tomatoes, peeled, seeded,
   and diced

In a medium bowl, whisk together the extra virgin olive oil, sherry vinegar, white wine vinegar, and salt and pepper to taste. Add the bell peppers and onion and stir together.

In a food processor, finely chop the almonds. Place the flour, eggs, and almonds in 3 separate bowls. Season the flour and eggs with salt and pepper. Dip the trout, one at a time, in the flour and pat off the excess. Dip in the egg and then lightly in the almonds.

In a large heavy frying pan, melt the butter with the olive oil over medium heat. Cook the trout until light golden on one side, 4 to 5 minutes. Turn the trout and continue to cook until golden and cooked through, 4 to 5 minutes longer.

To serve, add the tomatoes to the salad. Place a trout on each plate and top with the salad.

Rolled Swordfish Skewers with Tomatoes, Capers, and Lemon

Thin slices of swordfish rolled around a stuffing of dried tomatoes, capers, Parmigiano, garlic, and lots of lemon, threaded onto lemon-soaked bamboo skewers, and grilled look fantastic and taste even better. Take them hot from the grill, drizzle with lemony vinaigrette, and place them on a bed of wilted spinach . . . the results are memorable. You can get the skewers all made up and refrigerate until you're ready to grill them.

Serves 6

3 lemons
12 bamboo skewers
2^1/$_2$ to 3 pounds swordfish steaks, cut ^{3}/$_4$ inch
   thick, skin removed, cut into as large steaks
   as possible
3 tablespoons olive oil, plus extra for brushing
   the fish
^{1}/$_4$ cup minced yellow onion
3 garlic cloves, chopped
1^1/$_2$ cups fresh bread crumbs
^{1}/$_4$ cup capers, chopped
^{1}/$_2$ cup oil-cured Sun-Dried (page 13) or Oven-
   Dried Tomatoes (page 14), finely chopped
^{1}/$_4$ cup freshly grated Parmigiano-Reggiano
2 teaspoons grated lemon zest
2 tablespoons chopped fresh flat-leaf parsley
1 large egg, well beaten
Coarse salt and freshly ground black pepper
12 bay leaves, halved
^{1}/$_3$ cup extra virgin olive oil
^{1}/$_2$ teaspoon chopped fresh oregano

^{1}/$_2$ teaspoon chopped fresh thyme
2 large bunches spinach, washed and spun dry
6 lemon wedges

With a vegetable peeler, peel the lemons and set the peel aside. Juice the lemons. Soak the skewers in half of the lemon juice and reserve the remaining juice.

Cut the fish into 6 pieces about 3 × 3 inches. Cut each piece horizontally into 3 even slices. Chop any trimmings for the stuffing and reserve. Place each slice of fish between waxed paper and pound gently until it is about one third again as large.

Heat the olive oil in a large frying pan. Cook the onion, stirring until soft, about 7 minutes. Add any swordfish trimmings and the garlic and cook, stirring, for 2 minutes. Add the bread crumbs and stir over low heat for 30 seconds. Transfer to a bowl and add the capers, sun-dried tomatoes, Parmigiano, 1 teaspoon of the lemon zest, 1 tablespoon of the parsley, and the egg. Season to taste with salt and pepper.

Preheat an outdoor grill or the broiler.

Place the fish slices on a work surface in a single layer. Divide the stuffing evenly among the fish slices, placing it in the center. With oiled hands, roll up the slices of fish, squeezing them a bit so they hold together. Using 2 skewers, about 1 inch apart, thread 4 rolls alternately with 4 bay leaf halves and 3 or 4 strips of lemon peel. Repeat with the remaining ingredients and brush the rolls with olive oil.

To make the vinaigrette, in a small bowl, combine the extra virgin olive oil, the reserved lemon juice,

1 tablespoon hot water, the remaining 1 teaspoon grated lemon zest, 1 tablespoon parsley, the oregano, thyme, $3/4$ teaspoon salt, and $1/2$ teaspoon pepper and whisk well.

Cook the swordfish skewers over hot coals or under the broiler for about $1 1/2$ minutes per side, basting occasionally with the vinaigrette.

Heat a large skillet. Add the spinach and 1 teaspoon of the vinaigrette. Wilt the spinach slightly, 30 seconds.

Place the spinach on individual plates and place 2 skewers on top of each. Drizzle with the remaining vinaigrette and garnish with the lemon wedges.

Baked Bass with Herbed Tomatoes

One of the simple pleasures in life is taking the time to enjoy a weekend lunch, and here is the perfect dish to serve. Choose the freshest fish and bake it between layers of vine-ripened sweet tomatoes and lots of fresh herbs. Serve with crispy thin rounds of golden potatoes sautéed in olive oil and a bottle of crisp white wine.

Serves 6

$2 1/2$ to 3 pounds striped bass, gulf snapper, or
   other firm white fish fillets, skin and any
   bones removed and cut into 6 pieces
$1/4$ cup plus 1 tablespoon fresh lemon juice
$1/4$ cup plus 1 tablespoon extra virgin olive oil
Coarse salt and freshly ground black pepper
3 medium yellow onions, thinly sliced

2 tablespoons chopped fresh flat-leaf parsley
1 tablespoon chopped fresh oregano
1 tablespoon chopped fresh thyme
3 bay leaves
2 garlic cloves, thinly sliced
6 ripe red tomatoes, peeled and thinly sliced
$1/4$ cup dry white wine

Brush the fish with 2 tablespoons of the lemon juice and 1 tablespoon of the olive oil, sprinkle with $1/2$ teaspoon salt and $1/2$ teaspoon pepper, and let stand for 1 hour in the refrigerator.

Preheat the oven to 375°F.

Heat 2 tablespoons of the olive oil in a large frying pan over medium heat. Add the onions, parsley, oregano, thyme, and bay leaves and cook until the onions are soft and just beginning to turn golden, about 15 minutes. Add the garlic and cook, stirring, for 1 minute.

Spread half of the onions in the bottom of a large baking dish. Distribute half of the tomatoes over the onions and season with salt and pepper. Place the fish on the tomatoes. Place the remaining onions, then the remaining tomatoes on top and season with salt and pepper. Pour the wine over the tomatoes. Drizzle with the remaining 2 tablespoons olive oil and 3 tablespoons lemon juice. Cover with foil and bake for 15 minutes. Remove the foil and bake just until the fish is cooked and flakes, 15 to 20 minutes.

Serve directly from the baking dish.

Red-Hot Squid Salad

Perfect picnic food and easy to prepare! When you see fresh squid at your local fishmonger, buy it—the season is so short. Make the salad in the morning and refrigerate it until you're ready to pack the cooler. A loaf of bread, some sliced meats, a bottle of white wine, and you've got a meal. You can also add diced avocado, cured black olives, or chopped celery to the salad.

Serves 6

2 pounds fresh squid
6 green onions (white and 2 inches of the green part), cut into 1/4-inch slices
5 ripe plum tomatoes, diced
1 small yellow bell pepper, cored, seeded, and diced
1 small jalapeño, seeded and finely minced
2 tablespoons chopped fresh flat-leaf parsley, plus a few sprigs for garnish
1 teaspoon chopped fresh oregano
1 garlic clove, minced
1/4 cup extra virgin olive oil
3 tablespoons fresh lemon juice
Coarse salt and freshly ground black pepper
Lemon wedges

Wash the squid. Separate the bodies from the heads by tugging gently on the heads. Remove anything that is remaining on the insides of each squid, including the transparent quill bone in the body, and discard. Remove the tentacles by cutting them off just below the eyes. Remove the beak by turning the head inside out and pressing the center; discard. Remove the skin from the body by scraping it away with a knife. Slice the bodies into rings and leave the tentacles whole. Wash well and pat dry on paper towels.

Bring a large pot of salted water to a boil. Add the squid and simmer just until tender, about 10 seconds. Immediately remove and cool.

In a large bowl, combine the squid, green onions, tomatoes, bell pepper, jalapeño, parsley, and oregano.

In a small bowl, whisk together the garlic, olive oil, and lemon juice. Add the vinaigrette to the squid and vegetables and mix together. Season to taste with salt and pepper. Let sit in the refrigerator for at least 1 hour.

To serve, place the salad on a serving platter and garnish with lemon wedges and parsley sprigs.

Neapolitan Squid with Pine Nuts and Raisins

In September, Naples is dotted everywhere with red, as trays full of tomato paste dry in the Mediterranean sun. In Italy, tomato paste, or concentrato, made on a commercial basis is packaged and sold in small cans, tubes, or big metal tubs. Ideal for winter months, when just a tablespoon or two will give just the right lift to a dish, tomato paste has become synonymous with Naples. Just two tablespoons give this Neapolitan dish a welcome dose of rich, concentrated tart tomato flavor.

Serves 6

2 pounds fresh squid
3 tablespoons extra virgin olive oil
4 garlic cloves, crushed, plus 1 whole garlic clove
3 cups peeled, seeded, and chopped fresh or canned tomatoes
2 tablespoons tomato paste
$1/2$ cup cured black olives, such as Kalamata or Niçoise, pitted and chopped
$1/4$ cup golden raisins
$1/4$ cup pine nuts, toasted
2 tablespoons chopped fresh flat-leaf parsley
6 slices country-style bread

Wash the squid. Separate the bodies from the heads by tugging gently on the heads. Remove anything that is remaining on the insides of each squid, including the transparent quill bone in the body, and discard. Remove the tentacles by cutting them off just below the eyes. Remove the beak by turning the head inside out and pressing the center; discard. Remove the skin from the body by scraping it away with a knife. Slice the bodies into rings and leave the tentacles whole. Wash well and pat dry on paper towels.

Heat the olive oil in a large saucepan over medium heat. Add the crushed garlic and cook until golden, 2 minutes. Remove the garlic and discard. Using a food mill, puree the tomatoes directly into the pan. Add the tomato paste, $1/2$ cup water, the olives, raisins, pine nuts, and parsley and simmer over low heat for 10 minutes.

Increase the heat to medium, add the squid, stir together, cover, and simmer until the squid is tender, 1 to 2 minutes. Remove from the heat.

In the meantime, toast the bread until light golden on both sides. Rub with the whole garlic clove.

Spoon the squid into individual bowls and serve immediately, with the toasted bread on the side.

Moroccan Fish Tagine

In Casablanca, when my friend Fatima removed the cover of the fish tagine she was serving, I was overwhelmed by the heady aroma. A Moroccan tagine is both a conical earthenware cooking vessel and the stew cooked inside the vessel. It can be made with any combination of meats and vegetables, such as lamb with artichokes, preserved lemons, and olives or, as here, whole fresh fish with juicy ripe red tomatoes and preserved lemons. Serve with couscous or rice.

Serves 6

One 3½- to 4½-pound whole striped bass, gulf snapper, or other firm white fish, gutted and scaled, washed, and dried
1 tablespoon ground cumin
Large pinch of crushed red pepper flakes
Coarse salt and freshly ground black pepper
2 tablespoons fresh lemon juice
¼ cup olive oil
¼ cup plus 1 tablespoon chopped fresh cilantro, plus 5 whole sprigs
1 garlic clove, minced, plus 3 garlic cloves, crushed
4 medium ripe red tomatoes, peeled and sliced
1 green bell pepper, cored, seeded, and thinly sliced
1½ Preserved Lemons (page 171), pulp removed and skin thinly sliced

With a sharp knife, score the skin of the fish in a crisscross pattern, cutting through the skin. In a small bowl, mix together the cumin, red pepper flakes, 1 teaspoon salt, ¼ teaspoon pepper, the lemon juice, 2 tablespoons of the olive oil, the chopped cilantro, and the minced garlic. Rub the fish with the mixture. Place the crushed garlic and the cilantro sprigs in the cavity of the fish and let sit in the refrigerator, covered with plastic, for 1 hour.

Preheat the oven to 400°F.

Place half of the tomatoes, bell pepper, and preserved lemons in the bottom of a large baking dish. Season with salt and pepper. Place the fish on top. Arrange the remaining tomatoes, bell pepper, and preserved lemons on top. Drizzle with the remaining 2 tablespoons oil. Cover with foil and bake for 35 to 40 minutes.

Remove the foil and bake until the internal temperature of the fish is 140°F, 10 to 15 minutes longer.

Serve immediately, from the baking dish.

Preserved Lemons

If you are lucky enough to have Meyer lemons, the smooth, yellow-orange-skinned, sweeter lemons, by all means use them as a substitute.

Makes about 1 quart

8 lemons, washed
¹/₂ **cup coarse salt**
2 **cinnamon sticks**
4 **bay leaves**
Fresh lemon juice, as needed

Cut each lemon into quarters from the top to within ¹/₂ inch of the bottom, taking care to leave the 4 pieces joined at the stem end. Sprinkle the insides of the lemons with salt.

Place 2 tablespoons of the salt in the bottom of a canning jar and pack the lemons into the jar, pushing them down and adding the remaining salt, the cinnamon sticks, and the bay leaves as you go. If the level of lemon juice doesn't come almost to the top of the jar, add extra freshly squeezed juice as necessary, leaving some airspace. Close the jar and let the lemons sit in a warm place for 1 month, turning the jar upside down periodically to distribute the salt and juices.

To use the lemons, remove from the brine, discard the pulp, and wash the peel. Some white crystals will form on the top of the lemons in the jar; this is normal. The lemons can be stored at room temperature or refrigerated for up to 1 year.

Risotto alla Marinara

The secret to a great risotto is simple—top-quality ingredients and patience. In this one, use fresh shellfish, good stock, and the right rice.

Serves 6

1/2 pound squid
3/4 pound mussels, scrubbed and beards
    removed
3/4 pound clams, scrubbed
3 cups peeled, seeded, and chopped fresh or
    canned tomatoes
2 tablespoons olive oil
1 medium yellow onion, chopped
1/2 pound medium shrimp, peeled, deveined,
    and halved lengthwise
1 cup dry white wine
1 garlic clove, minced
2 tablespoons chopped fresh flat-leaf parsley,
    plus a few sprigs for garnish
1/4 teaspoon crushed red pepper flakes
1 1/2 cups arborio, vialone nano, or carnaroli rice
Coarse salt and freshly ground black pepper

Wash the squid. Separate the bodies from the heads by tugging gently on the heads. Remove anything that is remaining on the insides of each squid and discard. Remove the tentacles by cutting them off just below the eyes. Remove the beak by turning the head inside out and pressing the center; discard. Remove the skin from the body by scraping it away with a knife. Slice the bodies into rings and leave the tentacles whole. Wash well and drain.

Heat 2 cups water in a large frying pan over high heat. Add the mussels, cover, and simmer until they begin to open, 2 to 3 minutes. As they open, remove them from the pan and place in a bowl. Discard any unopened mussels. Repeat with the clams, cooking them for 3 to 5 minutes. Reserve the cooking liquid and strain if necessary.

Remove half of the clams and mussels from the shell, coarsely chop, and set aside.

In a small saucepan, heat 2 cups water and keep at just below a boil. Puree the tomatoes in a blender or food processor.

Heat the olive oil in a large frying pan over medium-high heat. Add the onion and cook until light golden, 10 minutes. Add the shrimp and the chopped mussels and clams and cook for 1 minute. Add the wine and cook until it has evaporated, about 3 minutes. Add the pureed tomatoes, the garlic, parsley, red pepper flakes, the reserved clam and mussel cooking liquid, and the clams and mussels still in the shell and reduce the heat to medium. Add the rice and stir. Cook, adding the simmering water a ladleful at a time to keep the risotto loose, until the rice has a chalky center, about 20 minutes. Add more water only after the previous addition has been absorbed.

Add the squid and continue to stir, adding hot water as necessary, until the rice is barely tender but still no longer chalky, 2 to 4 minutes. Season to taste with salt and pepper.

Garnish with parsley sprigs and serve immediately.

Fiery Steamed Mussels

Jet-black mussels steamed in a fiery hot tomato sauce with lots and lots of garlic and spices—the aromas alone will knock you out. The perfect dish to serve as a first course, or as a main course with plenty of crusty bread to soak up the irresistible juices. If you have any leftovers (which is highly unlikely), toss with linguine or fettuccine.

Serves 6

2 tablespoons extra virgin olive oil
1 small red onion, finely minced
4 garlic cloves, minced
1½ teaspoons ground cumin
1 teaspoon ground ginger
½ teaspoon ground turmeric
½ teaspoon sweet paprika
½ to 1 teaspoon harissa
Coarse salt and freshly ground black pepper
2 cups peeled, seeded, and chopped fresh or
    canned tomatoes
¾ cup Fish Stock (page 80) or bottled clam
    juice
3 pounds mussels, scrubbed and beards
    removed
¼ cup chopped fresh cilantro, plus whole
    sprigs for garnish
1 to 2 tablespoons fresh lemon juice

Heat the olive oil in a large skillet over medium heat. Add the onion and cook, stirring, until soft, about 7 minutes. Add the garlic, cumin, ginger, turmeric, paprika, harissa, and salt and pepper to taste. Cook, stirring constantly, for 2 minutes. Add the tomatoes and fish stock and simmer slowly, un-covered, for 15 minutes, until the sauce has thickened slightly. Remove from the heat and cool slightly.

In batches, puree the sauce in a blender until smooth. Return the puree to the pan and place the pan over medium-high heat. Add the mussels, cover, and simmer until the mussels begin to open, 2 to 3 minutes. As the mussels open, remove them with tongs and place in a serving bowl. Discard any mussels that do not open. Reduce the cooking liquid over high heat until reduced by one quarter. Add the cilantro and lemon juice.

Place the mussels in a bowl and pour the sauce over them. Garnish with cilantro sprigs and serve immediately.

Lemon Shrimp with Green Tomatoes

In late autumn, when most of the tomatoes in your garden are green because they just don't have enough sunshine to ripen on the vine, make this quick but terrific dish. The green tomatoes and lemon zest give the dish a distinct tartness against the creamy sweet crème fraîche. Serve steamed basmati or jasmine rice on the side or toss with cooked fettuccine.

Serves 6

1 tablespoon unsalted butter
1 garlic clove, minced
4 medium green tomatoes, peeled, seeded, and chopped
2 teaspoons finely grated lemon zest
2 pounds jumbo shrimp, peeled and deveined
1 cup crème fraîche
Fresh lemon juice to taste
Coarse salt and freshly ground black pepper
2 tablespoons snipped fresh chives

Melt the butter in a large frying pan over medium heat. Add the garlic and cook, stirring, for 1 minute. Add the tomatoes, lemon zest, and shrimp and simmer until the shrimp are almost firm, 5 minutes. Increase the heat to high, add the crème fraîche, and bring to a boil, stirring until the sauce thickens slightly, about 1 minute. Season with the lemon juice and salt and pepper to taste.

Place on a platter, garnish with the chives, and serve immediately.

Shrimp Tacos with Tomatillos and Pickled Jalapeños

Along with tomatoes, tomatillos belong to the nightshade family of vegetables. In fact, tomatillos resemble small tomatoes, except that they stay green and are encased in a thin parchment-like covering. They are pleasantly tart, and if you wrap them up in a crispy corn tortilla with shrimp and pickled jalapeños and drizzle it with sour cream and queso fresco, fresh white Mexican cheese, you'll be in Mexico.

Serves 6

1/2 cup plus 1 tablespoon corn oil
1 small yellow onion, minced
8 large tomatillos (about 1 pound), husks removed, rinsed, and chopped
3 garlic cloves, minced
2 tablespoons fresh lime juice
Coarse salt and freshly ground black pepper
1 pound large shrimp, peeled and deveined
12 corn tortillas
1/4 cup chopped pickled jalapeños
1/2 cup fresh cilantro leaves
1/2 cup sour cream
3 ounces queso fresco (optional)
Lime wedges

Heat 1 tablespoon of the oil in a large frying pan over medium-high heat. Add the onion and cook, stirring, until soft, about 7 minutes. Add the tomatillos and cook, stirring occasionally, until soft, about 10 minutes. Place the tomatillo mixture in a blender or food processor, add the garlic and lime juice, and process until smooth, 1 minute.

Season to taste with salt and pepper.

Return the mixture to the pan and set over medium-high heat. When the sauce is simmering, add the shrimp and cook until pink and curled, 2 to 3 minutes. Remove from the heat.

Heat the remaining $1/2$ cup corn oil in a large frying pan over medium heat. Add the tortillas, one at a time, and cook until lightly golden but still soft, about 15 seconds. Fold in half in the pan and continue to cook until almost crisp. Drain on paper towels.

To assemble, open the taco shells slightly. Fill with the shrimp mixture, jalapeños, cilantro leaves, sour cream, and queso fresco, if using. Serve immediately with lime wedges.

Deviled Lobster

During the summer from New Jersey to Santa Barbara, wherever there is the smallest patch of soil or sunny corner, you will find tomatoes growing. They get canned, they get squeezed, they get stewed into a spicy hot sauce that's baked with lobsters in an old-time favorite called "lobster fra diavolo." The sauce can be made ahead but the lobsters should be cooked at the last minute.

Serves 4

4 live lobsters (about $1 1/4$ pounds each)
2 tablespoons extra virgin olive oil
3 cloves garlic, thinly sliced
$3/4$ cup dry red wine
$3 1/2$ cups tomatoes, peeled, seeded, and chopped, fresh or canned
$3/4$ cup Fish Stock (page 80) or bottled clam juice
2 tablespoons red wine vinegar
20 fresh basil leaves, torn into small pieces
$1/2$ teaspoon chopped fresh oregano or marjoram
$3/4$ teaspoon crushed red pepper flakes
Coarse salt

Bring 4 quarts water to a boil in a large lobster or stock pot and add 2 tablespoons salt.

Add 2 lobsters, submerging them completely, and boil 4 minutes. Remove and cool under cold running water. Repeat with the remaining lobsters.

To split the lobsters, insert a knife into the point where the body meets the tail and cut the tail in half. Turn the lobster around and cut toward the front, cutting the lobster into 2 pieces.

Preheat the oven to 400°F.

In a saucepan, heat the olive oil over medium low heat. Add the garlic and cook until soft but not golden, 1 minute. Increase the heat to high, add the wine, and cook until almost evaporated, 3 to 4 minutes. With a food mill, puree the tomatoes directly into the pan. Add the fish stock, vinegar, basil, oregano, red pepper flakes, and salt to taste. Bring to a boil, reduce the heat to low, and simmer for 10 minutes. Taste and season with salt.

Divide the sauce into two 13 X 9-inch baking pans. Spread the sauce evenly over the bottom of the pans. Place the lobster halves cut side down on the sauce and bake until the lobsters are cooked, 15 minutes. If during the baking time, the lobsters look dry, add water.

To serve, place 2 lobster halves cut side up on each plate and drizzle with sauce from the pan. Serve immediately.

Grilled and Smoked Lobster with Curried Tomato Butter

For lobster lovers, here is the dish for summer entertaining. Make sure your grill is very hot, and place the halved lobsters on the grid just above the burning coals. Dousing the coals with water will impart a smoky flavor. These also make a spectacular first course; one lobster will do for two people.

Serves 6

2 medium ripe red tomatoes, peeled, seeded, and finely diced
7 tablespoons unsalted butter, at room temperature
1 shallot, minced
3/4 teaspoon curry powder
2 teaspoons minced fresh flat-leaf parsley
Coarse salt and freshly ground black pepper
6 live lobsters (1 1/4 to 1 1/2 pounds each)

Place the tomatoes in a paper towel–lined sieve and let drain for 1 hour.

Melt 1 tablespoon of the butter in a small saucepan over medium heat. Add the shallot and cook until soft, 4 to 5 minutes. Remove and place in a bowl.

Add the remaining 6 tablespoons butter, the tomatoes, curry powder, and parsley. Mash together well. Season to taste with salt and pepper.

Place one quarter of the butter in a saucepan and set aside. Place the remaining butter in a small bowl, covered with plastic. Set in the refrigerator until 15 minutes before you are ready to use it.

Prepare a fire in an outdoor grill.

Bring 4 quarts water to a boil in a lobster pot or large stockpot and add 2 tablespoons salt. Add 2 of the lobsters, submerging them completely, and boil for 4 minutes. Remove and cool under cold running water. Repeat with the remaining lobsters.

To split the lobsters, insert a knife into the point where the body meets the tail and cut the tail in half. Turn each lobster around and cut toward the front, cutting the lobster into 2 pieces.

Melt the curry butter in the saucepan and set aside. Place the lobsters on the grill, shell side down, cover them with a large metal bowl or the grill lid, and cook for 2 minutes. Throw 1/2 cup water on the coals to create smoke and continue to cook, covered, for 2 minutes longer. Remove the cover and drizzle with the melted butter. Place the cover back on top and cook for 2 minutes until the lobster is done.

Place the lobsters cut side up on a large serving platter. Dab the reserved curry butter onto the lobsters and serve immediately.

beef, veal, lamb, and pork

Steaks with Charred Tomato Salad

For your next barbecue, blacken tomatoes on a piping-hot grill, then chop and combine with red onions and basil oil to make a salad. Grill the steaks, top with the tangy salad, and serve.

Serves 6

8 medium ripe red tomatoes
1/2 cup chopped fresh basil, plus 20 basil leaves, thinly sliced
1/4 cup extra virgin olive oil
1 small red onion, thinly sliced
3 tablespoons red wine vinegar
Coarse salt and freshly ground black pepper
6 small market (rib-eye), porterhouse, or strip steaks (8 to 10 ounces each)

Cut the tomatoes crosswise in half and scoop out all of the seeds. Place the tomatoes cut side down on paper towels and let drain for 1 hour.

In a small saucepan, combine the chopped basil and olive oil. Heat over low heat just until the oil sizzles. Remove from the heat and let sit for 1 hour. Strain and discard the basil. (The oil can be made up to 1 day in advance.)

Preheat an outdoor grill.

Brush the cut sides of the tomatoes with 2 tablespoons of the basil oil. Place cut side down on the grill, 3 inches from the heat source, and grill until the flesh blackens, 4 to 5 minutes. Turn the tomatoes and char on the other side, about 1 minute.

Cut the tomatoes into 1-inch chunks and place in a bowl. Add the remaining basil oil, the red onion, vinegar, and thinly sliced basil. Season to taste with salt and pepper.

Oil the steaks and grill on one side until lightly browned, 4 to 5 minutes. Turn the steaks, season with salt and pepper, and continue to cook until medium rare, 4 to 5 minutes.

Remove the steaks from the grill and place on individual plates. Top with the charred tomato salad and serve immediately.

Brazilian Braised Beef with Tomato Sauce

This thick, intense tomato sauce gets its richness from braising the beef in it. Serve with crispy roasted potatoes and a simple salad for a satisfying main course. The stew can be made a couple of days ahead and refrigerated until ready to heat and serve; it can also be frozen for up to a month. This recipe was adapted from one created by the late Felipe Rojas-Lombardi, South American chef and cookbook writer.

Serves 6

6 garlic cloves, minced
1 tablespoon ground cumin
1 teaspoon dried oregano
1 tablespoon coarse salt
$^1/_2$ teaspoon freshly ground white pepper
$3^1/_2$ pounds beef chuck or eye of the round,
    trimmed of all fat and cut into large chunks

■ sauce
2 tablespoons olive oil
2 dried hot red chile peppers, seeded,
    or 1 teaspoon crushed red pepper flakes
3 large yellow onions, minced
4 garlic cloves, sliced
2 bay leaves
3 stalks celery, minced
1 carrot, grated
10 cups peeled, seeded, and chopped fresh or
    canned tomatoes
$1^1/_2$ cups Beef Stock (page 79)
Coarse salt and freshly ground black pepper

In a mortar and pestle pound the garlic, cumin, oregano, salt, and pepper to a smooth paste. Rub the mixture on the pieces of meat, place in a bowl, cover with plastic wrap, and refrigerate for 2 hours.

For the sauce, in a large heavy casserole, heat the olive oil over medium heat. Add the beef and cook, turning occasionally, until browned on all sides, 10 to 15 minutes. Remove the beef and set aside.

Add the chiles, onions, garlic, and bay leaves to the pot and cook, stirring occasionally, until the onions are light golden on the edges, 15 minutes. Add the celery and carrot and cook, stirring, for 5 minutes. Add the tomatoes, beef, and stock, cover, and simmer over low heat until the meat is tender and can be easily skewered, $1^1/_2$ to 2 hours.

Remove the cover and simmer until the sauce thickens slightly, 10 minutes longer. Season to taste with salt and pepper.

To serve, spoon the beef into a serving bowl and spoon the sauce over the top.

Hungarian Goulash

Peppers and tomatoes were introduced to Hungary during the Turkish invasion, and paprika, ground from dried sweet red peppers, has been an essential flavoring ever since. Goulash, the beef stew prepared with caraway seeds, bacon, garlic, and beer, relies upon best-quality, fresh, sweet Hungarian paprika. A dollop of sour cream is the finishing touch—it melts into the stew and gives the dish its creamy taste and texture. Serve with wide flat egg noodles, crispy roasted potatoes, or homemade egg dumplings. Make this a day or two ahead of time if you can so the flavors have time to meld.

Serves 6

2 garlic cloves, minced
$1/2$ teaspoon caraway seeds
Coarse salt and freshly ground black pepper
2 tablespoons unsalted butter
3 slices bacon, diced
3 medium yellow onions, coarsely chopped
$3^1/2$ pounds boneless beef chuck or round, cut into 1-inch pieces
3 tablespoons sweet paprika
4 cups beer
2 cups peeled, seeded, and chopped fresh or canned tomatoes
2 Hungarian wax peppers or 1 green bell pepper, cored, seeded, and cut into 1-inch pieces
1 dried hot cherry pepper or $1/4$ teaspoon crushed red pepper flakes
$1/3$ cup sour cream, at room temperature

In a mortar and pestle or spice grinder, mash together the garlic, caraway seeds, $3/4$ teaspoon salt, and $1/4$ teaspoon black pepper.

Melt the butter in a large heavy casserole over medium heat. Add the bacon and onions and cook until the onions are soft and the bacon is light golden, 7 to 10 minutes. Add the beef in batches and cook, stirring occasionally, until the beef is browned on all sides, 10 to 15 minutes.

Add the paprika and garlic mixture and cook, stirring, for 2 minutes. Increase the heat to high, add the beer and 3 cups water, and bring to a boil. Reduce the heat to low and simmer, covered, until the meat is almost tender, $1^1/2$ to 2 hours.

Add the tomatoes, wax peppers, and cherry pepper and simmer, uncovered, until the vegetables are tender and the sauce is thick enough to coat a spoon lightly, 20 to 30 minutes. Season to taste with salt and pepper.

To serve, ladle the stew into bowls and garnish with the sour cream.

Greek Beef Stew with Plenty of Onions

Adding sweet spices, like cinnamon sticks and cloves, to a beef stew might seem a bit odd, but it makes a traditional, very flavorful Greek dish called stifatho. Serve this on a chilly night with olive oil–flavored mashed potatoes or rice pilaf. Like many stews, this is even better if made a few days in advance and reheated just before serving.

Serves 6

1½ pounds pearl onions
¼ cup olive oil
4 garlic cloves, crushed
2½ pounds beef stew meat, cut into 1½-inch
    pieces and excess fat removed
1 cup dry red wine
¼ cup red wine vinegar
2 tablespoons tomato paste
2 cups peeled, seeded, and chopped fresh or
    canned tomatoes
2 bay leaves
1 cinnamon stick
4 whole cloves
Coarse salt and freshly ground black pepper

Bring a large saucepan of water to a boil. Add the onions and simmer for 30 seconds. Drain and cool. Peel the onions.

Heat 2 tablespoons of the olive oil in a deep frying pan over medium heat. Add the onions and cook, stirring occasionally, until golden brown, 12 to 15 minutes. Remove from the pan and set aside. Add the garlic and cook, stirring, until light golden, about 2 minutes. Remove the garlic and discard.

Add the remaining 2 tablespoons olive oil to the pan. Add the beef in batches and cook, turning occasionally, until browned on all sides. Add the red wine, red wine vinegar, tomato paste, tomatoes, bay leaves, cinnamon stick, and cloves and bring to a boil. Reduce the heat to low, cover, and simmer until the beef is almost tender, about 1 hour.

Add the onions and continue to simmer slowly until the meat is very tender and the sauce is thick, about 1 hour longer. Season to taste with salt and pepper. Remove the bay leaves and cinnamon stick.

Ladle the stew into bowls and serve immediately.

Chilasquilas

Gabriella Salas cooks with just the same love as her mother. She mixes the achiote paste, she picks thyme and oregano from her garden, she squeezes the onions, she smells the tomatoes. Her chilasquilas, Costa Rican beef turnovers, are smothered with a zippy tomato sauce scented with achiote. The smells fill the kitchen as we sit down to an unforgettable lunch with refried beans.

Fill the tortillas and make the tomato sauce in advance if you like. At the last minute, whip the egg whites for the batter and fry the turnovers.

Serves 6

2 tablespoons corn oil, plus oil for frying
1 pound flank steak
3 bay leaves
1 small yellow onion, chopped
Coarse salt and freshly ground black pepper
1 tablespoon Worcestershire sauce
$1/2$ teaspoon achiote paste
12 ripe plum tomatoes (about 2 pounds),
  seeded and diced
Pinch of sugar
Twelve 6-inch corn tortillas
2 large eggs, separated
2 large egg whites

Heat 1 tablespoon of the corn oil in a large frying pan over medium-high heat. Add the flank steak and sear until golden on both sides, 3 to 4 minutes total. Add 1 cup water, the bay leaves, and half the onion and bring to a boil. Immediately reduce the heat to low and simmer until the meat is tender,

adding water as necessary, about 1 hour. Strain then discard the liquid. Let the meat cool.

Shred the meat. Season with salt and pepper and Worcestershire sauce, and set aside.

Preheat the oven to 350°F.

Heat 1 tablespoon corn oil in a large frying pan over medium heat. Add the achiote paste and cook, stirring, for 1 minute. Add the remaining onion and cook, stirring occasionally, until soft, about 7 minutes. Add the tomatoes and simmer until the tomatoes are soft and most of the liquid has evaporated, 15 to 20 minutes. Season to taste with salt and pepper and the sugar. Set aside.

Wrap the corn tortillas in foil and warm in the oven for 10 minutes. Place one tortilla at a time on the work surface and cover half of it with some of the meat. Fold the other side over to form a half-circle turnover. Secure with a toothpick. Repeat with the remaining tortillas and beef.

Pour $1/4$ inch of corn oil into a frying pan and heat over medium heat. In the meantime, in a large bowl, whip the egg whites until they form stiff peaks. Add the egg yolks and whip for 5 seconds.

Dip the turnovers in the batter and fry until golden on both sides, 1 to 2 minutes per side. Drain on paper towels.

To serve, warm the tomato sauce while frying the tortillas. Place the turnovers on a platter and top with the sauce.

Tomato-Beef Chow Mein

Decades ago in San Francisco's Chinatown, spiral-bound cookbooks produced by small private clubs were the rage. This recipe is adapted from a 1920s "Circle and Square Club" cookbook.

Serves 6

1 pound flank steak
$^1/_4$ cup plus 2 tablespoons peanut oil
2 tablespoons soy sauce
2 tablespoons plus $^1/_4$ teaspoon cornstarch
1 tablespoon oyster sauce
2 tablespoons dry white wine
12 ounces fresh Chinese-style noodles
Coarse salt
1 small yellow onion, quartered
6 small ripe red tomatoes, peeled, seeded, and quartered
3 tablespoons brown sugar
$^1/_4$ cup rice vinegar
1 green bell pepper, cored, seeded, and cut into $^1/_2$-inch strips

Preheat the oven to 350°F.

Cut the flank steak into $1^1/_2$-inch-wide strips with the grain of the meat. Then cut each strip into thin slices, cutting across the grain. Place the beef in a bowl with 1 tablespoon of the peanut oil, the soy sauce, $^1/_4$ teaspoon of the cornstarch, the oyster sauce, and wine. Marinate, stirring occasionally, for 15 minutes.

Bring a large pot of salted water to a boil. Add the noodles and cook until done, 1 to 2 minutes. Drain.

Divide the noodles into three portions and place them in separate piles on a baking sheet or a work surface. Immediately heat 1 tablespoon of the oil in a large frying pan or wok. Spread one third of the noodles in the bottom of the pan. Cook, without stirring, until light golden and crispy, 2 to 3 minutes. Season with salt, turn, and cook on the other side until light golden and crispy, 2 to 3 minutes. Remove from the pan and drain on paper towels, then place on a baking sheet and keep warm in the oven. Repeat with the remaining noodles, using 2 more tablespoons of the oil.

Heat the remaining 2 tablespoons oil in a large frying pan over high heat. Add the beef and onion and cook until the meat is medium-rare, 2 to 3 minutes. Remove from the pan and set aside.

In a small bowl, stir together the remaining 2 tablespoons cornstarch and $^1/_3$ cup cold water. Add the tomatoes, sugar, vinegar, bell pepper, and $^1/_2$ teaspoon salt to the pan along with the cornstarch mixture and stir together until the pepper is almost soft, 2 to 3 minutes. Add the beef and onions and stir together for 30 seconds.

Divide the noodle cakes in half on 6 plates. Spoon the beef and tomatoes over the noodles and serve immediately.

Veal Shanks with Tomatoes, Orange, and Garlic

*M*ade *with veal or with lamb, either way, this is a dish you won't soon forget. Since the shanks have more muscle than most cuts, they tend to be tougher, but stewing them for a long time with tomatoes, chicken stock, and white wine renders them delicate, tender, and sumptuous. They're garnished just before serving with a healthy dose of chopped parsley, garlic, and orange zest, a variation of the classic* gremolata, *an Italian garnish made of parsley, garlic, and lemon zest. You can cook them a couple of days in advance and reheat just before serving.*

Serves 6

1/4 cup all-purpose flour
Coarse salt
3 veal shanks (about 2 pounds each), cut into
    1 1/2-inch slices
1/4 cup olive oil
6 sprigs fresh parsley
4 sprigs fresh thyme
1 medium yellow onion, cut into small dice
2 medium carrots, cut into small dice
2 stalks celery, cut into small dice
2 bay leaves
3 cups peeled, seeded, and chopped fresh or
    canned tomatoes
1 teaspoon grated orange zest
1/2 cup fresh orange juice
3 cups Chicken Stock (page 78)
2 cups dry white wine
Freshly ground black pepper

■ garnish
1 teaspoon grated orange zest
1/2 cup chopped fresh flat-leaf parsley
1 garlic clove, minced

Combine the flour and salt. Dust both sides of the veal shanks and tap off the excess. Heat 2 tablespoons of the oil in a large heavy casserole over medium-high heat. Add the veal and cook until golden brown on both sides, about 8 minutes. Cook the veal in batches so as not to crowd the pan. Remove and set aside.

Tie the parsley and thyme sprigs together with kitchen twine. Heat the remaining 2 tablespoons oil in the same pot. Add the onion, carrots, celery, parsley and thyme, and the bay leaves and cook until the vegetables are soft, about 10 minutes. Add the tomatoes and simmer for 5 minutes. Add the orange zest, orange juice, stock, and wine and simmer for 5 minutes. Add the veal shanks, reduce the heat to low, and simmer, covered, until the meat comes away from the bone, 1 1/2 to 2 hours. Season to taste with salt and pepper.

In the meantime, chop the orange zest, parsley, and garlic together.

When the veal is done, place it on a platter. If the sauce is too thin, simmer, uncovered, until it thickens. Spoon the sauce over the veal and top with the chopped orange zest, parsley, and garlic. Serve immediately.

Veal Bundles with Sausage and Herbs

To make these, thin veal scallopine are rolled around sweet pork sausage and fresh herbs, then stewed in tomato sauce. Serve with polenta, either creamy soft or fried into crispy triangles. You can make this two days in advance and reheat before serving.

Serves 4

12 slices veal scallopine (about 1½ pounds) or
    1½ pounds cut into 12 pieces
2 tablespoons extra virgin olive oil
1 small yellow onion, minced
2 garlic cloves, minced
3 tablespoons pine nuts
²/₃ cup fresh bread crumbs
1 tablespoon chopped fresh sage
½ teaspoon chopped fresh thyme
½ teaspoon chopped fresh rosemary
Coarse salt and freshly ground black pepper
10 ounces sweet bulk Italian sausage

■ sauce
2 tablespoons olive oil
2 medium yellow onions, chopped
½ cup dry red wine
2 tablespoons balsamic vinegar
1 teaspoon sugar
2 tablespoons tomato paste
½ teaspoon dried oregano
Pinch of crushed red pepper flakes
4½ cups peeled, seeded, chopped, and drained
    fresh or canned tomatoes
Coarse salt and freshly ground black pepper

Place each piece of veal between sheets of plastic or waxed paper and pound to ¼ to ³/₈ inch thick. Set aside.

Heat the olive oil in a medium frying pan over medium heat. Add the onion and cook, stirring, until soft, about 7 minutes. Add the garlic and pine nuts and cook, stirring, for 2 minutes. Add the bread crumbs and herbs and continue to cook, until light golden, for 2 minutes. Remove from the heat and season with salt and pepper. Add the sausage and mix well.

Spread the stuffing lengthwise down the middle of the veal cutlets, dividing it evenly among the cutlets. Fold the long sides over to partially cover the stuffing and roll up each cutlet. Cut kitchen string into eight 10-inch pieces and tie the veal parcels as if you were wrapping a present. Set aside.

For the sauce, heat the oil in a large sauté pan over medium heat and cook the onions, stirring, until soft, about 10 minutes. Add the red wine, balsamic vinegar, sugar, tomato paste, oregano, red pepper flakes, tomatoes, and salt and pepper to taste. Simmer slowly for 20 minutes, until the sauce is thickened slightly. Transfer to a blender or food processor and puree until smooth.

Return the sauce to the pan, add the veal rolls, cover, and simmer for 20 minutes, until cooked through and the veal is slightly firm to the touch.

Transfer the veal rolls to a warm platter and remove the strings. Pour the sauce over the rolls and serve immediately.

Braised Veal Meatballs with Artichokes, Olives, and Sage

*T*his dish of veal meatballs stewed with artichokes, olives, sage, and tomatoes is the inspiration of Paul Bertolli, chef at Oliveto Restaurant, in Oakland, California. The recipe is adapted from his memories of his Italian mother's cooking and it reeks of Tuscany. This is such a great recipe, when you make it, double it and serve one recipe the same day and freeze the remainder for another unforgettable dinner. Hot buttered homemade pappardelle make a perfect accompaniment.

Serves 6

> **B**etween the warm fruit held in one's hand in a garden patch and the despondent slough of my beldam's unswerving treatment of them there are myriad delicious things to do. Perhaps one of the most refreshing, to serve in summer either before or with grilled meats, or by itself for a good luncheon, is slices of ripe firm tomatoes which have been well sprinkled with herbs and olive oil on a large platter, and left to ruminate for a few hours. Before serving, what juice they have freed should be tilted out of the dish into a cup, for the cook to drink privately: The tomatoes will have held onto most of the oil, and their liquid will have mingled just enough with the herbs, and altogether it is a fine little nip, very strengthening!"
>
> From M. F. K. Fisher,
> *With Bold Knife and Fork*

2 tablespoons olive oil
3 medium yellow onions, minced
Coarse salt and freshly ground black pepper
20 small artichokes (about 3 pounds)
¼ cup plus 1 tablespoon fresh lemon juice
2 pounds ground veal
3 tablespoons chopped fresh flat-leaf parsley
½ teaspoon ground coriander
¼ cup freshly grated Parmigiano-Reggiano
2 large eggs
½ cup fresh bread crumbs
1 cup Chicken Stock (page 78)
½ cup dry white wine
1½ cups peeled, seeded, and chopped fresh or
    canned plum tomatoes
¾ cup green Spanish olives, pitted and very
    coarsely chopped
4 garlic cloves, minced
2 tablespoons chopped fresh sage

Heat the olive oil in a large frying pan over medium heat and cook the onions, stirring occasionally, until very soft, 15 to 20 minutes. Remove from the heat and season to taste with salt and pepper.

Preheat the oven to 450°F.

Pull off the outer leaves of each artichoke until you get to the light green, tender inner leaves. With a paring knife, trim the torn edges of the outer leaves. Cut the artichokes in half from top to bottom. For small artichokes, there is no need to remove the choke; if you are using larger artichokes, remove the choke with a spoon. Place the artichokes in a bowl of water with 2 tablespoons of the lemon juice.

In a large bowl, mix the veal, parsley, coriander, Parmigiano, eggs, bread crumbs, and $1/3$ cup of the cooked onions. Season with 1 teaspoon salt and $1/4$ teaspoon pepper and mix well. Make a small patty and cook it in a small frying pan, turning occasionally, until done, 5 to 8 minutes. Test and reseason the veal mixture as needed. Form it into about forty 1-inch meatballs. Place on a baking sheet, with space between the meatballs, and bake for 10 minutes. Remove and set aside. Reduce the oven temperature to 350°F.

Transfer the remaining onions to a baking dish and place the meatballs on top. Drain the artichokes, return to the bowl, and combine with the stock, wine, tomatoes, olives, garlic, sage, and the remaining 3 tablespoons lemon juice. Season with salt and pepper.

Distribute the artichoke mixture over the meatballs. Cover tightly with foil and bake until the artichokes are tender, about 1 hour.

Pour the liquid from the baking dish into a saucepan and reduce the liquid over high heat to 1 cup, 3 to 5 minutes. Pour the liquid over the meatballs and artichokes and serve immediately.

Tomatoes on the Easter Table?

An invitation to spend Greek Easter with Maria and Dimitri Likouressis, on the island of Zakynthos off the west coast of Greece, in the Ionian Sea, is a coveted one. Each year, they spit-roast lambs, brushing the meat with big switches of rosemary tied together like a giant paintbrush, doused in their house-made olive oil and fresh lemon juice. Maria makes tzatziki, the garlic, cucumber, and yogurt sauce redolent with garlic and mint, and Dimitri bakes bread in his beehive-shaped oven. The Easter table is packed with food, each dish tasting even better than the last.

Halfway through the meal, as everyone was complimenting the food and reaching for platters of seconds, Maria gave an apologetic look. "Thank you," she said, "but I have to tell you. . . . Everything on this table I have either made, or raised, or grown, except for the tomatoes. These are from the mainland; mine won't be ready for several weeks."

Lamb Stew with Zinfandel

Tomatoes, lamb, wild mushrooms, and pearl onions stewed in zinfandel wine make a gutsy dish for a snowy winter night. You can also use other red wines such as syrah, merlot, cabernet sauvignon, or pinot noir. A great make-ahead dish!

Serves 6

1 ounce dried wild mushrooms, preferably
    porcini
1$^1/_2$ tablespoons olive oil
3 pounds lamb stew meat, cut into 1$^1/_2$-inch
    pieces and trimmed of all fat
2 small carrots, cut into 1$^1/_2$-inch lengths, plus
    5 large carrots, cut into 1$^1/_2$-inch lengths
8 garlic cloves, crushed
1 large yellow onion, quartered
1$^1/_4$ cups zinfandel
3 sprigs fresh flat-leaf parsley
3 sprigs fresh thyme
2 bay leaves
1$^1/_2$ cups canned chopped tomatoes
4$^1/_2$ cups Lamb Stock (page 79) or Chicken
    Stock (page 78)
1 pound pearl onions
1$^1/_4$ pounds tiny red potatoes
1 pound wild or button mushrooms, cleaned
    and cut into 1-inch pieces
Coarse salt and freshly ground black pepper

Place the dried wild mushrooms in a small bowl and add 1$^1/_2$ cups boiling water. Let sit for 30 minutes, then strain the mushrooms and reserve the soaking water. If the water is sandy, pass it through a paper towel–lined strainer.

Heat the oil in a large heavy casserole over medium-high heat. Add the lamb, in batches, and cook, turning occasionally, until browned on all sides, 10 to 12 minutes; do not overcrowd the pan. Remove from the pan and set aside.

Add the small carrots, garlic, and yellow onion and cook until the vegetables are golden, about 7 minutes. Add the zinfandel and simmer until it has reduced by half, 3 to 4 minutes.

In the meantime, tie the parsley and thyme sprigs together with kitchen string. Add the herb bundle, bay leaves, dried mushrooms, reserved soaking liquid, the tomatoes, stock, and lamb and cook until the lamb is very tender, 1$^1/_2$ to 2 hours.

Cut an **X** in the root end of each pearl onion. Bring a saucepan of water, three-quarters full to the boil. Add the onions and simmer. Drain and cool the onions. Peel.

Add the pearl onions, potatoes, large carrots, and fresh mushrooms and simmer until the vegetables are tender, 20 minutes. Season to taste with salt and pepper.

Remove the herb bundle and bay leaves and discard. Ladle the stew into bowls and serve immediately.

Braised Lamb Shanks with White Beans

*N*othing *is more heartwarming in the winter than lamb shanks stewed in tomatoes with white beans. The meat falls from the bone and the beans melt in your mouth. You can make this a couple of days in advance and re-heat before serving.*

Serves 6

1 1/2 cups white kidney or cannellini beans
    (about 12 ounces), picked over and rinsed
3 tablespoons olive oil
6 lamb shanks (8 to 12 ounces each)
2 medium red onions, diced
2 large carrots, diced
6 garlic cloves, minced
1 1/2 cups dry red wine
1 1/2 cups Chicken Stock (page 78)
3 tablespoons tomato paste
1 1/4 cups peeled, seeded, and chopped fresh or
    canned tomatoes
1 teaspoon chopped fresh thyme
1 bay leaf
Coarse salt and freshly ground black pepper
1 tablespoon grated lemon zest
2 tablespoons chopped fresh flat-leaf parsley

Cover the beans with plenty of water and soak for at least 4 hours, or overnight. Drain.

Place the beans in a saucepan with enough water to cover by 2 inches. Simmer, uncovered, until the skins begin to crack and the beans are tender, 45 to 60 minutes. Drain.

In a large heavy casserole, heat the oil over medium heat. Add the lamb shanks and cook, turning occasionally, until golden brown on all sides, 10 to 12 minutes. Remove from the pan and set aside. Add the onions and carrots and cook until the onions are soft, 10 minutes. Add the garlic and stir for 1 minute. Add the wine, chicken stock, tomato paste, tomatoes, thyme, bay leaf, and lamb shanks, increase the heat, and bring to a boil. Reduce the heat to low and simmer, covered, until the shanks are very tender, 1 1/2 to 2 hours.

Add the beans, stir well, cover, and simmer slowly until the lamb begins to fall from the bones, about 30 minutes. Season with salt and pepper.

In a small bowl, combine the lemon zest and parsley. Place the lamb and beans on serving plates and garnish with the lemon and parsley.

Lamb Stew with Artichoke Hearts

During the early autumn, when artichokes and tomatoes are being harvested at the same time—kind of the last breath of summer—make this satisfying stew. You can make it a day or two in advance and reheat it, and any leftovers can be frozen for up to a month, for another meal.

Serves 6

6 medium artichokes
2 tablespoons fresh lemon juice
2 tablespoons unsalted butter
2 tablespoons olive oil
3 medium yellow onions, coarsely chopped
3 pounds lamb stew meat, preferably leg or
    shoulder, cut into 2-inch pieces and fat
    removed
Coarse salt
1 teaspoon sugar
1 1/2 tablespoons all-purpose flour
1/4 teaspoon chopped fresh thyme
1/4 teaspoon chopped fresh oregano
1/4 teaspoon chopped fresh savory (optional)
1/4 teaspoon chopped fresh marjoram (optional)
3 garlic cloves, minced
2 bay leaves
1 tablespoon chopped fresh flat-leaf parsley,
    plus whole leaves for garnish
1 cup dry white wine
2 1/2 cups peeled, seeded, and chopped fresh or
    canned tomatoes
1 1/2 to 2 cups Chicken Stock (page 78)
Freshly ground black pepper

Trim the artichokes by breaking off the outer leaves until you get to the tender, light green center leaves. Cut off the top half of each artichoke. With a paring knife, trim the torn edges of the outer leaves. Cut the artichoke in half from top to bottom. With a spoon, scoop out the hairy choke. As you work, drop the trimmed artichokes into a bowl of water with the lemon juice.

Melt the butter in a large frying pan over medium heat. Drain the artichokes and add them to the pan.

Cook them slowly, stirring occasionally, until tender but still slightly firm, 20 to 30 minutes. Remove from the pan and set aside.

Heat the olive oil in another large, deep frying pan over medium heat. Add the onions and cook, stirring occasionally, until light golden, 15 to 20 minutes. Remove with a slotted spoon and increase the heat to high. Season the pieces of lamb with salt and cook, in batches, turning occasionally,

> **B**y summer's end, in short, tomatoes are often viewed with a profound skepticism, for they illustrate the classic hallmarks of the phenomenon economists describe as 'declining marginal utility.' Which is their clever way of saying that the season's first tomato, plucked warm from the plant and eaten while one stands in the garden admiring tomatoes to come, is clearly preferable—though identical in every measurable respect—to the season's last."
>
> From Vladimir Estragon,
> *Waiting for Dessert*

until browned on all sides, 8 to 10 minutes; do not overcrowd the pan. Return all of the lamb to the pan, sprinkle with the sugar, and cook until the sugar melts, 2 to 3 minutes. Skim off any excess fat.

Sprinkle the lamb with the flour. Turn the pieces over again and when the flour has lightly browned, about 2 minutes, add the onions. Sprinkle the lamb and onions with the thyme, oregano, savory and marjoram if using, the garlic, bay leaves, and chopped parsley and stir together. Add the wine and cook until most of it has evaporated, 3 to 4 minutes. Add the tomatoes and stock and bring to a boil. Reduce the heat to low and simmer slowly, covered, until the lamb is tender, about 1½ hours. Check the lamb periodically and add water to keep it almost covered with liquid.

Transfer the lamb to a bowl. Skim the excess fat from the cooking liquid. Strain the liquid, return it to the pan, and simmer until it lightly coats a

spoon, 5 to 8 minutes. Add the meat and artichokes, season with salt and pepper, and simmer for 3 to 4 minutes.

Ladle the stew into wide soup bowls, garnish with parsley, and serve immediately.

So far as tomatoes are concerned, we have nothing to learn from the French. As it is an American plant—its original home being Peru—it is proper that Americans should have a greater number of varieties and improvements than any other country.

"The Germans are only just learning to like tomatoes; the English have made progress in this important branch of gastronomic education; the French revel in the tomato; and in Italian cookery it is an important ingredient; but in the United States tomato-eating amounts to a passion, a frenzy."

From Henry Finck, *Food and Flavor*

Grilled Lamb Burgers with Mint and Stewed Garlic Cloves

Spicy lamb burgers are a new twist on a very old American theme. Smothered with stewed tomatoes and whole garlic cloves, they make the centerpiece of a casual Saturday barbecue. Make the tomato sauce a day ahead, get the burgers prepped, and then at the last minute, just grill the bread and burgers and heat the sauce.

Serves 6

1½ pounds ground lamb
¼ cup finely minced red onion
2 garlic cloves, minced, plus 18 whole garlic cloves
¼ cup chopped fresh mint, plus 6 sprigs for garnish
3 tablespoons minced sun-dried tomatoes
½ teaspoon ground cumin
Coarse salt and freshly ground black pepper
2½ tablespoons olive oil
6 medium ripe red tomatoes, peeled, seeded, and chopped
6 slices country-style bread

In a medium bowl, combine the lamb, red onion, minced garlic, 2 tablespoons of the mint, the sun-dried tomatoes, cumin, 1 teaspoon salt, and pepper to taste. Form into 6 patties. Place on a plate and let sit in the refrigerator for 1 hour.

Preheat an outdoor grill.

Bring a small saucepan of water to a boil. Add the whole garlic cloves and simmer for 30 seconds.

Drain. Add more water to the saucepan, add the garlic cloves, and simmer until the garlic cloves are just soft, 5 to 10 minutes. Drain and set aside.

Heat 1 tablespoon of the olive oil in a frying pan over medium-high heat and add the tomatoes, the remaining 2 tablespoons mint, the garlic cloves, and salt and pepper to taste. Simmer until the juice from the tomatoes begins to evaporate, 5 to 10 minutes. Remove from the heat.

Brush the bread lightly on both sides with the remaining 1½ tablespoons olive oil. Grill the bread on each side until golden. Grill the lamb burgers for 3 to 4 minutes per side, until medium-rare.

Place a slice of grilled bread on each plate and top with a lamb burger. Spoon the tomato sauce on top and serve immediately, garnished with mint sprigs.

Lamb Kefta Tagine with Spiced Tomatoes

Kefta *are simply meatballs, and in North Africa they are highly spiced and stewed in a tomato sauce spiked with harissa, the peppery-hot condiment. Then eggs are broken onto the top and baked just until set. The result is a mixture of hot, sweet, and savory. The meatballs and tomato sauce can be prepared a day in advance.*

Serves 6

2 pounds ground lamb
$^1/_2$ cup chopped fresh flat-leaf parsley
1 cup chopped fresh cilantro, plus whole sprigs
    for garnish
2 medium yellow onions, minced
5 garlic cloves, minced
2$^1/_2$ teaspoons ground cumin
1 teaspoon paprika
$^1/_2$ teaspoon ground ginger
$^1/_2$ teaspoon ground cardamom
Coarse salt and freshly ground black pepper
$^1/_3$ cup dry bread crumbs
3 cups peeled, seeded, and chopped fresh or
    canned tomatoes
1 tablespoon tomato paste
$^1/_2$ teaspoon harissa, or to taste
$^1/_4$ teaspoon ground cinnamon
Pinch of saffron threads
1 teaspoon sugar
6 large eggs

In a large bowl, mix together the lamb, parsley, $^1/_2$ cup of the cilantro, half the onions and garlic, 2 teaspoons of the cumin, the paprika, ginger, cardamom, 1$^1/_4$ teaspoons salt, 2 teaspoons pepper, the bread crumbs, and $^1/_4$ cup water. Let stand for 1 hour.

In a blender or food processor, puree the tomatoes, tomato paste, the remaining $^1/_2$ cup cilantro, the remaining onions and garlic, the harissa, the remaining $^1/_2$ teaspoon cumin, the cinnamon, saffron, sugar, and salt and pepper to taste until smooth.

Transfer to a large ovenproof casserole and simmer for 30 minutes, until the sauce has thickened slightly. Season to taste with salt and pepper and additional harissa if needed. Remove from the heat.

Preheat the oven to 450°F.

Form the lamb mixture into 1-inch oval-shaped balls. Place on a baking sheet and bake for 10 minutes. Transfer the meatballs to the sauce and simmer until cooked through, 10 to 15 minutes (leave the oven on). Remove from the heat.

Break the eggs between the meatballs, keeping them separate. Cover the dish and bake until the egg whites are set but the yolks are still soft, 10 minutes.

Garnish with cilantro sprigs and serve immediately.

Pastitsio

This classic dish is kind of a Greek lasagne, layers of macaroni with tomatoes, lamb, and creamy-white béchamel sauce. All you need for a complete dinner is a simple green salad. Assemble this a couple of days in advance if you like, then bake just before serving. It's also perfect for a buffet, as it stays hot for a long time. Kefalotiri is a hard sheep's milk grating cheese available in well-stocked cheese markets.

Serves 10

1 pound elbow macaroni
4 tablespoons unsalted butter
1¼ cups freshly grated kefalotiri or
   Parmigiano-Reggiano
¼ teaspoon freshly grated nutmeg
½ teaspoon coarse salt
Freshly ground black pepper
3 large eggs, lightly beaten

■ tomato sauce
3 tablespoons extra virgin olive oil
1 large onion, chopped
6 garlic cloves, minced
1½ pounds ground lamb
2 cups peeled, seeded, and chopped fresh or
   canned plum tomatoes
½ cup tomato paste
2 teaspoons chopped fresh oregano
1 cup dry white wine
1 cup Chicken Stock (page 78)
¼ cup chopped fresh flat-leaf parsley
1 teaspoon sugar
Coarse salt and freshly ground black pepper

■ cream sauce
4 tablespoons unsalted butter
⅓ cup all-purpose flour
3 cups milk
¼ teaspoon freshly grated nutmeg
Coarse salt and freshly ground black pepper
1 large egg, lightly beaten

Bring a large pot of salted water to a boil. Add the macaroni and cook until tender, 8 to 11 minutes. Drain and return to the pot.

While the pasta is cooking, cook the butter in a small saucepan over medium-high heat until it foams and the bubbles subside, the solids turn brown, and it just begins to smoke, 4 to 6 minutes. Pour over the macaroni and stir together. Add ¾ cup of the grated kefalotiri, the nutmeg, salt, and pepper to taste and toss well. Let cool, then add the eggs and toss again. Set aside.

For the tomato sauce, in a large skillet heat the oil over medium heat. Add the onion and garlic and cook, stirring, until soft, about 7 minutes. Increase the heat to medium-high, add the lamb, and cook until the meat begins to brown. Add the tomatoes, tomato paste, oregano, wine, stock, parsley, sugar, and salt and pepper to taste, cover, and simmer slowly until the sauce thickens, about 20 minutes. Remove the cover and simmer slowly until the liquid is reduced by half, about 10 minutes. Remove from the heat and set aside.

For the cream sauce, in a medium saucepan, melt the butter over medium heat. Stir in the flour and cook, stirring, for 2 minutes. Add the milk all at once and bring to a boil, stirring constantly. Boil gently until the sauce thickens, about 1 min-

ute. Add the nutmeg and salt and pepper to taste, remove from the heat, and cool for 5 minutes.

Preheat the oven to 375°F. Butter a 13 × 9-inch baking dish.

Add the egg to the cream sauce. Add ¹/₂ cup of this sauce to the cooked meat sauce and stir well.

To assemble, spoon half of the macaroni evenly over the bottom of the baking dish and top with the meat sauce. Cover with the remaining macaroni. Pour the cream sauce over the top and spread to cover the macaroni completely. Sprinkle with the remaining ¹/₂ cup cheese. Bake until golden brown on top, about 50 minutes. Let stand for 10 minutes before cutting into squares to serve.

Eggplant Moussaka

When I first started making Greek food, moussaka was my first challenge. This masterful dish, a creamy tomato, eggplant, and lamb pie, can be assembled several days in advance and baked just before serving, or frozen for up to a month and baked still frozen; add an extra twenty to twenty-five minutes to the baking time.

Serves 8

2 large eggplants (about 1 pound each),
    unpeeled, cut into $1/4$-inch slices
Coarse salt
2 tablespoons olive oil, plus extra for brushing
    the eggplant
Freshly ground black pepper

■ tomato sauce
2 tablespoons olive oil
1 large yellow onion, chopped
4 garlic cloves, chopped
2 pounds ground lamb
$1^1/_2$ cups peeled, seeded, chopped, and drained
    fresh or canned tomatoes
2 tablespoons tomato paste
$1/_2$ cup dry white wine
3 tablespoons chopped fresh flat-leaf parsley
$1/_2$ teaspoon chopped fresh oregano
$1/_4$ teaspoon chopped fresh thyme
1 teaspoon sugar
$1/_4$ teaspoon ground cinnamon

■ cream sauce
3 tablespoons unsalted butter
$1/_4$ cup all-purpose flour
2 cups milk

$1/_8$ teaspoon freshly grated nutmeg
$1/_3$ cup plus 1 tablespoon freshly grated
    kefalotiri or Parmigiano-Reggiano
1 large egg, lightly beaten

Sprinkle the eggplant slices with salt and let sit in a colander to drain for 1 hour.

Preheat the oven to 450°F. Using 2 tablespoons of the olive oil, generously oil 2 baking sheets.

Rinse the eggplant and pat dry with paper towels. Place the eggplant in a single layer on the baking sheets and brush with oil. Season with pepper and bake, turning occasionally, until the eggplant is golden brown and tender, about 10 to 15 minutes. Stack on a plate. Reduce the heat to 350°F.

For the tomato sauce, heat the remaining 2 tablespoons olive oil in a frying pan over medium heat. Add the onion and garlic and cook, stirring, until soft, 7 minutes. Add the lamb and cook over high heat, stirring, for 3 minutes. Add the tomatoes, tomato paste, wine, parsley, oregano, thyme, sugar, cinnamon, and salt and pepper to taste. As soon as the liquid comes to a boil, reduce the heat to low and simmer, covered, for 30 minutes. Remove from the heat.

In the meantime, for the cream sauce, melt the butter in a medium saucepan over medium heat. Add the flour and cook, whisking constantly, for 2 minutes. Add the milk all at once and bring to a boil, stirring constantly. Let the mixture simmer slowly for 1 minute. Remove from the heat and add the nutmeg, 1 tablespoon of the cheese, and salt and pepper to taste.

To assemble, oil a 13 × 9-inch baking dish and place a layer of one third of the eggplant in the bottom. Top the eggplant with half of the meat sauce. Add another layer of eggplant and the remainder of the meat sauce. Top with the remaining eggplant. Stir the egg into the cream sauce and spread the sauce on top. Sprinkle with the remaining 1/3 cup cheese.

Bake until the moussaka bubbles around the edges, about 1 hour. Let stand for 10 minutes before cutting it into squares and serving.

Cypriot Pork and Eggplant Stew

From the island of Cyprus, this stew can be prepared very quickly and yet it's full of flavors that evoke the Mediterranean. The meat falls apart and the flavors of the pork, eggplant, and sweet tomatoes melt together in your mouth. Make it a couple of days ahead if you like, refrigerate, and reheat just before serving.

Serves 6 to 8

1/4 cup plus 1 tablespoon peanut oil
2 1/4 pounds pork stew meat, fat removed and
  cut into 2-inch cubes
1 large yellow onion, chopped
2 garlic cloves, crushed
3 cups peeled, seeded, and chopped fresh or
  canned tomatoes
2 tablespoons tomato paste

1 cup dry red wine
Coarse salt and freshly ground black pepper
2 medium eggplants (about 2 pounds total)
Fresh flat-leaf parsley sprigs

Heat 2 tablespoons of the peanut oil in a large frying pan over medium-high heat. Add the pork and cook, turning occasionally, until golden on all sides, 7 to 10 minutes. Remove from the pan and reserve in a bowl.

Reduce the heat to medium, add the onion and garlic, and cook, stirring, until the onion is soft, about 7 minutes. Add the tomatoes, tomato paste, red wine, and salt and pepper to taste and cook until the liquid reduces by one quarter, 8 to 10 minutes. Add the pork, reduce the heat to low, and simmer until the pork is almost tender, about 1 1/2 hours. Add water as necessary to maintain the same level.

In the meantime, cut the eggplant into 2-inch chunks. Sprinkle with salt and place in a colander. Allow the eggplant to drain for 30 minutes.

Rinse the eggplant under cold water and pat dry.

Heat the remaining 3 tablespoons peanut oil in a large frying pan over medium-high heat. Add the eggplant and cook, turning, until golden brown on all sides, 10 to 12 minutes.

Add the eggplant to the pork and stir together. Cover and cook until the pork is very tender, 45 to 60 minutes. Season to taste with salt and pepper.

To serve, spoon the stew into serving bowls and garnish with parsley sprigs.

Pork and Tomatoes with Sauerkraut

This hearty, robust dish is packed with flavor from the sweet tomatoes, tart sauerkraut, pungent juniper berries, and anise-like caraway seeds. It's perfect for a cold winter's night, served with boiled potatoes and a loaf of dark rye bread. And you can make it up to two days in advance and reheat just before serving.

Serves 6

1 tablespoon vegetable oil
2 pounds boneless pork, from the loin,
    shoulder, or butt, cut into $1^1/_2$-inch cubes
Coarse salt and freshly ground black pepper
3 pork sausage links (about 1 pound)
1 tablespoon unsalted butter
3 slices bacon, diced
1 large yellow onion, chopped
2 tablespoons juniper berries
2 bay leaves
1 teaspoon caraway seeds
3 cups peeled, seeded, and chopped fresh or
    canned tomatoes
3 cups prepared sauerkraut, rinsed and drained
1 cup Chicken Stock (page 78)
1 cup dry white wine

Heat the oil in a large heavy casserole over medium heat. Add the pork, season with salt and pepper, and cook, turning occasionally, until golden brown on all sides, about 15 minutes. Remove the pork from the pot and set aside.

Add the sausages and $1/_4$ cup water to the pot and cook, turning the sausages occasionally, until the water has evaporated, 8 to 10 minutes. Remove the sausages from the pan and cut each sausage on the diagonal into 4 pieces.

Melt the butter in the same pot. Add the bacon and onion and cook until the onion is soft and the bacon is light golden, 7 to 10 minutes. Pour off the excess fat. Tie the juniper berries in a square of cheesecloth and add to the pot, along with the pork, bay leaves, caraway seeds, and tomatoes. Bring to a boil, reduce the heat to low, and simmer until the pork is tender, $1^1/_2$ to 2 hours. Add water as necessary if the pan is dry.

In the meantime, in a large saucepan, combine the sausages, sauerkraut, chicken stock, and white wine and bring to a boil over medium-high heat. Reduce the heat to low and simmer, uncovered, until most of the liquid has evaporated, about 30 minutes.

When the pork is tender, add the sauerkraut and simmer for 10 minutes. Taste and season with salt and pepper.

Place in a serving bowl and serve immediately.

The art of cooking tomatoes lies mostly in cooking them enough. In whatever way prepared, they should be put on some hours before dinner."

From Sarah Rutledge, *The Carolina Housewife, 1847*

Barbecued Spareribs

Slather ribs with a zippy barbecue sauce and grill them over mesquite to get a smoky flavor—but watch them very closely during grilling, as they have a tendency to burn because of the sugar in the sauce. For even more smoky flavor, partially cover the ribs during the grilling. Serve with corn on the cob and coleslaw for a real Texas barbecue.

Serves 6

6 pounds pork spareribs, in 2 pieces
Coarse salt and freshly ground black pepper
1 tablespoon vegetable oil
1 small yellow onion, minced
2 cups peeled, seeded, chopped, and drained
    fresh or canned tomatoes
3 tablespoons Dijon mustard
$1/4$ cup packed brown sugar
$1/4$ cup fresh lemon juice
3 tablespoons soy sauce
2 tablespoons Worcestershire sauce
2 tablespoons hot pepper sauce, such as
    Tabasco
$1/4$ teaspoon ground allspice
$1/4$ teaspoon ground cloves
$1/4$ teaspoon ground ginger

Preheat the oven to 350°F.

Arrange the spareribs in a single layer on a baking sheet. Season well with salt and pepper, cover with foil, and bake until tender, $1^1/4$ to $1^1/2$ hours.

In the meantime, preheat an outdoor grill.

In a large saucepan, heat the oil over medium heat. Add the onion and cook, stirring, until soft, 7 minutes. Add the tomatoes, mustard, brown sugar, lemon juice, soy sauce, Worcestershire sauce, hot pepper sauce, allspice, cloves, ginger, salt and pepper to taste, and $1/4$ cup water. Bring to a boil, turn down the heat, and simmer slowly, uncovered, until the sauce thickens, 10 to 12 minutes. Remove from the heat.

Place the ribs on the grill 5 inches from the heat and brush generously with barbecue sauce. Partially cover the grill and cook the ribs for 5 to 10 minutes. Turn the ribs, baste them with more sauce, and continue to cook the ribs until golden brown, 5 to 10 minutes.

Remove the ribs from the grill and serve immediately.

Crispy Polenta with Pork Sausages and Puttanesca Sauce

Polenta, made earlier in the day or, better yet, a day or two in advance, is firm enough to cut into wedges and grill. Add some Italian pork sausages to the grill, then put the polenta and sausages together with puttanesca sauce, redolent with tomatoes, anchovies, garlic, hot red pepper, and capers, sprinkle the top with Parmigiano, and you've got a dish that is truly farmhouse Italian. Enjoy with a glass of red wine.

Serves 6

Coarse salt
1 1/4 cups polenta or coarse cornmeal
2 tablespoons unsalted butter at room
    temperature
1 cup freshly grated Parmigiano-Reggiano
Freshly ground black pepper
6 sweet Italian sausages (about 1 1/2 pounds)
1 recipe Puttanesca Sauce (page 31)

For the polenta, in a large saucepan bring 6 cups water and 1 teaspoon salt to a boil. Add the polenta in a slow stream, whisking constantly. Continue to whisk until the mixture thickens, then switch to a wooden spoon. Cook, stirring occasionally, until the polenta is thick enough for the spoon to stand up in the center of it, 15 to 20 minutes. Stir in the butter and 1/2 cup of the Parmigiano and season with salt and pepper. Pour into a lightly buttered 9-inch square baking dish. Chill for at least 1 hour or up to 3 days.

Preheat an outdoor grill.

Prick the sausages all over with a fork. Heat 1/2 cup water in a large frying pan. Add the sausages and cook until all the water has evaporated, about 5 minutes. Finish cooking the sausages on the grill, turning, until they are lightly browned and firm to the touch, about 5 minutes.

Cut the polenta into 6 pieces. Lightly brush the pieces with olive oil. Grill on both sides until hot throughout and lightly browned.

In the meantime, in a saucepan, heat the puttanesca sauce until hot and bubbling.

To serve, spread some puttanesca sauce on each plate. Top with the sausage and polenta. Sprinkle the top with the remaining 1/2 cup Parmigiano and serve immediately.

In the last twenty years the tomato has crossed its last frontier and conquered China."

From Raymond Sokolov,
Why We Eat What We Eat

---

chicken, duck, and rabbit

Chilean Chicken

Fennel, with its light, delicate licorice flavor, and tomatoes are the base for this casserole, or cazuela, as Chileans would say. This is more of a soup-stew, so serve it in a large tureen with rice and coarse bread to sop up the juices. For convenience, it can be made a couple of days in advance and reheated just before serving.

Serves 6 to 8

Two 3- to 3$\frac{1}{2}$-pound chickens
10 sprigs fresh thyme
6 sprigs fresh flat-leaf parsley
4 bay leaves
4 thin slices fresh ginger
3 tablespoons olive oil
2 garlic cloves, minced
7 medium ripe red tomatoes, peeled, seeded, and chopped
1 teaspoon ground fennel
1 cup dry sherry
Coarse salt and freshly ground black pepper
2 jalapeños, halved and seeded
2 pounds small red potatoes
6 medium fennel bulbs, quartered lengthwise, tops reserved and chopped

Wash the chickens and pat dry. Divide the thyme, parsley, bay leaves, and ginger between the cavities of the chickens. Truss the chickens.

Heat the olive oil in a large pot over medium heat. Add the garlic, tomatoes, and ground fennel. Simmer slowly, stirring occasionally, for 10 minutes. Add the sherry and cook until one quarter of the liquid has evaporated, 5 to 10 minutes. Add 8 cups water, 1 teaspoon salt, $\frac{1}{2}$ teaspoon pepper, and the jalapeños. Increase the heat to high and as soon as the liquid comes to a boil, reduce the heat to low, cover, and simmer for 15 minutes.

Place the chickens, side by side, in the broth and simmer, covered for 35 minutes.

Add the potatoes and fennel and cook until the chicken is cooked through and the potatoes and fennel are tender, 15 to 20 minutes.

Remove the chickens, remove the trussing strings, and discard the ginger, herb sprigs, and bay leaves. Cut the chickens into quarters and place them in a large serving tureen. With a slotted spoon, remove the vegetables from the broth and place around the chicken. Cover the chicken with foil to keep warm.

Increase the heat to high and reduce the broth by half, about 15 minutes. Season the broth with salt and pepper and ladle it around the chicken. Garnish with the reserved fennel greens and serve.

Arroz con Pollo

The Spanish casserole called arroz con pollo, *literally "rice with chicken," features saffron, tomatoes, chicken, long-grain rice, and peas all baked together. The most expensive spice, saffron is indispensable here, giving the dish a distinctive, pungent flavor and vibrant yellow color. You can assemble this dish ahead of time, then bake it just before serving.*

Serves 6 to 8

One 4-pound chicken, cut into 6 to 8 serving
    pieces, excess fat removed
$2^1/_2$ teaspoons chopped fresh oregano
Coarse salt
1 teaspoon freshly ground black pepper
2 tablespoons olive oil
1 large yellow onion, chopped
1 green bell pepper, cored, seeded, and diced
5 garlic cloves, thinly sliced
2 bay leaves
$1^1/_2$ teaspoons sweet paprika
$^1/_8$ teaspoon crushed red pepper flakes
3 cups peeled, seeded, and chopped fresh or
    canned tomatoes
$^1/_2$ cup dry white wine
1 teaspoon saffron threads
$1^3/_4$ cups long-grain white rice
1 cup fresh or frozen peas
2 tablespoons chopped fresh flat-leaf parsley

Dry the chicken pieces and rub with the oregano, 2 teaspoons salt, and the pepper. Let stand for 20 minutes.

Preheat the oven to 375°F.

Heat the oil in a large heavy casserole over medium heat. Add the chicken in a single layer and cook, turning once, until golden on both sides, 10 to 15 minutes. Remove the chicken and set aside. Drain off all but 2 tablespoons of oil from the pot and discard.

Add the onion, bell pepper, and garlic and cook until the onion is soft, about 7 minutes. Add the chicken, bay leaves, paprika, red pepper flakes, tomatoes, wine, 3 cups water, and the saffron. Bring to a boil, cover, and bake for 20 minutes.

Stir in the rice, peas, and salt to taste, return to the oven, and bake, covered, until the rice is cooked and all the liquid has been absorbed, about 20 minutes.

Remove from the oven and fluff the rice with a fork. Garnish with the parsley and serve immediately.

Chicken Oregano with Tomatillos

Oregano grows plentifully on the hillsides of southern Mexico, where it is often seen in dishes with tomatillos like this one of chicken stewed with onion, garlic, and smoky chipotle chiles. It can be made a day in advance and reheated just before serving. Serve with steamed rice.

Serves 6 to 8

2 tablespoons corn oil
Two 3-pound chickens, each cut into 6 to 8
    serving pieces, excess fat removed
1 small yellow onion, chopped
3 garlic cloves, minced
1¼ pounds fresh tomatillos, husks removed,
    rinsed, and coarsely chopped
3 pickled chipotle chiles, chopped
2 tablespoons chopped fresh oregano
¼ cup packed brown sugar
1½ cups Chicken Stock (page 78)
Coarse salt and freshly ground black pepper

Heat the oil in a large frying pan over medium heat. Add the chicken in a single layer and cook in batches, turning occasionally, until golden and it has rendered its fat, 10 minutes.

Remove the chicken and pour off all but 1 tablespoon oil from the pan.

Add the onion and garlic and cook until the onion is soft, about 7 minutes. Add the tomatillos, chipotle chiles, oregano, brown sugar, and chicken stock and simmer until the sauce thickens slightly, about 5 minutes. Add the chicken, cover, and simmer, turning the chicken occasionally, until the chicken is cooked through, about 30 minutes; if the sauce gets too thick, add more water as necessary. Season the sauce to taste with salt and pepper.

To serve, place the chicken on a platter and spoon the sauce over the top.

> **M**any foods we think of as Mediterranean, the ones we buy to remind us nostalgically of holidays in the sun, are comparative new-comers to Europe. As one historian has remarked, Herodotus—or Helen of Troy, for that matter—would not recognize their native haunts if they returned there today. Orange and lemon groves, peach orchards, eucalyptus forests, cypresses pointing the silver slopes of olive trees, would cast an unfamiliar shade. The color and taste of the food would seem alien, even Lorenzo the Magnificent never set eyes on the magnificent tomatoes, sweet peppers, and beans so ubiquitous in present day markets in Florence. In his day basil, the royal herb, was for keeping bedrooms free of flies; it had not yet encountered its soul mate, the tomato."
>
> From Jane Grigson,
> *Jane Grigson's Vegetable Book*

Stewed Chicken with Okra and Tomatoes

*W*hat could be better than chicken stewed with tomatoes, the meat almost falling from the bone? A stew like this one is best made midsummer, when the tomatoes are ripe on the vine and okra is coming into season. Always add okra at the last minute so it stays juicy. This is even better made a day or two in advance and reheated just before serving.

Serves 6 to 8

1/4 cup plus 1 tablespoon olive oil
1 1/4 pounds okra, washed and trimmed
Two 3 1/2-pound chickens, each cut into 6 to 8
    serving pieces, skin and excess fat removed
2 medium red onions, thinly sliced
5 cups peeled, seeded, and chopped fresh or
    canned tomatoes
2 garlic cloves, minced
1 tablespoon chopped fresh thyme
2 teaspoons ground cumin
4 whole cloves
1 cup Chicken Stock (page 78)
1 cup dry white wine
1 tablespoon red wine vinegar
Coarse salt and freshly ground black pepper
1/4 cup chopped fresh flat-leaf parsley

Heat 2 tablespoons of the olive oil in a large frying pan over medium heat. Add the okra and cook, stirring occasionally, until it changes color, 5 to 8 minutes. Remove from the pan and set aside. Drain all but 3 tablespoons of oil from the pan.

In the same frying pan, heat the remaining 3 tablespoons olive oil over medium heat. Add the chicken and cook until golden brown on both sides, 3 to 5 minutes per side. Remove from the pan and set aside. Drain all but 3 tablespoons of oil from the pan.

Add the onions and cook, stirring, until soft, about 7 minutes. Add the okra, tomatoes, garlic, thyme, cumin, cloves, chicken stock, and white wine, then add the chicken, cover, and simmer slowly until the breasts are tender, 25 minutes. Transfer the breasts to a platter and cover with foil to keep warm. Continue to cook the remaining pieces until the legs can be easily skewered, 15 to 20 minutes.

Return the chicken breasts to the pan and heat through. Season with the vinegar and salt and pepper. If the sauce is too thin, remove the chicken and reduce the liquid over high heat until it coats a spoon.

Add the parsley and stir together. Place the stew in serving bowls and serve immediately.

Chicken with Vinegar and Tomatoes

In Mexico, making the sauce of dried chiles, vinegar, spices, and tomatoes called adobo *is a simple process, but when chicken is stewed in it, the results are complex in flavor. You get tart, sweet, hot, and sour all in one bite. Serve this with mashed sweet potatoes. For convenience, it can be made two days in advance and reheated just before serving.*

Serves 6 to 8

1 tablespoon olive oil
Two 3- to 3½-pound chickens, each cut into
    6 to 8 pieces, excess fat removed
1 large yellow onion, minced
⅓ cup cider vinegar
3 tablespoons chili powder
2 teaspoons dried oregano
1 teaspoon ground cumin
1 teaspoon dried thyme
½ teaspoon ground cinnamon
¼ teaspoon ground cloves
¼ teaspoon ground allspice
6 garlic cloves, minced
3 cups peeled, seeded, and chopped fresh or
    canned tomatoes
Coarse salt and freshly ground black pepper

Heat the oil in a large frying pan over medium heat. Add the chicken in a single layer and cook in batches, turning halfway through, until light golden, 10 to 12 minutes. Remove the chicken and drain off all but 1 tablespoon oil from the pan.

Add the onion and cook until soft, about 7 minutes. Add the vinegar and simmer until it has reduced by half, about 2 minutes.

In the meantime, in a blender, puree the chili powder, oregano, cumin, thyme, cinnamon, cloves, allspice, garlic, and tomatoes until smooth.

Add to the pan and simmer for 5 minutes. Reduce the heat to low, add the chicken, cover, and simmer until the chicken is cooked through, 35 to 40 minutes.

Remove the cover and simmer over medium heat until the sauce has thickened, about 5 minutes. Season to taste with salt and pepper.

To serve, place the chicken on a platter and spoon the sauce over the top.

Moroccan Chicken with Tomato Marmalade

Honey *does wonders for bringing out the sweetness of tomatoes. Here, tomatoes and chicken are stewed with honey to make an exquisite Moroccan stew, or tagine. Serve with steamed couscous. You can make this a day in advance and heat just before serving.*

Serves 6 to 8

2 tablespoons unsalted butter
1 tablespoon olive oil
4 pounds chicken parts, excess fat removed
5 large ripe red tomatoes, peeled, seeded, and
   chopped
1 tablespoon tomato paste
1/2 teaspoon ground cumin
1/2 teaspoon saffron threads
1/4 teaspoon ground ginger
1 large yellow onion, grated
2 garlic cloves, minced
Coarse salt and freshly ground black pepper
1/4 cup honey
1 teaspoon ground cinnamon
1/4 cup sliced almonds, toasted
1 tablespoon sesame seeds, toasted

Melt the butter with the olive oil in a large casserole over medium heat. Add the chicken, tomatoes, tomato paste, cumin, saffron, ginger, onion, garlic, 1 cup water, 1 teaspoon salt, and 1/2 teaspoon pepper and bring to a boil. Reduce the heat to low, cover, and simmer until the chicken is starting to fall off the bone, 30 to 40 minutes. Add water as needed if the pot gets dry. Remove the chicken from the pot, cover with foil, and keep warm.

Add the honey and cinnamon to the pot and simmer, uncovered, over medium heat, stirring frequently, until the sauce is as thick as marmalade, 8 to 12 minutes. Add the chicken and simmer until the chicken is hot, 3 to 4 minutes. Season the sauce to taste with salt and pepper.

To serve, place the chicken on a platter, pour the sauce over it, and garnish with the almonds and sesame seeds.

Tomato-Saffron–Braised Chicken

You'll almost never find a recipe using saffron that doesn't also use tomatoes; the two marry well. Serve this hearty chicken braise with pasta, mashed potatoes, steamed basmati rice, or couscous. Make it a day in advance if desired and reheat just before serving.

Serves 4

2 tablespoons olive oil
One 3½- to 4-pound chicken, cut into 8 pieces,
    excess fat removed
1 small red onion, chopped
1 carrot, cut in half
2 bay leaves
1 teaspoon chopped fresh thyme
6 garlic cloves, minced
½ teaspoon saffron threads
½ cup dry white wine
2 cups Chicken Stock (page 78)
3½ cups peeled, seeded, and chopped fresh or
    canned tomatoes
One 2-inch piece orange zest, removed with a
    vegetable peeler
⅛ teaspoon cayenne
½ cup cured black olives, such as Niçoise or
    Kalamata, pitted and halved
2 tablespoons chopped fresh flat-leaf parsley
Coarse salt and freshly ground black pepper

Heat the olive oil in a large heavy casserole over medium heat. Add the chicken and cook, turning halfway through, until golden on both sides, 10 to 12 minutes. Remove from the pan and set aside.

Add the onion, carrot, bay leaves, and thyme and cook until the onion is soft, about 7 minutes. Add the garlic and stir for 1 minute.

Increase the heat to high, add the saffron and wine, and simmer until the wine reduces by half, about 1 minute. Add the stock, tomatoes, orange zest, cayenne, and chicken and cook until the juices run clear when the thigh of the chicken is pierced, 15 to 25 minutes. Remove the chicken and cover with foil to keep warm.

Simmer the sauce to thicken slightly, 5 to 10 minutes. Discard the bay leaves and orange zest. Put the chicken back in the pot, add the olives and parsley, and heat until the chicken is hot, 2 minutes. Season the sauce to taste with salt and pepper.

Place the chicken on a platter and spoon the sauce over the top. Serve immediately.

Chicken Cacciatore

"Hunter's-style" chicken is a classic American-Italian dish that varies from individual recipe to recipe. There is, however, one common denominator, tomatoes and chicken stewed together until the meat nearly falls from the bone. It's a great make-ahead dish.

Serves 6 to 8

¼ ounce dried wild mushrooms, preferably porcini
2 tablespoons olive oil
Two 3- to 3½-pound chickens, each cut into 6 to 8 serving pieces, excess fat removed
4 garlic cloves, sliced
1 cup dry red wine
4 cups peeled, seeded, and chopped fresh or canned tomatoes
2 green or red bell peppers, cored, seeded, and thinly sliced
1 pound fresh mushrooms, cleaned and halved
2 sprigs fresh thyme
2 bay leaves
Coarse salt and freshly ground black pepper

Put the dried mushrooms in a small bowl, pour 1 cup boiling water over them, and let stand until the water cools, about 30 minutes. Remove the mushrooms and reserve the mushroom water. If it is sandy, strain it through a cheesecloth-lined strainer. Coarsely chop the mushrooms.

Heat the olive oil in a large frying pan over medium heat. Add the chicken in a single layer and cook in batches, turning halfway through, until light golden, 10 to 12 minutes. Add the garlic and cook for 1 minute. Increase the heat to high, add the wine and the reserved mushroom liquid, and boil for 2 minutes. Add the tomatoes, bell peppers, fresh and dried mushrooms, thyme, and bay leaves, stir together, and simmer, covered, for 20 minutes.

Remove the cover and simmer until the sauce thickens and the chicken is cooked through, 10 minutes. Season to taste with salt and pepper. Remove the thyme and bay leaves and discard.

To serve, place the chicken on a platter and spoon the sauce over the top.

Ragout of Chicken, Sausage, and Red Peppers

This ragout of peppery hot sausage, chicken, and tomatoes cooked in one pot makes an easy yet substantial family dinner, but it can also be elevated for entertaining by serving it with "fancy" mashed potatoes flavored with chopped garlic, lemon zest, and parsley. To make things easy, it can be prepared a day in advance, stored in the refrigerator, and reheated just before serving.

Serves 6

1 pound spicy Italian pork sausage
3 tablespoons olive oil
6 chicken thighs, excess fat removed
1 medium yellow onion, quartered
2 red bell peppers, cored, seeded, and cut into
　1/2-inch strips
2 garlic cloves, minced
1 cup dry white wine
1 cup Chicken Stock (page 78)
2 1/2 cups peeled, seeded, and chopped fresh or
　canned plum tomatoes
Coarse salt and freshly ground black pepper
3 tablespoons chopped fresh flat-leaf parsley

Prick the sausage several times with the tines of a fork. Simmer in 1/4 cup water in a medium skillet, uncovered, until almost cooked through, 5 to 7 minutes. Remove the sausage and slice on the diagonal into 1/2-inch-thick slices. Set aside.

Heat the olive oil in a large frying pan over medium-low heat. Add the chicken thighs and cook, turning halfway through, until browned on both sides, about 10 minutes. Remove from the pan and set aside. Add the onion and peppers to the pan and cook, stirring occasionally, until soft, about 10 minutes. Add the garlic and cook for 1 minute. Turn the heat to high, return the chicken thighs to the pan, and add the wine. Bring to a simmer and reduce by one half. Add the chicken stock and tomatoes, cover, reduce the heat, and simmer slowly for 5 minutes. Remove the cover and simmer until the sauce has thickened, about 10 minutes. Add the sausage and cook for 2 minutes until completely cooked. Season to taste with salt and pepper.

Place the ragout on a large serving platter and garnish with the parsley. Serve immediately.

Chicken Creole

In the kitchens of New Orleans, Creole-style cooking has been a way of life for generations. A specialty of the American South, its roots are deeply planted in the traditions of African, Native American, Spanish, French, and English cooking. Serve this chicken in its sauce of tomatoes, bell peppers, onions, celery, and spicy hot pepper sauce with steamed white rice. You can make the dish a day in advance and heat just before serving.

Serves 6

2 tablespoons olive oil
1 large yellow onion, chopped
2 stalks celery, chopped
1 medium green bell pepper, cored, seeded, and diced
1/2 cup chopped fresh flat-leaf parsley, plus whole leaves for garnish
2 garlic cloves, chopped
3/4 cup Chicken Stock (page 78)
3 tablespoons red wine vinegar
2 cups peeled, seeded, and chopped fresh or canned tomatoes
2 tablespoons tomato paste
1 tablespoon brown sugar
1 teaspoon hot pepper sauce, such as Tabasco
Coarse salt and freshly ground black pepper
6 boneless, skinless chicken breasts
1/2 cup dry white wine

Heat 1 tablespoon of the olive oil in a large heavy casserole over medium heat. Add the onion, celery, bell pepper, and parsley and cook for 5 minutes.

Add the garlic and cook for 2 minutes until almost soft. Add the chicken stock, vinegar, tomatoes, tomato paste, brown sugar, hot pepper sauce, 1/2 teaspoon salt, and pepper to taste. Bring to a boil over high heat, reduce the heat to low, and simmer for 10 minutes.

Heat the remaining 1 tablespoon olive oil in a large frying pan over medium-high heat. Add the chicken breasts and cook until golden on both sides, 5 minutes total.

Add the white wine and tomato sauce to the chicken and simmer until the chicken is cooked through, about 10 minutes. Season to taste with salt and pepper. If the sauce is too thin, remove the chicken and keep warm. Reduce the sauce over medium-high heat until it thickens slightly.

To serve, place the chicken on a platter, spoon the sauce over it, and garnish with parsley.

Grilled Chicken with Corn, Pepper, and Tomato Relish

Relishes *like this one, with its sparkling fresh flavors of peppers, cherry tomatoes, corn, red onion, garlic, and red wine vinegar, are just the right colorful and flavorful touch for all kinds of grilled dishes, from skewers of pork and lamb chops to swordfish or tuna steaks to, of course, chicken. Make the relish a couple hours in advance if desired, but grill the chicken at the last minute.*

Serves 6

$^1/_2$ cup fresh corn kernels
1 cup assorted cherry tomatoes, halved
$^1/_2$ red bell pepper, diced
$^1/_2$ green bell or pasilla pepper, diced
$^1/_2$ yellow bell pepper, diced
$^1/_4$ teaspoon crushed red pepper flakes
1 small red onion, diced
2 garlic cloves, minced
3 tablespoons chopped fresh flat-leaf parsley,
     plus whole leaves for garnish
$^1/_4$ cup plus 1 tablespoon extra virgin olive oil
3 tablespoons red wine vinegar
1 tablespoon fresh lemon juice
Coarse salt and freshly ground black pepper
6 boneless, skinless chicken breasts (6 to 8
     ounces each)

Preheat an outdoor grill.

Bring a small saucepan of salted water to a boil. Add the corn and cook until tender, about 1 minute. Drain.

In a medium bowl, combine the corn, tomatoes, bell peppers, crushed red pepper flakes, red onion, garlic, parsley, olive oil, red wine vinegar, and lemon juice. Season to taste with salt and pepper.

Grill the chicken breasts 4 inches from the heat source, turning occasionally, until cooked through, 8 to 10 minutes. Season to taste with salt and pepper.

Cut each chicken breast on the diagonal into 4 to 5 slices. Arrange on serving plates and spoon the relish alongside, or pass separately in a bowl. Garnish with parsley and serve.

Chicken with Warm Tarragon-Tomato Vinaigrette

Tarragon, with its anise-like flavor, is a natural with tomatoes. Here, cherry tomatoes, fresh tarragon and tarragon vinegar, shallots, and olive oil are whisked together to make a warm vinaigrette and drizzled over chicken breasts. You can turn this into a sumptuous warm salad by tossing the sliced chicken with the vinaigrette and salad greens. This is a wonderful summer recipe, so simple that it is made in minutes.

Serves 6

1 1/2 tablespoons olive oil
6 boneless, skinless chicken breasts (6 to 8
    ounces each)
Coarse salt and freshly ground black pepper
3 tablespoons extra virgin olive oil
1 shallot, minced
2/3 cup Chicken Stock (page 78)
3 tablespoons tarragon vinegar, or more to taste
3 tablespoons chopped fresh tarragon
1 1/2 cups cherry tomatoes

Heat the olive oil in a large frying pan over medium heat. Add the chicken and cook, turning occasionally, until cooked through, 8 to 10 minutes. Season to taste with salt and pepper. Place on a platter and cover with foil to keep warm while you make the vinaigrette.

In the same pan, heat the extra virgin olive oil over medium heat. Add the shallot and cook until soft, about 3 minutes. Add the chicken stock and simmer until reduced by half, 1 to 2 minutes. Add the vinegar, tarragon, and tomatoes and stir just until warm, about 10 seconds. Remove from the heat and season with salt and pepper, and additional vinegar if needed.

Slice each chicken breast on the diagonal into 5 to 6 pieces. Fan them on individual plates. Drizzle the vinaigrette onto the chicken breasts and serve immediately.

Grilled Chicken Legs with Red Chile Paste

*T*his *simple dish is like a Mexican barbecue. Mild ancho chiles, with their gentle heat and rich flavor, give a fabulous jump-start to plain old chicken legs. You can marinate the chicken up to a day in advance. Serve the legs hot or cold with zippy coleslaw or potato salad.*

Serves 6

1 ancho chile
4 garlic cloves, minced
8 peeled, seeded, chopped, and drained fresh
    or canned plum tomatoes, or $2^1/_2$ cups
    canned plum tomatoes
$^1/_4$ cup fresh orange juice
1 tablespoon olive oil
Coarse salt and freshly ground black pepper
6 large chicken legs (8 ounces each), excess fat
    removed

Put the chile in a bowl, pour boiling water over it, and let sit until the water cools. Drain and remove the stem.

Place the chile in a blender with the garlic, tomatoes, orange juice, and olive oil. Blend to make a smooth paste, about 2 minutes. Season to taste with salt and pepper.

Place the chicken legs in a large baking dish and pour the red chile paste over them. Rub the legs so they are coated with the paste. Cover and let marinate for at least 2 hours, or overnight, in the refrigerator.

Preheat an outdoor grill.

Grill the chicken legs 4 inches from the heat source, brushing periodically with the marinade, until they are golden on one side, 10 minutes. Turn the chicken legs and grill, continuing to baste, until the legs are cooked through, 15 to 20 additional minutes.

Remove from the grill and serve hot, at room temperature, or cold.

> I f I live to be a hundred, I will never forget the bliss of smelling a tomato as it first appears, dwarf-green, pale, and slightly fuzzy, from its petal-like cocoon. Fragrant of dry leaves and rich dark loam. The gardener's joy is watching this globe grow daily. Fighting the beetle and borer, he knows that his table will be more sumptuous soon with the addition of this majestic juicy fruit—simply cut and dusted with salt and pepper. For a vine-ripened tomato requires nothing more. But don't tell basil I said so!"
>
> From Bert Greene, *Kitchen Bouquets*

Spicy Coconut-Lime Chicken

Lime, coconut, sesame, ginger, peanuts, chicken, and tomatoes all blend together in a sweet, sour, and spicy Indian-inspired dish. Thank you to my friend Brett Frechette for her friendship, encouragement, and this fantastic recipe. Serve this dish with steamed jasmine rice or Indian Tomato Rice (page 135).

Serves 6 to 8

1 teaspoon coriander seeds
1 teaspoon minced fresh ginger
1 tablespoon toasted sesame oil
2 garlic cloves, minced
1 teaspoon cayenne
8 green onions, minced
Grated zest of 1 lime
Juice of 4 limes
Juice of 1 lemon
$1/4$ cup soy sauce
2 tablespoons rice wine vinegar
2 tablespoons molasses
$1/2$ cup coconut milk
$1/2$ cup raw peanuts plus 2 tablespoons coarsely
  chopped raw peanuts
$1/4$ cup chopped fresh cilantro, plus whole
  sprigs for garnish
2 pounds boneless, skinless chicken breasts,
  cut into thin strips
2 tablespoons peanut oil
$1/3$ pound sugar snap peas
1 cucumber, peeled, halved seeded, and cut
  into $1/2$-inch diagonal slices
3 cups red or yellow cherry tomatoes, halved

In a blender or spice grinder or a large mortar and pestle, puree or pound the coriander seeds, ginger, sesame oil, garlic, cayenne, half of the green onions, the lime zest, lime and lemon juice, soy sauce, vinegar, molasses, coconut milk, and the $1/2$ cup peanuts until smooth. Add chopped cilantro and mix together.

Put the chicken in a bowl, pour three quarters of the marinade over it, and marinate for 2 hours in the refrigerator. Reserve the remaining marinade.

Heat the oil in a large skillet over medium-high heat. Add the chicken and cook, stirring frequently, until cooked through, 6 to 8 minutes. Remove from the pan. Add the sugar snap peas and 2 tablespoons water and cook, stirring, until bright green but still crunchy, 1 to 2 minutes. Add the cucumber and cook just until warm. Add the reserved marinade, the chicken, and tomatoes and stir together until the tomatoes are warm.

Serve immediately, garnished with cilantro sprigs, 2 tablespoons peanuts, and the remaining green onions.

Smoky Chipotle Duck

This Mexican-inspired duck is steamed for an hour to remove excess fat, then braised in a zingy sauce of smoky hot chipotle chiles, sweet tomatoes, thick slices of onion, and lots of spices. Serve with steamed rice and black beans. Or, strip the meat from the bones and use as the filling with rice and beans in burritos or enchiladas. Make a day in advance and store in the refrigerator until you are ready to reheat and serve.

Serves 8

Two 5-pound ducks
6 garlic cloves
2 teaspoons ground cumin
8 black peppercorns
4 whole cloves
$2/3$ cup chopped onion plus 6 large yellow
    onions, thickly sliced
4 tablespoons corn oil
20 fresh or canned plum tomatoes, peeled and
    sliced
1 recipe Chipotle Sauce (page 37)
Coarse salt and freshly ground black pepper

Prick the bottoms of the ducks with the tines of a fork in several places. Pour 1 inch of water into a large pot and bring to a boil. Add the ducks, breast side up on a rack, cover, and steam for 1 hour. Watch the water level closely.

In the meantime, in a mortar and pestle or blender, pound or process the garlic, cumin, peppercorns, cloves, chopped onion, and 6 tablespoons water to a smooth paste.

In a large frying pan, heat the oil over medium heat. Add the sliced onions and cook until soft, about 10 minutes. Add the spice paste and cook over low heat, stirring occasionally, for 10 minutes. Increase the heat to medium-high, add the tomatoes and 2 cups water, and simmer for 3 minutes. Add the chipotle sauce and simmer for 2 minutes. Remove from the heat.

Cool the ducks enough to handle and cut each into 8 serving pieces. Add the duck to the tomato sauce, stir well to coat with sauce, cover, and simmer slowly until the duck is tender, 45 to 60 minutes. Check the pan periodically and add water as necessary so the pan doesn't get dry.

If needed, remove the cover and simmer to reduce the sauce so it thickens slightly. Season to taste with salt and pepper.

To serve, place the duck on a serving platter and spoon the sauce over the top.

Stewed Rabbit with Cherry Tomatoes

This dish comes from the island of Ischia, off the coast of Naples, where it is served with roasted potatoes seasoned with lemon and rosemary. If rabbit isn't to your liking or is unavailable, substitute chicken. Make this a day in advance and reheat just before serving if you like.

Serves 6

3 tablespoons olive oil
8 garlic cloves, crushed
Two 2¹/₂-pound rabbits, each cut into 4 pieces
2 cups dry white wine
5 cups red cherry tomatoes (about 1¹/₂ pounds), halved
12 fresh basil leaves, torn into small pieces, plus a few sprigs for garnish
Coarse salt and freshly ground black pepper

Heat the olive oil in a large heavy frying pan over medium heat. Add the garlic cloves and cook until light golden, 2 minutes. Remove the garlic and discard.

In batches, add the rabbit and cook until golden on all sides, 8 to 12 minutes. Return all the rabbit to the pan, add the wine, and simmer until it reduces by half, about 10 minutes. Add the tomatoes, basil, 2 cups water, ¹/₂ teaspoon salt, and ¹/₄ teaspoon pepper. Bring to a boil, reduce the heat to low, and simmer slowly, uncovered, until the rabbit is tender when pierced with a fork, 35 to 40 minutes. Transfer the rabbit to a warm serving platter and cover with foil.

Reduce the liquid in the pan over high heat until it coats a spoon, 5 to 8 minutes. Season to taste with salt and pepper.

To serve, pour the sauce over the rabbit and garnish with basil sprigs.

Paulo's Stewed Rabbit

This Tuscan farmhouse favorite uses the acidity from tomatoes to tenderize rabbit, which can sometimes be tough. By the end of the cooking time, the meat falls from the bone. Serve with boiled or golden-roasted potatoes. You can make the stew a couple days before serving and store it in the refrigerator, or freeze it for up to a month.

Serves 6

1 carrot, diced
1 stalk celery, diced
1 medium yellow onion, diced
3 cups dry red wine
1½ tablespoons chopped fresh thyme
1½ tablespoons chopped fresh sage
1½ tablespoons chopped fresh flat-leaf parsley, plus whole leaves for garnish
1 tablespoon chopped fresh oregano
3 bay leaves
¼ cup extra virgin olive oil
Two 2½- to 3-pound rabbits, each cut into 6 pieces; reserve the livers
1 tablespoon unsalted butter
3 cups Chicken Stock (page 78)
1½ cups peeled, seeded, and chopped fresh or canned plum tomatoes

In a large bowl, combine the carrot, celery, onion, red wine, thyme, sage, parsley, oregano, bay leaves, and 2 tablespoons of the olive oil. Mix well, add the rabbit, and let marinate in the refrigerator for 24 hours.

The next day, strain the marinade and reserve both the solids and liquid, separately from the rabbit. Dry the rabbit. Dice the reserved livers.

In a large heavy casserole, melt the butter with the remaining 2 tablespoons olive oil over medium heat. Add the reserved marinade solids and the liver and cook until the vegetables are soft, about 10 minutes. Reduce the heat to medium-low, add the pieces of rabbit, and cook, turning, until golden brown, about 10 minutes. Add half of the reserved marinade liquid (discard the rest), the chicken stock, and tomatoes and simmer, covered, for 30 minutes. Remove the cover and simmer until the sauce thickens slightly, about 5 minutes.

Place the rabbit on a platter and spoon the sauce over the top. Garnish with parsley and serve immediately.

side dishes

Fried Green Tomatoes

Pick *tomatoes when they are still tart, crunchy, and green. Serve this Southern classic with the Tomato Mayonnaise with a Kick as a first course or as a side dish to simple grilled meat or fish. The tomatoes can be breaded several hours in advance.*

Serves 6

5 or 6 medium green tomatoes, cut into ¹/₂-inch
   slices
Coarse salt
1 cup all-purpose flour
3 large eggs, beaten
2 tablespoons milk
1¹/₂ cups yellow or white cornmeal
2 teaspoons chopped fresh sage, plus a few
   sprigs for garnish
1 teaspoon chopped fresh thyme, plus a few
   sprigs for garnish
1 teaspoon chopped fresh oregano, plus a few
   sprigs for garnish
1 green onion, minced
Freshly ground black pepper
¹/₄ cup olive oil
1 recipe Tomato Mayonnaise with a Kick
   (page 40)

Place the tomatoes in a single layer on paper towels and salt lightly. Let sit while you prepare the breading.

Preheat the oven to 375°F.

Place the flour in a bowl. Combine the eggs and milk in a separate bowl. Combine the cornmeal, sage, thyme, oregano, and green onion in a third bowl. Season all three with salt and pepper. With paper towels, dry the tomatoes. One by one, place the tomato slices in the flour and tap off the excess. Next dip in the egg mixture to coat completely, then dip in the cornmeal and tap off the excess.

Heat 2 tablespoons of the olive oil in a large skillet over medium-low heat until rippling. Cook the tomato slices in batches, in a single layer, until they are golden on both sides and the walls of the tomatoes are fork-tender, 10 to 12 minutes. Remove from the pan and drain on paper towels, then place the tomato slices on a baking sheet and keep warm on the top rack of the oven until all of the tomatoes are cooked.

To serve, place the tomatoes on a plate. Garnish with herb sprigs and serve with the mayonnaise.

Warm Cherry Tomatoes

Dishes that are simple to prepare with lots of exploding flavors and colors are invaluable to the hurried cook. So when your garden is dripping with cherry tomatoes, pick a big basket full of all colors and shapes and serve as an accompaniment to grilled lamb chops and oven-roasted red potatoes. This is an almost-instant recipe that can only be done at the last minute.

Serves 6

1 tablespoon extra virgin olive oil
4 cups assorted cherry tomatoes
1 garlic clove, minced
1 tablespoon chopped fresh flat-leaf parsley
Coarse salt and freshly ground black pepper

Heat the olive oil in a large skillet over medium heat. Add the tomatoes and garlic and stir together until well mixed and warm, 1 to 2 minutes. Add the parsley and stir together. Season to taste with salt and pepper.

To serve, place in a bowl.

Tomatoes' Setback

Tomatoes were assigned to the potato family when tomatoes and potatoes arrived in England about the same time. The potato's misfortune may have negatively influenced the tomato's rise in culinary circles. Soon after introducing the potato to Queen Elizabeth, Sir Walter Raleigh planted the tuber and invited his peers to enjoy a repast featuring potatoes in each course. Unfortunately, his servant cooked the toxic foliage causing acute stomachaches. That set the potato, and possibly tomato, back many, many years."

From Robert Hendrickson,
The Great American Tomato Book

Tomato, Red Onion, and Potato Gratin

Who can resist the comfort of potatoes? Layered with slices of fresh tomato and topped with Fontina cheese, this gratin is the epitome of comfort food. You should bake the gratin as soon as you have assembled it, or the potatoes will turn brown, but it will stay hot for at least half an hour once it is taken from the oven.

Serves 6

1¼ pounds red or waxy potatoes
¾ cup Chicken Stock (page 78)
1 medium red onion, thinly sliced
Coarse salt and freshly ground black pepper
4 garlic cloves, thinly sliced
1 tablespoon chopped fresh thyme
2 medium ripe red tomatoes, thinly sliced
1 cup coarsely grated Fontina cheese (about 4
    ounces)
1¼ cups heavy cream

Preheat the oven to 375°F. Grease a 2½-quart gratin or baking dish.

Cut the potatoes into ⅛-inch slices and place in a bowl of cold water.

Place the chicken stock in a saucepan and reduce over high heat by half. Set aside.

Sprinkle the onion over the bottom of the baking dish. Season with salt and pepper. Drain the potatoes and layer half of them, overlapping them like shingles, over the onion. Sprinkle half of the garlic over the potatoes. Season with salt and pepper and half of the thyme. Next, layer the tomatoes over the potatoes. Sprinkle with half the cheese. Season with salt, pepper, garlic and the remaining thyme and garlic. Then layer the remaining potatoes over the top and season with salt and pepper. Combine the reduced chicken stock and the cream and pour the mixture over the potatoes. Sprinkle with the remaining cheese. Cover with foil and bake for 40 minutes.

Remove the foil and with a large spoon, press down on the potatoes to moisten the top. Continue to bake until the potatoes are tender when pierced with a knife and the top is golden brown, 30 to 40 minutes.

Serve directly from the dish, either hot or warm.

Gratin Niçoise

Plum tomatoes are the best choice for this gratin; they are less juicy and have more pulp than regular round tomatoes. I often make layered vegetable casseroles at the height of summer with all of the fresh vegetables from my garden. As an alternative, use a cup of crumbled goat cheese and a quarter cup of Parmigiano-Reggiano in place of just Parmigiano, with equally delicious results. This can be assembled one day in advance and baked before serving.

Serves 8

6 small Japanese eggplants (about 1 pound), cut
    diagonally into $1/4$-inch slices
3 tablespoons extra virgin olive oil
Coarse salt and freshly ground black pepper
2 garlic cloves, minced
2 teaspoons chopped fresh oregano
1 cup freshly grated Parmigiano-Reggiano
4 small zucchini (about $1^1/4$ pounds), cut
    diagonally into $1/4$-inch slices
6 ripe plum tomatoes, thinly sliced
2 yellow bell peppers, roasted (see page 13),
    peeled, seeded, and cut into $1^1/2$-inch strips
$1^1/2$ cups Chicken Stock (page 78)

Preheat the oven to 375°F.

Brush both sides of the eggplant slices with the olive oil and place on a baking sheet. Season with salt and pepper. Bake the eggplant, turning occasionally, until soft and golden, 15 to 18 minutes. Remove from the oven and set aside; leave the oven on.

In a small bowl, combine the garlic, oregano, and Parmigiano-Reggiano.

Oil a 3-quart gratin or baking dish. Place one quarter of the eggplant at one end of the dish. Next, place a layer of one quarter of the zucchini on top of the eggplant, overlapping slightly like shingles. Continue with one quarter of the tomatoes and then one quarter of the bell peppers. Continue in the same manner, using the remaining eggplant, zucchini, tomatoes, and peppers. Season with salt and pepper. Pour the stock over the vegetables and sprinkle with the cheese mixture.

Bake in the upper third of the oven until most of the liquid is absorbed and the vegetables are tender, 60 to 70 minutes.

Serve either hot or warm.

---

n New York every corner grocery, even in the poorer quarters, has its constant supply. Apparently, all classes, rich and poor alike, are bound to have their tomatoes daily, be their price five cents a pound or twenty-five or more."

From Betty Wilson,
Cooks, Gluttons, and Gourmets

Baked Grapes and Green Tomatoes

In October, all around the Tuscan countryside, when the vines are dripping with Sangiovese grapes and the tomatoes are still green, this unusual dish is served with mixed grilled meats or roasted chicken. For her inspiration, thanks to Sammie Daniels, a California transplant now living in Tuscany. In place of Italian Sangiovese grapes, Sammie recommends using other sweet grapes like Concord.

Serves 6

4 medium green tomatoes, cut into 1/2-inch slices
1/4 cup extra virgin olive oil
Coarse salt and freshly ground black pepper
4 cups ripe red grapes
1 cup dry bread crumbs

Preheat the oven to 375°F. Oil a 2 1/2-quart baking dish.

Layer half of the tomatoes in the bottom of the baking dish. Drizzle with 2 tablespoons of the olive oil and season with salt and pepper. With your hands and using gentle pressure, squeeze half of the grapes onto the tomatoes. Repeat with the remaining tomatoes, seasoning them with salt and pepper, and grapes. Sprinkle the top with the bread crumbs and drizzle with the remaining 2 tablespoons olive oil.

Bake until the tomatoes are soft, the juices are bubbling around the edges, and the bread crumbs are golden, 40 to 50 minutes.

Let cool for 10 minutes and serve.

Baked Tomatoes and Onions

This simple old-time baked gratin is served in Australia for Sunday dinner with roast lamb. It can be assembled in advance and baked just before serving. Sue Condos of Melbourne, Australia, deserves a big thanks for the recipe.

Serves 6

8 large ripe red tomatoes, peeled and sliced
2 large yellow onions, thinly sliced
Coarse salt and freshly ground black pepper
1 cup fresh bread crumbs
3 tablespoons unsalted butter

Preheat the oven to 400°F. Oil a 2 1/2-quart baking dish.

Layer a single layer of tomatoes in the bottom of the baking dish. Layer a single layer of onions on top of the tomatoes. Season as you go with salt and pepper. Continue to layer the tomatoes and onions, finishing with a layer of tomatoes. Cover the top with the bread crumbs and dot with the butter, distributing it evenly.

Bake until the bread crumbs are golden brown and crisp, the juices are bubbling, and the onions are tender, 50 to 60 minutes.

Let sit for 10 minutes before serving.

Ratatouille

Every vegetable that is in Provence goes into ratatouille, the quintessential vegetable stew of eggplant, tomatoes, zucchini, onions, and bell peppers. This recipe was inspired by Lulu Peyraud, an extraordinary cook, friend, and owner of the incomparable Domaine Tempier Winery in Bandol. Lulu grills the peppers in her kitchen fireplace first, then stews them with the other ingredients. If you are leery of using so much olive oil, just brush the eggplant with oil and bake it in a 375°F oven until golden, fifteen to twenty minutes. Ratatouille can be made a day in advance, but bring it to room temperature or reheat to serve.

Serves 6

2 medium eggplants (about 1 pound each), cut
   into 1-inch cubes
Coarse salt
¼ cup plus 2 tablespoons olive oil
2 medium yellow onions, cut into quarters
6 garlic cloves, minced
4 small zucchini (about 1 pound), cut into
   ¾-inch slices
3 medium ripe red tomatoes, peeled, seeded,
   and quartered
3 yellow or red bell peppers, roasted (see page
   13), peeled, seeded, and cut into 1-inch
   strips
2 bay leaves
¼ cup chopped fresh flat-leaf parsley
½ teaspoon chopped fresh thyme
Freshly ground black pepper
1 tablespoon red wine vinegar

Place the eggplant in a colander and sprinkle with salt. Let sit for 30 minutes. Rinse the eggplant and pat dry with paper towels.

Heat 3 tablespoons of the olive oil in a large frying pan over medium heat. Add the eggplant and cook until golden, 15 to 18 minutes. Remove and set aside.

Heat the remaining 3 tablespoons olive oil in another large frying pan over medium heat. Add the onions and cook until light golden, about 20 minutes. Add the garlic and zucchini and cook, stirring occasionally, for 5 minutes. Add the eggplant, tomatoes, bell peppers, bay leaves, parsley, thyme, and salt and pepper to taste and simmer slowly for 20 minutes.

Add the red wine vinegar and stir together, then season to taste with salt and pepper.

To serve, place the ratatouille in a serving bowl.

Caponata

Caponata is a zesty Sicilian vegetable stew that celebrates the height of summer with all of its freshness. In
this recipe, the eggplant is deep-fried, but if you prefer,
you can toss it with two tablespoons olive oil and bake in
a 375°F oven, turning occasionally, until golden, fifteen
to twenty minutes. Serve caponata at room temperature as
a relish with grilled bread, or as a salad on the side of
grilled steaks, chicken, or fish.

Makes 6 cups; serves 6

2 eggplants (about 2 pounds total)
Coarse salt
Olive oil
1 large yellow onion, diced
1 red bell pepper, cored, seeded, and diced
2 stalks celery, diced
3/4 cup cured green olives, pitted and coarsely
    chopped
2 tablespoons capers
1/4 cup red wine vinegar
1/4 cup tomato paste
1 teaspoon sugar
5 cups peeled, seeded, and chopped fresh or
    canned tomatoes
1/4 cup pine nuts, toasted
Freshly ground black pepper

Peel the eggplants in vertical strips, so they are
striped. Cut the eggplant into 1/2-inch cubes. Place
in a colander and sprinkle with salt. Let drain for
30 minutes.

Rinse the eggplant and dry with paper towels.
Heat 1 inch of olive oil in a deep heavy saucepan
over medium-high heat. Add the eggplant in
batches and cook, turning occasionally, until tender
and golden, 3 to 5 minutes. Remove with a slotted
spoon and drain on paper towels.

Transfer 2 tablespoons of the oil to a large frying
pan and heat over medium heat. Add the onion,
bell pepper, and celery, cover, and cook until soft, 8
to 10 minutes. Remove the cover and cook until
the vegetables start to turn golden brown, 6 to 8
minutes. Add the olives, capers, red wine vinegar,
tomato paste, sugar, and tomatoes and cook until
the liquid has evaporated, 20 to 30 minutes.

Add the eggplant and pine nuts and stir well. Season to taste with salt and pepper. (Caponata can be
made 2 days in advance and stored in the refrigerator.)

Beans, "Cherries," and Summer Savory

There is something about the bright flavors of warm cherry tomatoes bursting in your mouth. Use all colors and sizes of cherry tomatoes here, red, yellow, yellow pear, green, and orange. Add some beans, both green and yellow, and flavor the dish with summer savory. This simple recipe is perfect served with grilled steaks, chicken breasts, or trout.

Serves 6

Coarse salt
³/₄ pound green beans, trimmed
³/₄ pound yellow beans, trimmed
1 teaspoon unsalted butter
1 teaspoon olive oil
2 tablespoons chopped fresh summer savory,
    plus sprigs for garnish
3 cups assorted cherry tomatoes

Bring a large saucepan of salted water to a boil over medium-high heat. Add the beans and cook until tender, 4 to 6 minutes. Drain and rinse under cold water. (This can be done 1 day in advance; refrigerate until ready to proceed.)

In a large frying pan, melt the butter with the olive oil over medium heat. Add the beans and savory and cook, stirring frequently, until hot, 2 minutes. Add the cherry tomatoes and cook until the tomatoes are warm, about 1 minute; do not break their skins.

To serve, place the beans and tomatoes on a platter and garnish with savory sprigs.

A world without tomatoes is like a string quartet without violins. . . . In this world of uncertainty and woe, one thing remains unchanged: Fresh, canned, pureed, dried, salted, sliced, and served with sugar and cream or pressed into juice, the tomato is reliable, friendly, and delicious. We would be nothing without it."

From Laurie Colwin, "Tomatoes," *Gourmet,* August 1992

Late-Harvest Green Beans and Tomatoes

Green *beans are so tender and sweet at the beginning of the season, but later, when they are more mature and tougher, it's sometimes hard to know what to do with them. Try stewing late-autumn beans with tomatoes and garlic: The beans will get soft, and the flavors melt together. This is a perfect make-ahead dish; just heat it up when you're ready to serve.*

Serves 6

2 tablespoons olive oil
1 small yellow onion, chopped
4 garlic cloves, thinly sliced
1 pound green beans (tender or mature), ends removed
2¼ cups peeled, seeded, and chopped fresh or canned tomatoes
Coarse salt and freshly ground black pepper

Heat the olive oil in a large frying pan over medium heat. Add the onion and cook, stirring occasionally, until soft, 7 minutes. Add the garlic and stir for 1 minute. Increase the heat to high, add the beans and tomatoes, and bring to a simmer. Reduce the heat to low, cover, and cook until the beans are very tender and soft, 30 minutes.

Remove the cover and cook until most of the liquid has evaporated, about 10 minutes. Season to taste with salt and pepper.

Serve hot or warm.

Okra and Tomato Stew

Okra is a vegetable that people either love or hate. Usually it's the texture that puts people off. But stew it with tomatoes, pearl onions, and cilantro for a new twist on an old theme, and you'll find some new fans. Serve with roasted chicken. This stew can be prepared a day in advance, without the cilantro. Before serving, bring to room temperature and add the cilantro.

Serves 6

1/2 pound pearl onions
3 tablespoons olive oil
1 1/2 pounds okra, stems removed
4 garlic cloves, minced
1 1/4 cups peeled, seeded, and chopped fresh or
     canned tomatoes
Coarse salt and freshly ground black pepper
1 tablespoon coriander seeds
2 tablespoons fresh lemon juice
1/4 cup chopped fresh cilantro

Bring a small pot of water to a boil. Add the onions and simmer for 1 minute. Drain the onions, cool, and peel.

Heat the olive oil in a large skillet over medium heat. Add the onions and cook, shaking the pan periodically, until golden, about 15 minutes. Reduce the heat to low, add the okra, and cook, stirring occasionally, for 5 minutes. Add the garlic and cook for 1 minute. Add the tomatoes, 1 cup water, and salt and pepper to taste. Cover and simmer slowly until the okra is very tender, 20 to 30 minutes.

In the meantime, in a mortar and pestle or a spice grinder, coarsely grind the coriander seeds. Add to the stew with 1 tablespoon of the lemon juice. Simmer until the liquid has reduced by half, 5 to 7 minutes. Remove from the heat and stir in the chopped cilantro. Season to taste with the remaining lemon juice and salt and pepper.

Serve hot, warm, or at room temperature.

Fennel Stewed with Tomatoes

Fennel is often mislabeled as anise, causing some people who don't like the flavor of licorice to avoid it at all costs. But fennel is sweeter and more delicate than anise, and this simple fennel stew with tomatoes has converted many sworn fennel-haters into devoted fennel-lovers. Together, the two ingredients come alive. Make this a couple of days ahead and heat gently to serve.

Serves 6

3 tablespoons olive oil
1 large yellow onion, chopped
3 garlic cloves, thinly sliced
3 small fennel bulbs (about 1 pound), trimmed
    and cut lengthwise in half
1¼ cups peeled, seeded, and chopped fresh or
    canned tomatoes
½ cup dry white wine
2 bay leaves
½ teaspoon chopped fresh thyme
Coarse salt and freshly ground black pepper

Heat the olive oil in a large frying pan over medium heat. Add the onion and cook until soft, about 7 minutes. Add the garlic and cook, stirring, for 1 minute. Add the fennel and cook for 5 minutes. Add the tomatoes, wine, bay leaves, thyme, and ½ cup water. Cover and simmer until the fennel is very tender, 40 to 50 minutes. Season to taste with salt and pepper.

To serve, place in a serving dish.

Fava Beans and Tomatoes

Along the Eastern Mediterranean, from Turkey to Egypt, fava beans are stewed with tomatoes to make this spicy, relatively low-fat side dish to serve with grilled lamb chops or chicken breasts. Buy young tender fava beans— they will be so sweet they will remind you of sweet English peas. Make several hours in advance and reheat just before serving, or serve at room temperature.

Serves 6

2 tablespoons olive oil
2 medium yellow onions, chopped
4 garlic cloves, minced
4 pounds young tender fava beans in the pod,
    shelled (about 4 cups), unpeeled
¼ cup plus 1 tablespoon chopped fresh cilantro
½ teaspoon crushed red pepper flakes
3 cups peeled, seeded, and chopped fresh or
    canned tomatoes
1 teaspoon fresh lemon juice
Coarse salt and freshly ground black pepper

In a large saucepan, heat the olive oil over medium heat. Add the onions and cook until they begin to turn golden brown, about 12 minutes. Add the garlic and stir for 2 minutes. Reduce the heat to low, add the fava beans and cilantro, and cook, stirring occasionally, for 2 to 3 minutes. Add the red pepper flakes and tomatoes, partly cover, and simmer until the sauce has thickened, 30 to 40 minutes.

Add the lemon juice and season to taste with salt and pepper. Serve warm or at room temperature.

Stewed Tomatoes and Eggplant

This simple autumn vegetarian stew of eggplant and vine-ripened tomatoes is flavored with lots of garlic and basil. The tomatoes and eggplant are cooked separately to retain their individual flavors, then combined just before serving. Serve alongside skewers of well-seasoned pork or lamb at your next barbecue. Perfect for entertaining, it's another one that you can make a day in advance, and you can serve it hot, warm, or at room temperature.

Serves 6

2 eggplants (about 2 pounds), cut into 1-inch
    cubes
Coarse salt
$1/4$ cup olive oil
4 garlic cloves, thinly sliced
4 medium ripe red tomatoes, peeled, seeded,
    and chopped
Freshly ground black pepper
20 fresh basil leaves, torn into small pieces,
    plus basil tops for garnish

Place the eggplant in a colander and sprinkle with salt. Let sit for 30 minutes.

Preheat the oven to 400°F.

Rinse the eggplant under cold water and pat dry with paper towels. Toss the eggplant with 3 tablespoons of the olive oil and place in a single layer on a baking sheet. Bake until golden and tender, 15 to 20 minutes. Remove from the oven and set aside.

Heat the remaining 1 tablespoon olive oil in a large frying pan over medium heat. Add the garlic and cook, stirring, for 1 minute. Do not let the garlic brown. Add the tomatoes and simmer until thickened and reduced to a sauce, 20 to 30 minutes. Add the eggplant and season to taste with salt and pepper.

To serve, toss the stew with the basil leaves and place in a serving bowl. Garnish with the basil tops.

Warm Indian Tomatoes with Spicy Chiles

This is the essence of simplicity—these spicy Indian tomatoes take less than ten minutes from start to finish. I serve them with steamed basmati or jasmine rice and a small bowl of yogurt alongside to cool the heat. You can adjust the amount of chiles to your own particular taste. If fresh coconut is available, by all means use it.

Serves 6

2 tablespoons unsalted butter
4 green onions, thinly sliced
2 teaspoons cumin seeds
2 teaspoons black mustard seeds
$3/4$ teaspoon ground turmeric
4 garlic cloves, minced
1 jalapeño, seeded and minced
6 large ripe red tomatoes, quartered
1 teaspoon sugar
$1/4$ cup grated unsweetened coconut
$1/2$ cup plain yogurt
Coarse salt and freshly ground black pepper
3 tablespoons chopped fresh cilantro

Melt the butter in a large saucepan over medium heat. Add the green onions, cumin seeds, mustard seeds, turmeric, garlic, and jalapeño and stir for 15 seconds. Add the tomatoes and stir until the tomatoes are hot, 2 to 3 minutes. Remove the pan from the heat.

Add the sugar, coconut, and yogurt and stir together. Season to taste with salt and pepper. Place in a serving bowl and garnish with the cilantro.

beverages, ketchup, condiments, and a few desserts

Tomato Juice

There's nothing like a glass of ice-cold, freshly made tomato juice, far better than anything you'd ever buy in a bottle or can. And it just takes a big batch of the most flavorful tomatoes available and a little effort. Use it for Bloody Marys or add a squeeze of lemon to each glass and serve with cucumber and tomato sandwiches for a late-summer lunch. This can also be made with yellow tomatoes.

Makes 6 cups

5 pounds ripe red tomatoes, cored and
   quartered
1 small red onion
1 stalk celery with leaves
Sugar
Coarse salt and freshly ground black pepper

Place the tomatoes, onion, and celery in a large pot set over medium heat. Cover and cook, stirring occasionally, until the tomatoes are soft, about 30 minutes. Let cool. Remove the onion and celery and discard.

Pass the tomatoes through a food mill fitted with the fine blade or a fine sieve. Discard the solids. Measure the juice and return it to the cleaned pot. For each 4 cups tomato juice, add 1 teaspoon sugar, 1 teaspoon salt, and pepper to taste. Stir the tomato juice over medium heat to dissolve the sugar and salt. As soon as they are dissolved, remove the juice from the heat and cool.

Taste and season with salt. Chill, and serve within 3 days.

Easy Does It

Everybody has his own special technique for getting ketchup out of the bottle. Some smack the bottom of the bottle with their palms, others give it a gentle coaxing with a knife inserted into the neck of the bottle, while others, those in the know apparently, tap the neck several times with the side of their hands. When it does finally come out of the bottle, it comes rolling out at a good twenty-five miles a year, about three-thousandths of a mile an hour. But who's counting? To calculate the speed of the flow, there is a device called a Bostwickometer, a special chute-like contraption that measures the speed at which ketchup travels.

The Best Bloody Mary

For years, this poor drink has been relegated as merely the cure for hangovers. How unfair! A good Bloody Mary is refreshing, packs a real punch, and is even somewhat healthy (especially if it is really a Virgin Mary, without the vodka). For a great variation on a classic theme, make a Bloody Caesar by substituting a cup of bottled clam juice for one cup of the tomato juice and using lime juice in place of lemon.

Serves 6

2 lemon wedges
2 tablespoons celery salt
Coarse salt and freshly ground black pepper
8 jiggers 100-proof vodka (1½ cups)
2 tablespoons fresh lemon juice
2 teaspoons Worcestershire sauce
1 teaspoon Tabasco sauce
1 tablespoon prepared horseradish
4 cups Tomato Juice (page 234) or commercial tomato juice
6 small stalks celery with leafy tops

To prepare the glasses, rub the rims with the lemon wedges. On a saucer, combine the celery salt, 1 teaspoon salt, and ¼ teaspoon black pepper. Invert the glasses and dip the rims into the celery salt mixture. Set the glasses aside and reserve the celery salt.

In a pitcher, combine the vodka, lemon juice, Worcestershire sauce, Tabasco, horseradish, tomato juice, and a large pinch of the celery salt mixture. Season to taste with salt and pepper.

To serve, fill the glasses with ice and pour in the Bloody Mary mixture. Stick a stalk of celery in each glass and serve immediately.

Sparkling Tomato Juice

Tomato juice and sparkling water garnished with cucumbers, mint, and lemon make a refreshing and almost-no-calorie drink.

Makes 6 cups; serves 6

2 cups Tomato Juice (page 234) or commercial tomato juice
3 cups sparkling water
1 cup springwater
½ English cucumber, peeled, seeded, and coarsely chopped, plus 6 cucumber slices
1 tablespoon chopped fresh mint
2 tablespoons fresh lemon juice
6 lemon slices

Combine the tomato juice, sparkling water, springwater, chopped cucumber, mint, and lemon juice in a pitcher. Stir together and let sit for 1 hour in the refrigerator. Strain.

Serve chilled, garnished with the lemon and cucumber slices.

Golden Mary

Mix yellow vine-ripened tomatoes with tequila, cilantro, garlic, ginger, and lime juice for one of the best drinks ever. These are a snap to make, but make sure you make a big batch—served over crushed ice, they go quickly.

Serves 6

2 lime wedges
Coarse salt and freshly ground black pepper
Large pinch of ground cumin
8 jiggers best-quality tequila (1½ cups)
¼ cup fresh lime juice
1 tablespoon minced fresh ginger
¼ cup chopped fresh cilantro
4 cups Tomato Juice (page 234), made with
    yellow tomatoes
6 green onions, trimmed
6 yellow cherry tomatoes, split

To prepare the glasses, rub the rims with the lime wedges. On a saucer, combine 1 tablespoon salt, ¼ teaspoon black pepper, and cumin. Invert the glasses and dip the rims into the salt mixture. Set the glasses aside.

In a blender, puree the tequila, lime juice, ginger, cilantro, and tomato juice until smooth. Season to taste with salt and pepper.

To serve, fill the glasses with ice cubes and pour in the drink mixture. Stick a green onion in each glass and a cherry tomato on the rim. Serve immediately.

Tomato "Martini"

This clear, concentrated tomato nectar takes only minimal effort if you start it a day in advance. Drain crushed ripe tomatoes overnight and serve the juice in iced martini glasses garnished with colorful cherry tomatoes, diced cucumbers, and fresh mint. This is a favorite of Paul Bertolli, chef at Oliveto's in Oakland.

Serves 6

6 pounds ripe red tomatoes, quartered
Coarse salt
18 assorted cherry tomatoes
¼ English cucumber, peeled, seeded, and finely
    diced
2 teaspoons chopped fresh mint

Place the tomatoes in a bowl and with your hands, crush them well. Place the tomatoes in a cheesecloth-lined fine strainer set over a large bowl. Let the tomatoes drip for 24 hours in the refrigerator.

About an hour before serving, press the tomatoes slightly with your hands to extract more liquid and continue to drain for 1 hour.

Bring a saucepan of water to a boil. Using a knife, make a cross in the bottom of each tomato. Add the tomatoes to the water and simmer until the skins curl around the crosses, 5 to 10 seconds. Remove the tomatoes and place in a bowl of ice water. Drain and peel.

Taste the essence and season with salt. Pour the essence into glasses. Distribute the tomatoes, cucumbers, and mint among the glasses. Serve immediately.

Fresh Tomato Ketchup

Is there any other word in the American vocabulary that is so familiar to all of us and yet it has two distinctly different common spellings? All sizes, shapes, and kinds of ketchup line the grocery store shelves today—the array is mind-boggling. This homemade version is a flavorful variation on the theme. You will need to sterilize the jars and process them for twelve minutes in a boiling-water bath.

Makes 4 $^1/_2$-pint jars or 4 cups

5 pounds ripe red tomatoes, quartered
3 medium red onions, finely chopped
1 red bell pepper, cored and seeded
1 garlic clove, thinly sliced
1 tablespoon black peppercorns
1 tablespoon mustard seeds
1 tablespoon allspice berries
2 teaspoons whole cloves
2 teaspoons celery seeds
1 thin slice fresh ginger
1 cinnamon stick
2 bay leaves
$^1/_2$ cup packed dark brown sugar
1 teaspoon sweet paprika
$^1/_4$ teaspoon ground mace
1 cup cider vinegar
1 teaspoon coarse salt
Large pinch of cayenne

To sterilize the jars, wash them in hot soapy water. Rinse well. Bring a large pot of water to a boil. Add 4 $^1/_2$-pint jars and lids and boil 1 minute. Remove with tongs and drain.

Place the tomatoes, onions, bell pepper, and garlic in a large pot. Bring to a boil over high heat, reduce the heat to medium-low, and simmer, stirring occasionally, until the vegetables are very soft, about 30 minutes. Pass through the finest blade of a food mill to make a semi-smooth puree. Alternatively, puree in the blender until smooth and pass through a fine strainer. Place the puree back in the cleaned soup pot.

Place the peppercorns, mustard seeds, allspice berries, cloves, celery seeds, ginger, cinnamon stick, and bay leaves on a piece of cheesecloth and tie it up to form a bag. Add to the tomatoes, along with the brown sugar, paprika, mace, cider vinegar, salt, and cayenne. Simmer slowly, stirring frequently, until the ketchup is very thick, $1^1/_2$ to 2 hours. Remove the cheesecloth bag and discard.

While the ketchup is still hot, pour into the sterilized jars, leaving $^1/_4$ inch of headroom. Seal and process in a boiling-water bath for 12 minutes. Remove and cool.

Barbecue Sauce

Everybody has his or her own favorite barbecue sauce, and the controversy rages: should it contain molasses, ginger, mustard . . . ? In America, how to make the perfect barbecue sauce can be the cause of a family argument, a cook-off, or a showdown. This one is great for marinating pork or beef ribs or chicken, perfect for summer grilling.

Makes about 1 1/2 cups

1 tablespoon vegetable oil
1 small yellow onion, minced
1 cup tomato puree
1/4 cup Dijon mustard
1/4 cup fresh lemon juice
1/4 cup packed brown sugar
2 tablespoons Worcestershire sauce
2 tablespoons hot sauce, such as Tabasco
1/2 teaspoon ground allspice
1/2 teaspoon ground ginger
Coarse salt and freshly ground black pepper

In a large saucepan, heat the vegetable oil over medium heat. Add the onion and cook, stirring, until soft, about 7 minutes. Add the tomato puree, mustard, lemon juice, brown sugar, Worcestershire sauce, hot sauce, allspice, ginger, 1/4 cup water, and salt and pepper to taste. Bring to a boil, turn down the heat, and simmer slowly, uncovered, until the sauce thickens, 5 to 10 minutes.

The sauce can be refrigerated for up to 3 days or frozen for up to 1 month.

Pickled Tomatoes

Years ago, I went to a class that Mary Sue Milliken and Susan Feniger, of Border Grill in Los Angeles, were teaching in San Francisco. I still remember the flavors of their food—and I became hopelessly and forever hooked on these Indian-inspired, spicy, pickled tomatoes. These can be served as soon as they are cool, but they are best when they have mellowed for two or three days.

Makes 6 to 8 cups

8 small ripe red tomatoes, peeled and
    quartered
12 green onions, thinly sliced diagonally
2 serrano or jalapeño peppers, halved and
    thinly sliced diagonally
1 tablespoon crushed black peppercorns
1 tablespoon black mustard seeds
1/3 cup grated fresh ginger
8 garlic cloves, minced
2 teaspoons ground turmeric
2 tablespoons ground cumin
2 teaspoons sweet paprika
1/3 cup olive oil
1/2 cup balsamic vinegar
1/4 cup red wine vinegar
1 1/2 tablespoons coarse salt
1/3 cup packed light brown sugar

Place the tomatoes, green onions, and chiles in a serving bowl.

In a small bowl, combine the black peppercorns, mustard seeds, ginger, garlic, turmeric, cumin, and paprika.

In a large saucepan, heat the olive oil until it is almost smoking. Add the combined spices and stir vigorously for 2 to 3 minutes. Pour this mixture over the tomatoes, green onions, and chiles and stir together.

In a small saucepan, bring the balsamic and red wine vinegar, salt, and sugar to a boil over high heat. Immediately pour the vinegar over the tomatoes, green onions, and chiles. Stir together, mixing well, and cool to room temperature.

Ketchup Comes to America

E very culture around the world had a variation of the earliest forms of ketchup made by the fermentation and salting process. Some countries used fish in the fermentation process, while others used soybeans along with vinegar, wine, brandy, or liquor. These sauces [were] used to preserve and flavor food or even disguise the taste and smell. One such fish sauce, *ke-tsiap,* was a spicy pickled-fish condiment used in seventeenth-century China. It is thought to be the precursor to the name "ketchup."

In the 1700s, North America, so influenced by Britain, continued to use England's popular mushroom, fish, and walnut ketchups. In 1727, a non-tomato ketchup recipe, believed to be the first recipe recorded in English, included anchovies, shallots, white wine vinegar, white wines, and a myriad of spices such as horseradish, lemon peel, ginger, and cloves. The first-known tomato ketchup recipe in America was published in 1812 by Philadelphia physician, scientist, and horticulturist James Mease, although multiple versions of tomato ketchup were undoubtedly made before that time. Mease's recipe resembled [the] tomato sauce made by French Creole refugees from Haiti. Unlike previous ketchups, this recipe did not strain the tomatoes, which made it thicker than its predecessors, or add many spices.

Another recipe from around the same time called for slicing and salting the tomatoes and allowing them to stand for two days before reducing them and adding spices. The author suggested using a "spiritus liquor" to prevent mold!

In the early years, recipes for tomato ketchup were considered secret and confidential information by manufacturers. Around 1900, competition was so great and ketchup [so] readily available, a gallon cost twenty to sixty cents. A decade later, more than 138 brands of ketchup were produced. Today more than one hundred brands are produced, not to mention regional and gourmet brands.

From Andrew Smith, *Pure Ketchup*

Green Tomato Pickle

When summer comes to a raging halt and you still have green tomatoes on the vine, here's one solution. Pick firm green tomatoes, cut them into wedges, and pickle them in vinegar and salt with garlic, herbs, and black pepper for a few weeks. When you crave a hint of summer, open up a jar and serve them with grilled meats, over pasta, or tucked into sandwiches. If processed for longer storage, they will keep in a cool dark place for several months. Once you've opened the jar, however, store in the refrigerator and use within two weeks. But they don't need to be processed—just store in the refrigerator and eat within seven to ten days.

Makes 4 pints

1¹/₂ cups tarragon vinegar
1¹/₂ cups white wine vinegar
¹/₂ cup coarse salt
³/₄ cup packed brown sugar
¹/₂ teaspoon crushed red pepper flakes
3 pounds green tomatoes, cut into wedges
1 small head cauliflower (about 1 pound), cut
    into small florets
1 teaspoon black peppercorns
1 teaspoon white peppercorns
8 sprigs fresh tarragon
8 garlic cloves, thinly sliced

Wash and sterilize the jars (see page 237).

In a large saucepan, combine the tarragon vinegar, white wine vinegar, salt, brown sugar, crushed pepper flakes, and 1 cup water and bring to a boil over high heat; boil for 2 minutes. Add the tomatoes and cauliflower florets, cover, and simmer until the vegetables are hot but still crunchy, about 30 seconds.

Pack the tomatoes, cauliflower florets, black and white peppercorns, tarragon sprigs, and garlic into the sterilized jars. Bring the vinegar solution to a boil and pour it into the jars, leaving ¹/₄ inch headspace. Cover and seal.

For longer storage, process in a boiling-water bath, completely submerged, for 10 minutes. Place in a cool dark place and let sit for 2 weeks before serving. Alternatively, just seal the jars and refrigerate; use within 7 to 10 days.

Sweet Spiced Yellow Tomato and Golden Raisin Chutney

There are thousands of tomato chutney recipes. This one, using the best vine-ripened backyard tomatoes, represents the best of summer. The golden yellow-hued chutney meets its match in grilled pork tenderloin or duck breasts.

Makes about 3 cups

3 pounds yellow tomatoes, peeled, seeded, and chopped
1 large yellow onion, minced
1 cup golden raisins
1 cup packed light brown sugar
1 cup cider vinegar
3 tablespoons grated fresh ginger
2 jalapeños, seeded and chopped
1 teaspoon mustard seeds
$^3/_4$ teaspoon ground cumin
$^1/_4$ teaspoon ground allspice
$1^1/_2$ teaspoons coarse salt

Wash and sterilize three half-pint jars (see page 237).

In a large saucepan over medium-high heat, combine the tomatoes, onion, raisins, sugar, vinegar, ginger, jalapeños, mustard seeds, cumin, allspice, and salt. Bring to a boil, stirring occasionally. When the sugar has dissolved, reduce the heat to low and simmer until the mixture thickens, 30 to 45 minutes.

Ladle the hot chutney into jars, leaving $^1/_4$ inch of headspace. Cover and seal. (If processing is desired for longer shelf life, process the covered jars in a boiling-water bath for 15 minutes.)

Today's Ketchup Is Thicker!

 Before 1906 commercial ketchup was thinner, 5 to 15 percent pulp compared to our 25 to 35 percent pulp we have today. Then the narrow-neck bottles became the industry standard. It reduced the amount of air that came in contact with the ketchup, turning the ketchup a dark, unappetizing color. However, it was hard to pour thick ketchup through a narrow mouth. Heinz went so far as to incorporate the slow-pouring ketchup into an advertising blitz, but later went on to repackage their ketchup in a wider-mouth bottle.

"Heinz was also the one to develop single-serving ketchup pouches perfect for fast food eateries. The public loved them and sales of single-serve packets grew from half a million cases to five million cases in ten years. In 1983, they introduced plastic squeezable bottles, and in the 1990s, 60 percent of all ketchup brands are sold in plastic containers. Today ketchup can be found in the smallest individual packets all the way up to whopping sixty-four-ounce plastic bottles."

From Andrew Smith, *Pure Ketchup*

Tomato-Date Chutney

Sweet and tangy, this relish gives a real lift to lamb chops, pork chops, or your favorite Indian-style curry dish. The recipe was inspired by Marcella Friel, who likes to use the dried tomato halves packed in bulk as opposed to the tomato halves packed in oil. The flavors of the chutney get even better if you make it several days in advance; store it in the refrigerator until you are ready to use it. You will find unsweetened coconut in any health food store.

Makes 1½ cups

½ cup dried tomato halves (about 12 pieces)
⅓ cup pitted dried dates
3 tablespoons grated and unsweetened dried coconut
¼ cup fresh lemon juice
1 tablespoon grated fresh ginger
½ teaspoon ground fennel
½ teaspoon ground coriander
3 tablespoons chopped fresh flat-leaf parsley
¼ teaspoon coarse salt
⅛ teaspoon cayenne

Soak the tomatoes and dates in 1 cup boiling water for 5 minutes. Drain, reserving the soaking liquid. Chop the tomatoes.

Combine the tomatoes, dates, coconut, lemon juice, ginger, fennel, coriander, parsley, salt, and cayenne in a bowl and stir together. Moisten the mixture as needed with the soaking liquid to attain a thick paste. Cover and refrigerate until ready to serve.

Italian Green Tomato Jam

The last time I left Italy, my chef friend Giovanna Ascari gave me a small jar of jam. It was perfect for boiled meats, as an accompaniment to thin shavings of Parmigiano-Reggiano, or as a filling for hot rolls. The jam keeps for months in the refrigerator and needs no processing.

Makes 1½ to 2 cups

5 pounds green tomatoes
4 cups sugar
Peel of 2 lemons, removed with a vegetable peeler

Halve the tomatoes crosswise and squeeze out the juice through a strainer. Discard the seeds. Reserve the juice. Cut the tomatoes into 1-inch pieces, place in a bowl with the sugar, tomato juice, and lemon peel and let sit overnight at room temperature.

The next day, place the mixture in a saucepan and bring to a boil over high heat. Reduce the heat to medium and simmer for 10 minutes. With a slotted spoon, transfer the tomatoes to a clean bowl. Reduce the juice until very thick, 20 to 30 minutes. Pour the tomatoes and juice back into the bowl and stir together. Let sit overnight at room temperature.

For the next 1 or 2 days, repeat the simmering process until the tomatoes are quite dry and the juice is thick.

Pour the mixture into sterilized (see page 237) jars and store in the refrigerator for at least 1 month before using.

Tomato and Lemon Preserves

When your garden is bursting with tomatoes at the height of summer, make a batch of these preserves. Then, on a cold winter's morning, spread the sweet and tart preserves on hot scones, toasted English muffins, or toast for a perfect breakfast. No need to process the preserves in a water bath, just sterilize the jars and seal. The preserves are fine for up to six months.

Makes 4 cups

4 pounds small ripe red or yellow tomatoes, or
   a combination, peeled and cored
4 cups sugar
Eight 2-inch strips lemon peel, removed with a
   vegetable peeler
1 lemon, thinly sliced

Wash and sterilize the jars (see page 237).

Place the tomatoes, sugar, and lemon peel in a bowl. Stir together, being careful not to break the tomatoes. Cover with plastic wrap and let stand in the refrigerator overnight.

The next day, drain off the juice and place it in a saucepan. Discard the lemon peel. Bring to a boil and continue to boil until the mixture reaches the thread stage (215°F). Add the tomatoes and sliced lemon and cook until the jam is clear and thick, 10 to 20 minutes.

Fill the sterilized jars with the mixture and seal.

Tomato Tartar Sauce

For grilled or crispy batter-fried fish, give old-fashioned tartar sauce a face-lift with a few spoonfuls of tomato paste. This will keep in the refrigerator for up to a week.

Makes 1 1/2 cups

1 recipe Mayonnaise (page 38)
2 1/2 tablespoons tomato paste
2 green onions (white and green parts), thinly
   sliced
2 tablespoons capers
1/4 cup minced gherkins
1 teaspoon Dijon mustard
2 teaspoons fresh lemon juice
1/2 teaspoon sweet paprika
Pinch of cayenne
Coarse salt and freshly ground black pepper

In a bowl, stir together the mayonnaise and tomato paste until well mixed. Add the green onions, capers, gherkins, mustard, lemon juice, paprika, and cayenne. Season to taste with salt and pepper. Refrigerate until ready to use.

Sun-Dried Tomato Tapenade

Sun-dried tomatoes are available sun- or oven-dried, sometimes packed in oil. The ones packed in oil are sweeter, more flavorful, and ready to use straight from the jar.

Makes 1¹/₂ cups

3 anchovy fillets, soaked in cold water for 10 minutes, drained, patted dry, and mashed with a fork
1 cup cured black olives, such as Niçoise or Kalamata, pitted
2 garlic cloves, minced
3 tablespoons capers, chopped
¹/₄ teaspoon grated lemon zest
¹/₂ teaspoon herbes de Provence
2 tablespoons fresh lemon juice
¹/₂ cup oil-cured Sun-Dried Tomatoes, finely chopped, 2 tablespoons oil reserved (page 13)
Coarse salt and freshly ground black pepper

Place the anchovies, olives, garlic, capers, lemon zest, and herbes de Provence in the bowl of a food processor. Pulse a few times until a rough paste. Add the lemon juice, tomatoes, and the 2 tablespoons reserved oil. Pulse a couple of times. Season to taste with salt and pepper. Store in the refrigerator until ready to use, or for up to several days. Bring to room temperature before using.

What's Inside Has Not Changed

Not since New Coke–Classic Coke spent a billion dollars to change its image on the can has any company followed suit in such a major way. Not until Heinz Ketchup. This is the stuff that has graced every American table and refrigerator for years, used to slather on hamburgers, french fries, and meat loaf. They didn't change the bottle size or shape, not even the sweet-tart tomato sauce inside. Nope, instead all they did was to update the label. For the first time in fifty-six years, the H. J. Heinz Co. traded in the classic black lettering for a more colorful eye-catching label. The white background was replaced by images that creep towards the next millenium. There is a smiling sun wearing headphones on one label, a moppy-haired cook in a chef's hat squirting ketchup in the direction of a big chunky hamburger, and an overstuffed picnic basket being carried off by a crew of ants.

" 'We're not really changing the icon,' " Heinz's chairman, Anthony F. X. O'Reilly said. " 'We're adjusting it for our main audience, which is children.' "

From James Barron,
"Overhauling a Classic Condiment," *The San Francisco Chronicle,* 3 July 1996

Tomato Upside-Down Spice Cake

This old-timey tomato cake is one my great-grandmother used to make with heirloom tomatoes from her garden. Much ahead of her time, she didn't know that the tomatoes she grew would be chic one hundred years later.

Serves 8 to 10

■ topping
4 tablespoons unsalted butter
$1/4$ cup packed brown sugar
2 teaspoons grated fresh ginger
2 small ripe red tomatoes, peeled, seeded, and
  thinly sliced

■ cake
$1^1/2$ cups all-purpose flour
2 teaspoons baking powder
Large pinch of salt
1 teaspoon ground ginger
$1/2$ teaspoon ground cloves
$1/4$ teaspoon ground cinnamon
$1/4$ teaspoon ground mace
8 tablespoons (1 stick) unsalted butter, at room
  temperature
$3/4$ cup sugar
$1/2$ cup molasses
2 large eggs, separated
1 teaspoon vanilla
$1/2$ cup milk

1 cup heavy cream
1 tablespoon confectioners' sugar
A few drops of vanilla

Preheat the oven to 350°F. Butter a 9-inch round cake pan.

For the topping, melt the butter, brown sugar, and ginger in the cake pan over medium-low heat. Cover with a single layer of the tomato slices. If you have more tomatoes, reserve for another use.

For the cake, sift the flour, baking powder, salt, ginger, cloves, cinnamon, and mace together.

Cream the butter and sugar together in a large bowl. Add the molasses, then add the egg yolks one yolk at a time, beating well after each addition. Add the vanilla and mix well. Add the milk alternately with the dry ingredients, beating well after each addition.

Beat the egg whites until stiff. Fold the whites into the cake batter. Spread the batter over the tomatoes and bake until a skewer inserted into the center comes out clean, 45 to 50 minutes.

Let the cake cool for at least 15 minutes, then run a knife around the edges of the pan to loosen it. Turn the cake over onto a serving platter and let it sit, still in the pan, for another 5 minutes. Remove the pan.

To serve, whip the cream and flavor with the confectioners' sugar and vanilla.

Cut the cake into wedges and serve the cream on the side.

Love-Apple Chocolate Cake

Odd as it may seem, for years, tomatoes have been added to chocolate cakes with great results. My grandmother would pulverize green or red tomatoes and add them to her cakes with thick, rich, and chocolatey results. Frost with your favorite chocolate icing.

Serves 8 to 10

4 ounces bittersweet chocolate, finely chopped
1/2 cup plus 1 tablespoon half-and-half
3/4 cup packed light brown sugar
2 cups sifted cake flour
1 teaspoon baking soda
1/4 teaspoon salt
8 tablespoons (1 stick) unsalted butter, at room
  temperature
3/4 cup granulated sugar
2 large eggs, separated
2 medium ripe red tomatoes, peeled, seeded,
  chopped, drained, and pureed (about 1 cup)
1 teaspoon vanilla

Preheat the oven to 350°F. Butter and flour two 9-inch round cake pans.

Place the chocolate, 1/2 cup of the half-and-half, and the brown sugar in a bowl set over a pan of boiling water, or in a double boiler. Do not let the water touch the bottom of the pan. Stir occasionally until the mixture is smooth, 5 minutes. Remove from the heat.

Sift the flour, baking soda, and salt together.

In a large bowl, cream the butter and granulated sugar until light and fluffy. Add the egg yolks one at a time, beating well after each addition.

In a small bowl, mix together the tomato puree, the remaining 1 tablespoon half-and-half, and the vanilla. Add to the butter mixture alternately with the flour. Mix in the chocolate mixture.

Beat the egg whites until stiff but not dry. Fold into the batter.

Pour into the prepared pans, dividing it evenly. Bake until a skewer inserted into the center comes out clean, about 25 minutes. Cool on a wire rack.

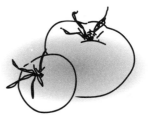

I n America, in the fifties, convenience food was all the rage. Backed by a tremendous amount of marketing and promotion, canned Campbell's tomato soup was at its pinnacle, and Campbell's was sending out cooking pamphlets, doing store demonstrations, and distributing cookbooks filled with recipes like this one for tomato soup cake. From *Campbell's Cooking with Soup:*

"Tomato soup gives a wonder-what-it-is flavor and rosy color to cakes and cookies. Once tried, these are the unusual cake specialties you will want to make again and again. Some women win blue ribbons at fairs with tomato soup cakes; others bake them for holiday gifts. Most women make them just for the pleasure of baking an easy cake with fascinating flavor—a little spicy, a little tangy, and altogether special. Cake mix users will find that spicy cakes made with tomato soup have more than extra flavor.

Rosy Chiffon Cake

Serves 8 to 10

2 1/4 cups sifted cake flour
1 1/2 cups sugar
3 teaspoons baking powder
1 teaspoon baking soda
1 1/2 teaspoons allspice
1 teaspoon ground cinnamon
1/2 teaspoon ground cloves

1 can (10 3/4 ounces) condensed tomato soup
1/2 cup salad oil
1/4 cup water
5 egg yolks
1 cup egg whites (7 to 8)
1/2 teaspoon cream of tartar

Preheat oven to 325°F. Sift together flour, sugar, baking powder, soda, and spices into mixing bowl. Make a well in flour mixture; add soup, oil, water, and egg yolks; beat until smooth. Beat egg whites with cream of tartar together in large mixing bowl until they form very stiff peaks. Pour egg yolk mixture gradually over whites, gently folding with rubber spatula until completely blended. Pour into ungreased 10-inch tube pan. Bake at 325°F for 65 to 70 minutes or until top springs back when lightly touched. Remove from oven and turn pan upside down over neck of funnel; let cool at least 1 hour. Loosen cake around edge and tube of pan with spatula; remove from pan and glaze if desired."

Italian Green Tomato Tart

Mincemeat, a rich, spicy autumn preserve, is usually made with green tomatoes, apples and other fruits, spices, ground meat or "mince," and suet—a solid white beef or sheep fat. I have omitted the mince and used butter in place of suet. Serve the tart warm, in its rich cornmeal crust, during the autumn months for an unforgettable dessert. Make the pastry and "mincemeat" a day or two in advance if you like. Then assemble and bake the tart the day you want to serve it.

Serves 8

■ filling
5 medium green tomatoes (about 1³/₄ pounds),
    chopped
Coarse salt
³/₄ cup packed brown sugar
³/₄ cup golden raisins
3 tablespoons unsalted butter
1 teaspoon ground cinnamon
¹/₂ teaspoon freshly grated nutmeg
¹/₄ teaspoon ground cloves
2 teaspoons grated lemon zest
3 tablespoons fresh lemon juice
1 large tart apple, such as McIntosh or
    Gravenstein, peeled and chopped

■ pastry
10 tablespoons (1¹/₄ sticks) unsalted butter, at
    room temperature
³/₄ cup granulated sugar

3 large egg yolks
1¹/₂ cups all-purpose flour, plus more if needed
¹/₂ cup plus 2 tablespoons cornmeal or polenta
¹/₄ teaspoon salt

1 cup heavy cream
Confectioners' sugar
¹/₄ teaspoon vanilla

For the filling, sprinkle the tomatoes lightly with salt and let stand for 1 hour.

Place the tomatoes in a large saucepan, cover with cold water, bring to a boil, and boil for 5 minutes. Drain and return the tomatoes to the pan. Add the brown sugar, raisins, butter, and ¹/₂ cup water. Bring to a boil over high heat. Reduce the heat to low and simmer for 20 minutes, adding water as necessary so the bottom doesn't scorch.

Add the cinnamon, nutmeg, cloves, lemon zest, lemon juice, and apple. Bring to a boil over high heat, reduce the heat to medium, and cook, stirring occasionally, until the mixture is thick, about 20 minutes. Cool.

For the pastry, in a stand mixer, using the paddle, cream the butter and sugar until light and fluffy, 1 to 2 minutes. Add the egg yolks one at a time, beating thoroughly after each addition. Sift the flour, cornmeal, and salt into the creamed mixture and beat on low speed until the dough comes together. Turn out onto a floured surface and knead lightly, adding a little flour if needed, until the dough is no longer sticky. Shape into a disk, wrap in plastic, and let rest in the refrigerator 20 minutes.

Preheat the oven to 375°F.

Cut the dough in half and return half to the refrigerator. Press the remaining dough into a fluted 9-inch tart pan with a removable bottom. Build up the sides with the trimmings. Flute the edges.

Spoon the mincemeat into the tart shell and spread it evenly. Roll out the remaining dough ¼ inch thick. With a small heart-shaped cookie cutter, cut as many shapes as possible from the dough. Place them on top of the mincemeat, starting on the outside, overlapping the shapes slightly in concentric rings and covering the entire top. Bake the tart for 35 to 40 minutes, until golden. Cool 20 minutes on a rack.

Whip the heavy cream to soft peaks and flavor with confectioners' sugar to taste and the vanilla. Serve warm or at room temperature.

Tomato Sorbet

Sorbets or sorbettos like this are often served in fancy French or Italian restaurants as an appetizer or between courses to cleanse the palate. Adding sugar to the mix, coupled with the sweetness of the tomatoes, means you can do the same with this one—or serve it as dessert. You can make the sorbet mixture a day in advance and freeze it then, but for the smoothest texture, freeze it just before serving. Thanks to Emma Afra of Rome for her help and inspiration.

Makes 1 generous quart

8 ripe red tomatoes (about 3^1/$_2$ pounds), peeled,
    seeded, and coarsely chopped
One 2-inch piece lemon peel, removed with a
    vegetable peeler
^{1}/$_4$ cup fresh lemon juice
1^1/$_3$ cups sugar
Pinch of coarse salt
1 large egg white

Put the tomatoes through a food mill fitted with the finest blade into a bowl, or use a food processor and then strain. Add the lemon peel, lemon juice, sugar, and salt. Stir with a wooden spoon until the sugar dissolves.

In another bowl, beat the egg white until stiff. Add to the tomato mixture and stir together. Remove the lemon peel and discard. Freeze the mixture in an ice cream machine. Place in the freezer until ready to serve.

growing tomatoes

How to Grow the Perfect Tomato?

Happily for the millions of us who devour tomatoes, they are prolific plants, averaging about four pounds per plant. Almost anyone can raise a crop of mouthwatering tomatoes, whether you plant hybrids or heirlooms, cherries, or slicers, in raised beds or containers. A few key steps will help you select appropriate varieties for your own environment, increase your yield, and enhance the flavors of the tomatoes that you grow.

Know Your Microclimate

Know what your local weather is inclined to do. Remember that tomatoes love a sunny (but not blazing) warm climate and need to be sheltered from wind. Indeed, they can grow as perennials in a tropical climate, but most of us grow them as annuals, pulling them up at the end of the year. Compare varieties for growing season, harvest time, and growing requirements. Wherever you live, plant tomatoes in the ground after any chance of frost, and when nighttime temperatures are consistently above 55°F. Your local county or university extension agent can provide valuable information about microclimates.

If you do call your county extension office, ask them about the soil in your area. This information will give you insight into common local diseases or pests. They will be familiar with what varieties grow successfully in your area. Consider testing the soil; gardening supply catalogs sell soil testers.

Sow Your Own Seeds

So you like a certain tomato variety and you want to grow it again next year? What you need to do is save the seeds of almost any tomato and your chances are pretty good—as long as the tomato isn't a hybrid! Hybrids are a controlled cross between two different parent lines bred to reproduce the best characteristics of both. Hybrid seeds frequently revert back to one or the other ancestor and produce inferior fruit.

Pick a tomato that is fully ripe. Cut it crosswise in half and squeeze the seeds and liquid that surrounds them into a bowl or a glass jar uncovered in a warm place. Let the mixture sit for several days, stirring occasionally, until it ferments. How will you know? The mixture will divide and leave you with the "extraneous materials" on top; the good seeds will fall to the bottom. Discard the top matter, rinse the seeds, and let dry on a plate. When they are completely dry, store in an airtight container in a cool place until next growing season.

Plant a Variety of Tomatoes

Decide what tomatoes to plant according to your needs. Are you interested in tomatoes for salads, slicing tomatoes for sandwiches, or in cooking, canning, or making tomato sauce for winter use? Do you prefer reds that pack more punch than the yellows and pinks? Ideally, planting an assortment will give you a variety of options and let you have a colorful medley as well. A mix of early- (50 days to harvest), mid- (65 to 80 days), and late- (80+ days) season tomatoes will provide tomatoes that ripen throughout your entire growing season. Planting a variety also lets you experiment to find out what grows well for you.

Space

Consider the amount of space that you have available when choosing your plants. The indeterminate varieties of tomatoes need room, lots of room. They put out long branches or vines, as well as long roots, and keep going until they are pulled up or are killed by a frost. Staking or using cages to train the vines is particularly advisable for the indeterminate type of tomato plant. Indeterminate tomatoes ripen at various stages and produce abundantly throughout the entire growing season.

If space is limited, determinate tomatoes are a good choice. They are especially suitable for container and window box gardens. Determinate tomatoes are also referred to as bush tomatoes because of their small to medium size, ranging from about one and a half to four and a half feet. Staking

---

To Stake or Not to Stake

The advantage of staking tomatoes is that the plant's growth is controlled without being restricted. The vines can be trained and gently tied to the wire cage or stakes, allowing the offshoots to grow. The foliage produced shades the tomatoes as they grow and protects them from sunscald. The disadvantage is that it does become difficult to see all the leaves to check for insects and diseases.

If you tie the main stem of tomato plants to a sturdy stake and pinch off the offshoots, you will be able to plant more, placing them closer together, and move more freely between the plants. Fruit production will be somewhat less, however, and be more susceptible to the hot sun.

Whichever technique you use, make sure your stakes are sturdy. Buy substantial wood stakes about six feet long. Insert them before you begin transplanting your tomatoes to avoid root damage, and place them about one foot apart.

---

is advisable to keep the fruit off the ground. Determinate tomato plants yield one crop that ripens simultaneously during a short season.

Hybrid or Heirloom?

Diseases and pests are always a concern in a successful garden. Hybrid tomatoes, and other hybrid vegetables, have been developed to resist disease and adapt to shorter growing seasons. Abbreviations for what they are resistant to or tolerant of are listed on the seed package or in the catalog description. Hybrids are sturdy, disease-resistant productive plants, but the tomatoes often lack the full flavor that home gardeners strive for.

Recently, interest in heirloom tomatoes, also called old-fashioned or open-pollinated tomatoes, has increased greatly. Seed companies that offer heirloom seeds and plants are flourishing. Because heirloom plants generally do not have the disease resistance of hybrids, attention to healthy, disease-free soil is essential.

Growing Guidelines

Whether you get a jump start on the growing season by starting your plants indoors or plant seeds directly in the ground, optimum germination soil

> From him [in reference to his oldest friend in the world, George], I learned the basics: that tomatoes are likely to ripen faster if the plants are grown along a sheltered south wall; that seedlings planted in hillocks of earth are less likely to be washed out in late-spring rains; and most important of all, that cow manure is best when it is well rotted. None of those powdered, deodorized fertilizers for our garden, George decreed. Instead, a trip to the local dairy with burlap bag and rubber gloves, so that we could pick our compost fresh!"
>
> From Bert Greene, *Kitchen Bouquets*

temperatures lie between 75 and 85 degrees. A soil thermometer comes in handy for this. The best temperatures for seedling growth are daytime temperatures between 70 and 75 degrees and nighttime temperatures between 60 and 65 degrees.

Seedlings benefit from a hardening-off phase to get them accustomed to outdoor conditions before being placed in the soil. Keep them in a sunny place during the day, and cover the young plants at night if there is any chance of frost or chilly temperatures.

Prepare the soil by digging down about ten to twelve inches and adding organic materials or compost and any fertilizer or nutrients. Use a light hand with nitrogen additives, which will give great foliage, but few tomatoes. Place the stakes or whatever type of support you choose at this time. You will avoid disturbing the root system later on.

Place the plant deep in the soil with only the first, true leaves above the ground. Water tomatoes consistently and evenly, but moderately, and preferably early in the day. Avoid watering them from

> Keep a journal of what tomatoes (or other vegetables) you've planted where. Note growing patterns, care, problems, and which ones were your favorites for next year's planting. Your journal will come in handy when you're browsing through seed catalogs in the depth of winter. Take it out and read it when the days are short, snow covers the ground, and winter is carrying on much too long: It will remind you of what's to come.

overhead, because dirt can splash on the leaves and promote fungus problems. Once the plant has blossoms, cut back on watering. Check the soil with your finger or with a water gauge.

Tips

- Maintain soil pH of 6.0 to 7.0.

- Carefully tie each tomato plant to a cage or stake as it grows.

- Pinch off sideshoots or new leaf growth between the leaves and trunk.

- Pinch off the top of the plant once it has four blossoms to curb its growth so it will produce fruit and not foliage.

- For easier and more effective watering, use tubes or juice or coffee cans with one end open and the other pierced with several holes. Insert a tube or can in the ground by each tomato stem, letting it stick up a couple of inches above the ground so it will be easy to find later. Watering tubes help channel water toward the roots.

- Planting flowers such as nasturtiums, poppies, and marigolds near your tomato plants attract insects that eat tomato aphids and other pests

Growing in Containers

Cherry and currant tomatoes are good for containers or hanging baskets. If you can set up a container against a sunny wall with a trellis, the plant will grow up the trellis. Some small varieties won't need any staking or support. Choose containers about twelve inches deep and twelve inches wide, with good drainage. Place your containers or hanging baskets where tomatoes will get six hours of sun. Remember that the soil in hanging baskets dries out more quickly than the soil around plants in the ground so frequent watering will be necessary.

Tomatoes' Challenges

There are a few pesky problems that can interfere with your tomato-growing experience. The ones described below are the most common pests and diseases. The abbreviations given in parentheses are listed on the seed packages.

- Hornworms are caterpillars that blend so well with the coloring of the leaves that you really have to look closely. If you aren't diligent in your care, what you may eventually see are the leaves they have stripped and destroyed.

- Nematodes (N) are minute worms that assault the roots and cause root knot.

- Black hopping beetles are tiny, flea-like insects that munch round holes in the leaves.

- Fusarium (F) and verticillium (V) wilt are fungal diseases. Fusarium wilt can ultimately kill the plant, as the leaves turn yellow and die. Verticillium wilt usually doesn't happen until the plant has fruit, but, again, the leaves turn yellow and die. These fungal infections are spread through infected soil, debris, and seeds. There is no cure for these diseases. The affected plants should be destroyed, not recycled into your compost.

- Alternaria rot (A) is a fungal disease affecting injured or weakened fruit, which causes decay around the stem and on the skin of the tomato.

- Tobacco mosaic (T) is a viral disease that can actually spread by exposure to tobacco smoke or from the unwashed hands of a smoker handling the plant.

- Blossom drop happens when the temperatures go beyond or drop below the ideal day and evening temperatures.

- Blossom end rot appears at the ends of the tomatoes as a leathery, black spot. Sudden changes in watering habits, poor drainage, or too much nitrogen or not enough calcium in the soil can contribute to blossom end rot.

- Badly misformed or scarred fruit called catfacing is a deformity caused by cool and/or wet weather during pollination. The tomatoes don't look great, but they taste fine.

- Splitting of ripe or nearly ripe tomatoes is probably caused by irregular watering or too much sun.

Never tug or pull a tomato from the vine—a gentle twist will do. A perfectly ripe tomato should almost fall from the vine into your hands.

tomato varieties

Just to Name a Few

Match up tomatoes best suited to your climate, space, and needs, but have fun experimenting with different varieties each year. Below are a few favorites from the hundreds of varieties of tomatoes available today.

Early-season tomatoes: 50 to 65 days until harvest

Mid-season tomatoes: 65 to 80 days until harvest

Late-season: 80 to 110 days or more until harvest

Ace: Large, firm red heirloom; determinate; mid-season.

Azoychka: Small yellow Russian heirloom; determinate; late-season.

Beefsteak: Also known as Red Ponderosa or Crimson Cushion; large ribbed fruit; indeterminate; late-season.

Black Prince: Deep garnet medium-size fruits on small plants from Siberia; indeterminate; mid-season.

Bradley: Midsize pink fruit; strong determinate; highly productive in short period of time; late-season.

Brandywine: Dark pink heirloom, now available in yellow and red; ultimate beefsteak or slicing tomato; indeterminate; mid- to late-season.

Burpee's Pixie Hybrid: Red cherry; determinate—excellent for containers or small gardens; early-season.

Burpee's Supersteak Hybrid: Red super-size slicer; indeterminate; mid-season.

California Sun Hybrid: Red fruit; dwarf indeterminate; mid-season.

Carmello: French midsize; indeterminate; heavy yield, high weight-to-size ratio; mid-season.

Caro Rich: Deep orange American heirloom; highest in vitamin A, lowest in acid; determinate, needs no trellising; late-season.

Celebrity: Red midsize hybrid; determinate; highly disease resistant and adaptable; mid-season.

Chello Hybrid: Bright yellow cherry; determinate, small bushy plant; early-season.

Cherokee Purple: Midsize dusky pink/rose and purple heirloom; indeterminate, with short vines; late-season.

Costoluto Genovese: Large deeply ridged deep-red multipurpose Italian heirloom; indeterminate; mid- to late-season.

Dad's Mug: Squarish large pink, meaty heirloom; indeterminate; late-season.

Dona: Midsize deep-red French hybrid; indeterminate, vigorous plants; early-season.

Dorothy's Green: Large chartreuse heirloom beefsteak; indeterminate; late-season.

Early Cascade: Midsize red, growing in clusters; indeterminate; prolific throughout season; early-season.

Early Girl: Midsize red slicing tomato; indeterminate; more disease resistant than previous generations; early-season.

Enchantment: Crimson three-inch plum tomato; indeterminate; mid-season.

Eva Purple Ball: Small, juicy pink heirloom; indeterminate; mid-season.

First Lady II: Midsize; indeterminate; full-season producer; early season—extra early.

Floragold Basket: Dwarf yellow cherry; determinate, perfect for hanging baskets; late-season.

Gold Nugget: Oval yellow nuggets; determinate; early-season.

Goldie: Large gold heirloom; indeterminate, with vigorous vine growth; late-season.

Great White: Large white, juicy beefsteak; indeterminate, with heavy foliage; late-season.

Green Bell Pepper: Pepper-shaped fruit with mottled green striping; good for stuffing; indeterminate; mid-season.

Green Grape: Yellow-green cherry heirloom; determinate; mid-season.

Green Zebra: Heirloom with green flesh, green-striped skin; indeterminate; mid-season.

Hawaiian: Heat-tolerant hybrid; indeterminate; mid-season.

Husky Cherry Red: Red cherry clusters; dwarf indeterminate, developed for home gardens; early-season.

Husky Gold: Gold midsize; dwarf indeterminate, good for open and small gardens and for containers; mid-season.

Husky Pink: Midsize; dwarf indeterminate; mid-season.

Mandarin Cross: Large golden-orange Japanese fruit; indeterminate; mid-season.

Marvel Striped: Large heirloom in red, yellow, and orange with orange and red striations inside; indeterminate; late-season.

Micro-Tom: Crouton-sized fruit; dwarf determinate, grows five to eight inches tall; late-season.

Milano: Deep red long pear-shaped plum, good for tomato paste; determinate; early-season.

Old German: Large yellow-with-red-streaks heirloom; indeterminate; mid-season.

Orange Cherry: Bright orange heirloom; indeterminate; good in hot climates; mid-season.

Orange Pixie Hybrid: Large orange cherry; determinate; early-season, extra early.

Oregon Spring: Juicy, nearly seedless midsize to large; determinant; good in cool climates; early-season.

Palestinian: Midsize dark pink heirloom; indeterminate; mid-season.

Pineapple Tomato: Very large heirloom plants with red and yellow fruit; indeterminate; late-season.

Pink Girl: Pink midsize; indeterminate; mid-season.

Principe Borghese Italian Drying: Small egg-shaped Italian heirloom; good for drying; indeterminate; mid-season.

Pruden's Purple: Dark-pink-skinned heirloom with crimson flesh and creamy texture; indeterminate; late mid-season.

Red Cherry Large: Firm round cherry; indeterminate; prolific; mid-season.

Red Currant: South American heirloom with tiny fruit; indeterminate; mid-season.

Ruby Pear: Grape-sized ruby-red Chinese hybrid; indeterminate; mid-season.

Ruffled Tomato: Yellow "pleated" fruit; good for stuffing; indeterminate; mid-season.

Salsa: Round red French midsize; semi-indeterminate (plant size is limited, but produces all season); mid-season.

San Francisco Fog: Midsize red; indeterminate, tall plant; mid-season.

San Marzano: Red; good for cooking; indeterminate; mid-season.

San Remo Sauce Tomatoes: Large elongated, heavy fruit; indeterminate; good for drying, sauces, and salsa; mid-season.

Southern Night: Russian heirloom, with round blackish-red fruit; determinate; late-season.

Stupice: Small red smooth-skinned heirloom from Czechoslovakia; indeterminate, cold-tolerant; early- to mid-season.

Sun Gold: Orange cherry; indeterminate, tall plants with long strands of fruit; early-season.

Super Italian Paste: Deep orange-red banana-pepper–shaped meaty heirloom; indeterminate; mid-season.

Supersweet 100 and Sweet 100: Red cherry; indeterminate; early-season.

Thessaloniki: Large red Greek; indeterminate; mid-season.

White Bush: Midsize white; dwarf determinate, no staking needed; mid-season.

White Queen: Large white heirloom beefsteak; indeterminate; late-season.

Yellow Bell: Bright yellow solid heirloom; indeterminate; good for ketchup, sauces, and preserves; early-season.

Yellow Cherry: Bright yellow; indeterminate; mid-season.

Yellow Pear: Miniature pear-shaped clear yellow American heirloom; indeterminate; mid-season.

Yellow Stuffer: Yellow stuffing tomato; indeterminate; mid-season.

seed
s🍅urces and
organizations

Abundant Life Seed Foundation
P.O. Box 772
Port Townsend, Washington 98368

Bountiful Gardens by Ecology in Action
18001 Shafer Ranch Road
Willits, California 95490

The Cook's Garden
P.O. Box 535
Londonderry, Vermont 05148
Phone: 802–824–3400; Fax: 802–824–3027

Garden State Heirloom Seed Society
P.O. Box 15
Delaware, New Jersey 07833
Annual membership includes access to members'
seed listings and other publications.

Heirloom Seed Project
Landis Valley Museum
2451 Kissel Hill Road
Lancaster, Pennsylvania 17601
Catalog, $4 (Canada, $5)

Heirloom Seeds
P.O. Box 245
West Elizabeth, Pennsylvania 15088
Catalog, $1, refundable toward first purchase

Johnny's Selected Seeds
Foss Hill Road
Albion, Maine 04910
Phone: 207–437–4301

Maine Seed Saving Network
P.O. Box 126
Penobscot, Maine 04476
Membership

The Natural Gardening Company
Complete Organic Gardening Source
217 San Anselmo Avenue
San Anselmo, California 94960
Phone: 707–766–9303; Fax: 707–766–9747
Hybrid and heirloom tomatoes

Nichols Garden Nursery
1190 North Pacific Highway
Albany, Oregon 97321
Phone: 503–928–9280

Ornamental Edibles
3622 Weedin Court
San Jose, California 95132
Phone: 408–946–SEED (7333)

Pinetree Garden Seeds
Route 100
New Gloucester, Maine 04260
Phone: 207–926–3400

Santa Barbara Heirloom Seedling Nursery
P.O. Box 4235
Santa Barbara, California 93140
Phone: 805–968–5444; Fax: 805–562–1248

Seed Savers Exchange
3076 North Winn Road
Decorah, Iowa 52101
Phone: 319–382–5990

Seeds of Change
P.O. Box 15700
Santa Fe, New Mexico 97506–5700
Phone: 505–438–7052

Seeds of Diversity Canada
P.O. Box 36 Station Q
Toronto, Ontario
Canada M4T 2L7
Membership

Tomato Festivals

The Spaniards take a pasting every August 28, as the date marks the Tomato Battle, when the entire town of Buñol, in eastern Spain, is turned red. Valencians and tourists alike pelt each other with tons of tomatoes at the annual Tomatina Festival. This peculiar celebration of the tomato began fifty years ago as a diversion when the town had banned bullfighting in 1932.

For one day in late summer each year, Boston's City Hall Plaza is cleared to host the annual Tomato Festival. Slicing tomatoes and cherry tomatoes are judged, tomatoes are sold, tomatoes are tasted and compared. Participating growers from across the state include large-scale farmers, those who operate farm stands, and those who participate in local farmers' markets. Surprisingly, for a small state, Massachusetts sustains a five-million-dollar tomato crop. All proceeds from the festival support the preservation of open-space land in Massachusetts.

Every year at Heronswood in Melbourne, Australia, during late February or early March, they celebrate the tomato harvest with an Heirloom Tomato Festival. As many as a hundred and fifty varieties of heirloom tomatoes are showcased over the week.

The Little River Tomato Fest takes place each September in Carmel Valley, California. Gary Isben, the host, offers a tasting of his many, many varieties of home-grown heirloom tomatoes and a country barbecue with live music and hundreds of tomato dishes to sample.

Shepherd's Garden Seeds
30 Irene Street
Torrington, Connecticut 06790
Phone: 860–482–3638

Smith & Hawken
117 East Strawberry Drive
Mill Valley, California 94941
Phone: 800–776–3336

Southern Exposure Seed Exchange
P.O. Box 170
Earlysville, Virginia 22936
Phone: 804–973–4703
Catalog, $2

Terra Edibles
Box 63
Thomasburg, Ontario
Canada K0K 3H0
Catalog, $1

Territorial Seed Company
20 Palmer Avenue
Cottage Grove, Oregon 97424
Phone: 541–942–9547

Tomato Growers Supply Company
P.O. Box 2237
Fort Myers, Florida 33902
Phone: 941–768–1119
Hybrid and heirloom tomatoes and peppers

Tomato Seed Company
P.O. Box 1400
Tyron, North Carolina 28782

Totally Tomatoes
P.O. Box 1626
Augusta, Georgia 30903
Phone: 803–663–0016; Toll-free fax:
888–477–7333

Turtle Tree Seed Farm
5569 North County Road 29
Loveland, Colorado 80538
Catalog, $1

W. Atlee Burpee Company
300 Park Avenue
Warminster, Pennsylvania 18974
Phone: 800–333–5808; Fax: 800–487–5530

index